THE
GENESIS OF
JUSTICE

ALSO BY ALAN M. DERSHOWITZ

Psychoanalysis, Psychiatry, and Law
(with Jay Katz and Joseph Goldstein)

Criminal Law: Theory and Practice
(with Joseph Goldstein and Richard D. Schwartz)

The Best Defense

Reversal of Fortune: Inside the von Bülow Case

Taking Liberties:
A Decade of Hard Cases, Had Laws, and Bum Raps

Chutzpah

Contrary to Popular Opinion

The Advocate's Devil

The Abuse Excuse: And Other Cop-Outs, Sob
Stories, and Evasions of Responsibility

Reasonable Doubts

The Vanishing American Jew: In Search of Jewish
Identity for the Next Century

Sexual McCarthyism: Clinton, Starr,
and the Emerging Constitutional Crisis

Just Revenge

THE
GENESIS OF
JUSTICE

Ten Stories of Biblical Injustice that Led to the Ten Commandments and Modern Law

---

ALAN M. DERSHOWITZ

WARNER BOOKS

A Time Warner Company

Warner Books, Inc., 1271 Avenue of the Americas,
New York, NY 10020
Visit our Web site at www.twbookmark.com

w A Time Warner Company

Printed in the United States of America
First Warner Books Printing: March 2000
10 9 8 7 6 5 4 3

Library of Congress Cataloging-in-Publication Data

Dershowitz, Alan M.
    The Genesis of justice : ten stories of biblical injustice that led to the Ten
Commandments and modern law / Alan M. Dershowitz.
        p.   cm.
    Includes bibliographical references and index.
    ISBN 0-446-52479-4
    1. Justice—Biblical teaching.   2. Bible O.T. Genesis—Criticism,
interpretation, etc.   I. Title.
BS1235.6.J8D47 2000
222'.1106—dc21   99-050220

Book design by Giorgetta Bell McRee

I lovingly dedicate this book to my mother, Claire Dershowitz, and to my late father, Harry Dershowitz, who provided me with my background in the Bible and with the freedom to raise questions. They were the genesis of my interest in both the Bible and justice.

Genealogy of the Major Biblical Characters Discussed in
*The Genesis of Justice**

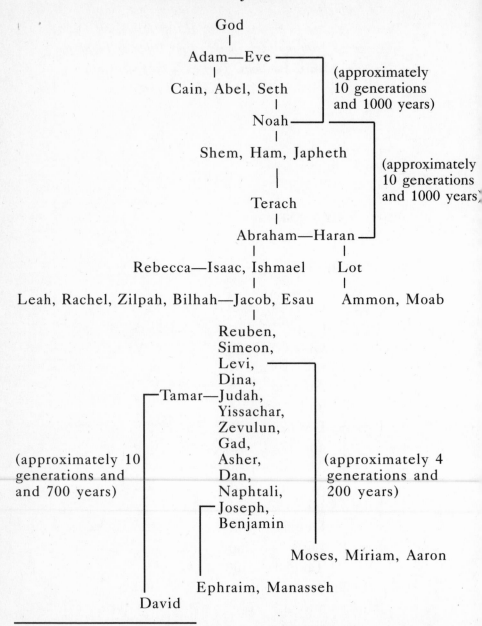

God
|
Adam—Eve ⎤
| (approximately
Cain, Abel, Seth   10 generations
| and 1000 years)
Noah ⎦
|
Shem, Ham, Japheth
| (approximately
| 10 generations
Terach   and 1000 years)
|
Abraham—Haran
| |
Rebecca—Isaac, Ishmael   Lot
| |
Leah, Rachel, Zilpah, Bilhah—Jacob, Esau   Ammon, Moab
|
Reuben,
Simeon,
Levi,
Dina,
Tamar—Judah,
Yissachar,
Zevulun,
Gad,
(approximately 10   Asher,   (approximately 4
generations and   Dan,   generations and
and 700 years)   Naphtali,   200 years)
Joseph,
Benjamin

Moses, Miriam, Aaron

Ephraim, Manasseh
David

---

*These estimates were derived from Archbishop James Ussher's traditional dating system from the seventeenth century. This dating system has not been without its critics (see Mordecai Cogan, "Chronology," *The Anchor Bible Dictionary*, ed. David Noel Freedman, New York: Doubleday, 1992, vol. 1, pp. 1002–1011, for a discussion of alternative dating systems). The Bible itself rarely is specific about the time between major events. Accordingly, scholars have had to extrapolate from the ages of biblical figures and other sparse data provided by the text.

Throughout this book, the original Hebrew names are used interchangeably with their Anglicized counterparts.

Table of Contents

Acknowledgments

This book was begat by a long line of patriarchs, matriarchs, friends, and relatives. First and foremost are my parents and grandparents who imbued me with a love of the Bible and Jewish learning. My teachers, whom we too often treated with disrespect, provided me with the basic tools for understanding the Bible. I apologize to them for taunting them and misbehaving in their classes. I know they will be surprised that I learned anything, but believe it or not, I really did. My Yeshiva friends, many of whom are still my friends, were and remain an important part of my education. The students in my Bible seminar at Harvard Law School helped me test my theories and hone my interpretative skills. My friends on Martha's Vineyard, who joined my wife and me for the weekly Bible class, contributed brilliant insights. My friends, colleagues, and relatives in Israel, who shared their perspectives with me, helped to broaden my approach. Special appreciation to my friends and colleagues who reviewed the manuscript and pointed out its numerous mistakes.

I owe an enormous debt to the countless biblical commentators who, over the millennia, have elaborated, explained, challenged, translated, and kept alive the words of the Bible. Everyone who reads the Bible today stands on the shoulders of giants.

A special word of appreciation to the Morton Foundation and to Morton and Rosalind Davis, for helping to defray the expenses of my research trip to Israel, and to the Gruss Foundation, for providing research support at Harvard.

My usual thanks to my wife, Carolyn, my mother, Claire, my in-laws, Dutch and Mortie, my children Elon, Jamin, and Ella, my daughter-in-law, Barbara, my grandchildren, Lori and Lyle, my brother, Nathan, my sister-in-law, Marilyn, my nephew, Adam, my niece, Rana, my brother-in-law, Marvin, my sister-in-law, Julie, and my nephews, Isaac and Jonah—all of whom contributed in different ways. My thanks as well to my friends, Murray and Malkie Altman, Bernie and Judy Beck, Zolly and Katie Eisenstadt, Carl and Joan Meshenberg, Hal and Sandy Miller-Jacobs, Josh and Rochelle Weisberger, Barry and Barbara Zimmerman, Tsvi Groner, Martin Levine, Alan Rothfeld, Ken and Gerry Sweder, Israel Ringel, Michael and Jackie Halbreich, Alex MacDonald, Maureen Straford, Naomi Foner, Jeffrey Epstein, Maureen White, Jerry Davidson, Joanne and Tom Ash, and Lisa Foster.

Among my friends and colleagues who reviewed the manuscript, I wish to single out Madeline Kochen who educated me, corrected me, and provided unique insights into the intrepretative processes of Jewish law, about which she is truly a master.

It is especially gratifying for me to work with students. Among those who helped me on this project have been Aharon Friedman, Talia Milgrom-Elcott, and Meron Hacohen.

Thanks also to Jessica Papin for her extraordinary

editorial assistance, to Helen Rees for her guidance and support, and to Larry Kirshbaum for his enthusiasm about this project. This book could not have been produced without the help of Maura Kelley, John Orsini, Audrey Lee, and Manny Lim. Thanks also to the librarians at Harvard Law School and at the Harvard Divinity School for their assistance.

A note of appreciation to Everett Fox for permitting me to use his extraordinary translation of Genesis, which is as true to the ancient rhythms of the Torah as it is to the contemporary eye.

The responsibility for my misinterpretations, misunderstandings, and other mistakes is entirely my own. I am sure that if I had paid more attention in Hebrew school, I would not have made them.

PART I

WHY GENESIS?

Would you give a young person a book whose heroes cheat, lie, steal, murder—and get away with it? Chances are you have. The book, of course, is Genesis. And you are right to encourage your child to read it—with some guidance. It is the best interactive moral teaching tool ever devised: Genesis forces readers of all ages to struggle with eternal issues of right and wrong.

There is a fundamental difference between the Five Books of Moses, especially the first book, Genesis, and the New Testament and Koran. The New Testament and the Koran teach justice largely through examples of the perfection of God, Jesus, and Mohammed. Christian or Muslim parents can hand their children the New Testament or the Koran and feel confident they will learn by example how to live a just and noble life. The parables and teachings may require some explanation,[1] but on the whole, the lessons to be derived from the lives of Jesus and Mohammed are fairly obvious. Who can quarrel with the Sermon on the Mount, or with Jesus' reply to those who would stone the adulteress on the Mount of Olives, or with the parable of the good Samaritan?[2] The same is true with Mohammed. The Koran describes his life as exemplary and Mohammed himself as "of a great moral character." If you pattern your behavior after Jesus or Mohammed, you will be a just person.

In sharp contrast, the characters in the Jewish Bible—even its heroes—are all flawed human beings. They are good people who sometimes do very bad things. As Ecclesiastes says: "There is not a righteous person in the whole earth who does only good and never sins."[3] This tradition of human imperfection begins at the beginning, in Genesis. Even the God of Genesis can be seen as an imperfect God, neither omniscient, omnipotent, nor even always good. He "repents" the creation of man, promises not to flood the world again, and even allows Abraham to lecture Him about injustice.[4] The Jewish Bible teaches about justice largely through examples of injustice and imperfection.[5] Genesis challenges the reader to react, to think for him- or herself, even to disagree. That is why it is an interactive teaching tool, raising profound questions and inviting dialogue with the ages and with the divine.

What lessons in justice are we to learn from the patriarch Abraham's attempted murder of *both* his sons? Or from God's genocide against Noah's contemporaries and Lot's townsfolk? Generations of commentators have addressed these questions, and rightfully so. They need addressing. These stories do not stand on their own. Reading the Old Testament,* and especially the Book of Genesis, must be an active experience. Indeed, the critical reader is compelled to struggle with the text, as Jacob struggled with God's messenger. A midrash describes how man "toils much in the study of the Torah."[6] Maimonides believed that Torah study is so demanding that husbands engaged in this exhausting work should be obliged to have sex with their wives only "once a week, because the study of Torah weakens their strength." For comparative purposes, rich men who don't work must have sex with their wives "every night," and ordinary laborers "twice a week."[7] Whether or not we agree that biblical scholarship should interfere with our sex lives, it is certainly true that we are invited by the ambiguities of the text to question, to become angry, to disagree. Perhaps that is why Jews are so contentious, so argumentative, so "stiff-necked," to use a biblical term. I love reading the Torah precisely because it requires constant reinterpretation and struggle.

I first thought about justice when, as a child, I studied the Book of Genesis. To this day, I remember the questions it raised better than the answers given by my rabbis. To read Genesis, even as a ten-year-old, is to question God's idea of justice. What child could avoid wondering how Adam and Eve could fairly be punished for disobeying God's commandment not to eat from the "Tree of the Knowing of Good and Evil," if—before eating of that tree—they lacked all knowledge of good and evil? What inquisitive child could simply accept God's decision to destroy innocent babies, first during the flood and later in the fire and

*I use the terms "Old Testament" and "Jewish Bible" interchangeably, without intending any theological implications.

brimstone of Sodom and Gomorrah? How could Abraham be praised for his willingness to sacrifice his son? Why was Jacob rewarded for cheating his older twin out of his birthright and his father's blessing?

I first encountered these questions as an elementary-school student in an Orthodox Jewish day school (yeshiva) during the 1940s and 1950s. My teachers, mostly Holocaust survivors from the great rabbinic seminaries of Europe, encouraged the sorts of mind-twisting questions posed by the rabbis over the centuries, without fear of apostasy. These were old questions, asked by generations of believers. Each question had an accepted answer—an answer that strengthened faith in the divine origin of the text and in the goodness of God and His prophets. Sometimes there were multiple answers, occasionally even con-flicting ones, but they were all part of the canon. Some of them required a stretch—even a leap of faith. But none, at least none that were acceptable, encouraged doubt about God's existence or goodness.

If a skeptical student asked a question outside of the canon, the teacher had a ready response: "If your question were a good one, the rabbis before you, who were so much smarter than you, would have asked it already. If they did not think of it, then it cannot be a good question." The teachers even had an au-thoritative source for their pedagogical one-upman-ship. The Talmud recounts the story of the great teacher Rabbi Eliezer, who was teaching the follow-ing principle:

> If a fledging bird is found within fifty cubits [about seventy-five feet] ... [of a man's prop-erty], it belongs to the owner of the property.

> If it is found outside the limits of fifty cubits, it belongs to the person who finds it.
>
> Rabbi Jeremiah asked the question: "If one foot of the fledging bird is within the limit of fifty cubits, and one foot is outside it, what is the law?"
>
> It was for this question that Rabbi Jeremiah was thrown out of the house of study.[8]

I would occasionally ask impertinent questions that got me tossed out of class. I remember upsetting a teacher by asking where Cain's wife came from, since Adam and Eve had no daughters. A classmate was slapped for wondering how night and day existed before God created the sun and the moon. My teachers dubbed these questions *klutz kashas*—the questions of a "klutz," or ignoramus. But I persisted in asking them, as did many of my classmates. I continue to ask them in this book.

Following my bar mitzvah, I began to deliver *divrei Torah*—talks about the weekly Bible reading—at the Young Israel of Boro Park Synagogue, which my family attended. My mother found a copy of one of these talks among some old papers, and it was amazing to discover that even back then I was thinking about some of the issues addressed in this book, arguing that rules without reason are antithetical to liberty and that the first seeds of democracy are planted when lawmakers see the need to justify their commands.[9] The talk my mother found was about the Bible portion called Chukkat,* which deals with a category of laws for which the rabbis could find no basis

---

*An excerpt from my talk of June 16, 1956, is reprinted in the endnotes on p. 21. The "ch" in Chukkat is pronounced like the first syllable in "Hasid" or "chutzpah."

in reason. They were divine orders to be followed blindly, simply because God issued them. These *chukim* were distinguished from *mishpatim*, which were laws based on reason and experience. The word *"mishpat"* comes from the same root as the words "justice" and "judge" and so *mishpatim* (the plural of *mishpat*) were based on principles of justice, whereas *chukim* needed no justification.[10]

As I will try to show in this book, the unique characteristic of the Bible—as contrasted with earlier legal codes—is that it is a law book explicitly rooted in the narrative of experience. The God of Genesis makes a covenant with humans, thereby obligating Himself to justify what He commands—at least most of the time. The Bible reflects the development of law from unreasoned *chok* to justified *mishpat*. Abraham's argument with God over the fate of Sodom and Gomorrah—the first instance in religious history of a human being challenging God to be just—marks an important watershed in the development of democracy.

These and other stories of justice and injustice had a powerful effect on my young mind. They encouraged me to view the world in a skeptical and questioning manner. If Abraham could challenge God, surely I could challenge my teachers. When my high school principal refused me permission to take a statewide exam for a college scholarship on the ground that no one with my low grades stood a chance of winning, I challenged his action and won both the opportunity to take the test—and the scholarship itself. The Bible had empowered me to pursue justice. I imagine these Bible stories must have had similar effects on the minds of other inquiring students, Christian, Muslim, and Jew alike!

I read Genesis as an invitation to question everything, even faith. It taught me that faith is a process rather than a static mind-set. The Book of Genesis shows that faith must be earned, even by God. Jacob expressly conditions his faith on God complying with His side of the bargain—of the covenant. As a child, I trivialized this unique relationship between God and His people by inventing conditions of my own: I would be faithful if God would bring a World Series championship to Brooklyn. I spent many a faithless day until 1955, when the Dodgers finally beat the Yankees—and promptly moved to Los Angeles. God works in mysterious ways.

As I grew older I continued to ponder the wonderful stories of Genesis. They leap into my mind whenever I think about contemporary issues of justice and injustice, as if they are hard-wired into my consciousness. As a law professor, I have always used biblical narratives in classes as sources of analogy and reference, since most students have some familiarity with Adam, Eve, Cain, Abel, Abraham, Sarah, Jacob, Moses, David, Job, Jesus, and Mohammed.

In the fall of 1997 I decided to offer a Harvard Law School seminar on the biblical sources of justice. I was flabbergasted at the amount of interest. Approximately 150 students applied for the 20 places in the seminar. The classes themselves were exhilarating, as Jews, Christians, Muslims, atheists, and agnostics explored the sacred texts in search of insights about justice and law. In the spring of 1998 I spent several months in Israel, reading biblical commentaries and discussing them with a wide assortment of scholars from differing perspectives. In the fall of 1998 I taught the seminar again, focusing on the narratives of Genesis and

Exodus. And in the summers of 1998 and 1999 I led a Bible study group on Martha's Vineyard in which we explored the ethical implications of several biblical stories.

My students have included religious fundamentalists who take every word of Scripture literally. "God said it. I believe it. Case closed," read a bumper sticker I saw in the law school parking lot. At the other extreme I have taught atheists, agnostics, and some who have never even opened a Bible in their lives. As one woman told me: "Until now, I've thought of the Bible as a book I see in a hotel room drawer while I'm looking for stationery."

Some of my students view the Bible as great literature, akin to Shakespeare, Homer, and Dostoyevsky. I regard it differently, as a holy book in which many people believe and for which some have been willing to die—and kill. Whether or not one believes the Bible was written or inspired by God and redacted by humans, it cannot, in any view, be read as just another collection of folktales, short stories, or historical accounts. It is a sacred text, and Scripture must be read differently from secular literature if it is to be fully appreciated. We read Shakespeare to glory in his mastery of language and to share his remarkable understanding of the human condition. Yet we do not look to Hamlet or Othello as templates for moral behavior. We identify with the struggles Shakespeare's characters undergo, while recognizing that Shylock and Lear are the creations of a brilliant human mind. The Bible, on the other hand, purports to be the word of God and the moral guide to all behavior. We are supposed to act on it, not merely ponder its insights. No one was ever burned at the stake for misinterpreting *Macbeth*.

In preparing for my classes on the Bible, and in writing this book, I have tried to reread the biblical texts afresh. For purposes of the Harvard classes, I am neither Jew nor Christian nor Muslim. I take no position on divine versus human or singular versus multiple authorship. Each student is encouraged to bring his or her tradition to the reading of the texts. Nor do I take a position on the "truth" of the various commentators, who are deemed "authoritative" by different religions. We study many commentators, judging them by their contribution to the discussion and the insights they provide, without regard to their doctrinal presuppositions.

I found particular inspiration in a statement made by the great medieval commentator Ibn Ezra, a Spanish Jew of the twelfth century who was familiar with Greek, Christian, and Islamic philosophy and wrote one of the most brilliant and enduring commentaries on the Bible. Ibn Ezra once said that "anyone with a little bit of intelligence and certainly one who has knowledge of the Torah can create his own midrashism."[11] Midrashim, or the singular midrash, are interpretations of the biblical text by the use of illustrative stories, explanations, commentaries, and other forms of exegesis. There is a traditional saying in Judaism, "There are seventy faces to the Torah," which means there is no one correct interpretation of a biblical narrative.[12] A contemporary scholar has suggested that many of these faces "were latent; and as generation after generation found expression for some or other of these aspects, they revealed again and anew the Torah which Moses received on Sinai."[13]

It is in this spirit that I join this dialogue among generations. Every generation has the right, indeed the duty, to interpret the Bible anew in the context of contemporary knowledge and information. Eight centuries ago the most revered of Jewish commentators, Maimonides, insisted on studying ancient and current writers, both within and outside of his own religion, because he believed that "one should accept the truth from whatever source it proceeds."[14] Maimonides read widely among Greek and Arab writers and was particularly influenced by Aristotle, while fundamentally disagreeing with his concept of God. Norman Lamm, the president of Yeshiva University, has reiterated this eclectic perspective: "No religious position is loyally served by refusing to consider annoying theories which may well turn out to be facts. . . . Judaism will then have to confront them as it has confronted what men have considered the truth throughout generations. . . . [I]f they are found to be substantially correct, we may not overlook them. We must then use newly discovered truths the better to understand our Torah—the 'Torah of truth.'"[15]

It is in the nature of midrashic interpretation that it "keeps its gates open. It never closes a debate."[16] Nor does it exclude any from participation in this never-ending discussion of the Bible. The "quest" (*drash*) continues, "untamed" and "unabated" in its spirit of free inquiry.[17] One of my uncles, who is a rabbi and a professor in Israel, has traced our family name and believes that it derives from the Hebrew word *"doresh"* or *"drash,"* which means "to seek interpretations," particularly of the Bible. Our family apparently has a long history of being *darshanim*, people who interpret sacred texts. There is no way, of course, to be certain of this derivation, but I would be proud to be part of such a tradition. The generations of my family whom I have known certainly lend support to my uncle's theory, though not all my relatives would agree with the questioning tone and content of this book.

Unlike others who have written about the Bible, I do not bring to the project a lifetime of biblical study. Instead I bring a lifetime of legal studies and practice coupled with a solid grounding in the Bible. In my forty years as a lawyer, I have thought constantly about the Bible and how it has impacted on the law. My teaching and practice have been informed by biblical as well as secular sources. Now it is time for me to write about this fascinating relationship, which has played such an important part in my own personal and professional life.[18]

I try to use my legal, political, and personal experiences to raise new questions about ancient sources and to provide new insights into old questions. I make no claim of being "right." Nor do I claim any religious or other authority. My goal is simply to stimulate discussion among believers, nonbelievers, skeptics, and others who share my fascination with the enduring influence of this book called the Bible.

Most people who write about the Bible have an agenda, sometimes overt, more often hidden. They seek to prove or disprove the divine origin of the Bible, the superiority or inferiority of one particular religious approach to the text, or some point about the history of the Scriptures. In reading many of the traditional commentaries, I have observed that they fall into several categories.

First, there are the "defense lawyers." Like any

good lawyer defending a client, they rarely ask a question unless they already know the answer. In this case, the answer must prove the goodness of God, the consistency of the text, and the divine origin of the Bible. These defense lawyers search for "proof texts" that will corroborate what they already know to be true. As one midrash confidently assures its readers: "Whenever you find a point [apparently] supporting the heretics, you find the refutation at its side."[19] The most prominent among the defense lawyer commentators is Rashi, a brilliant and tireless eleventh-century French Jew whose full name was Rabbi Solomon ben Isaac. Rashi, who lived through the Crusades, wrote exhaustive commentaries on the Bible and the Talmud, generally limiting himself to narrow textual interpretation and reconciliation rather than broad philosophical or theological elaborations.

Next, there are the "Socratic" commentators, who seem prepared to ask the difficult questions and acknowledge that they do not always have the perfect answers. These commentators are willing to leave some matters unresolved and to express occasional doubt, because the correct interpretation may be inaccessible to their generation or hidden in coded language. Ultimately, even the most open-minded of these commentators is not prepared to make the leap of doubt or faithlessness, though they demand that others make a comparable leap of faith. The most prominent of the Socratic commentators is Maimonides, who studied Greek philosophy and who believed that scientific knowledge was consistent with biblical truth. His writings endure not only as biblical interpretation but also as stand-alone philosophical works.

Then there are the subtle skeptics. Although they proclaim complete faith, any discerning reader can sense some doubt—doubt about God's justice, doubt about God's compliance with His covenant, even occasional doubt about God's very existence. These commentators employ veiled allusion, hypothetical stories, and mock trials to challenge God and to wonder why His people have suffered so much. It is no sin, according to these skeptics, to *feel* doubt. After all, human beings are endowed with the capacity, if not the need, to doubt. The sin is to *act* on these doubts. Judaism is a religion in which theological purity is not as important as observance of the commandments. When God gave the Jews the Torah, the people said they would "do and listen" (*na'aseh v'nishmah*). This response—placing "doing" before "listening"—has been interpreted to justify theoretical skepticism as long as it is accompanied by devout behavior.[20] Among the prominent skeptics is Rabbi Levi Yitzchak of Berditchev, an eighteenth-century Hasidic master who actually filed a religious lawsuit (a *din Torah*) against God for breaking His covenant with the Jewish people.[21]

Throughout most of history it has been assumed that the Jewish Bible was written or inspired by God and that it was given to the Jewish people at Sinai as a single document. During the Middle Ages some traditional commentators wondered about textual inconsistencies that suggested multiple authors or later additions. Moses describes his own death. Places and peoples are mentioned that did not come into existence until well after the Torah was supposed to have been given at Sinai. For example, in a passage describing Abraham's journey, the Bible states, "The

Canaanite was then in the land."* Ibn Ezra wonders about the historical accuracy of that statement, offers a possible interpretation, and then hedges his bet: "Should this interpretation be incorrect, then there is a secret meaning to the text." He cautions, "Let one who understands it remain silent."[22] A commentator on Ibn Ezra suggests a reason for the rather cryptic warning: Ibn Ezra realizes the clause about the Canaanites is an anachronism but is loath to engender doubt among his readers. The solution: silence! Many biblical scholars now acknowledge that the Book of Deuteronomy appears to have been written later than the other four books and that the different styles within the first books suggest multiple authorship, subsequent editing, and redaction.

The question of who wrote the Bible has been hotly debated by academics for more than a century. Though I am familiar with this literature and have used it in my classes, *this* book is not part of *that* debate.[23] Instead *The Genesis of Justice* speaks not to the who but to the how: How are we to understand the stories of apparent injustice that are supposed to teach us about justice? In order to join that millennia-old debate, I have chosen to accept the assumptions of its historic participants about the divine nature of the text. For purposes of this book, it does not matter whether Genesis was dictated to Moses by God or compiled by an editor from multiple sources. What *does* matter is that it has been considered a sacred text for more than two millennia. This does not, of course, require a literal fundamentalist approach. As Ibn Ezra put it: "[I]f there appears something in the Torah that is intel-

*Genesis 12:6.

14

lectually impossible to accept or contrary to the evidence of our senses, then we must search for a hidden meaning. This is so because intelligence is the basis of the Torah. The Torah was not given to ignoramuses."[24]

Pope John Paul II has made a similar point:

> Fundamentalism also places undue stress upon the inerrancy of certain details in the biblical texts, especially in what concerns historical events or supposedly scientific truth. It often historicizes material which from the start never claimed to be historical. It considers historical everything that is reported or recounted with verbs in the past tense, failing to take the necessary account of the possibility of symbolic or figurative meaning. . . .
>
> Fundamentalism likewise tends to adopt very narrow points of view. It accepts the literal reality of an ancient, out-of-date cosmology, simply because it is found expressed in the Bible; this blocks any dialogue with a broader way of seeing the relationship between culture and faith. Its relying upon a non-critical reading of certain texts of the Bible serves to reinforce political ideas and social attitudes that are marked by prejudices—racism, for example—quite contrary to the Christian gospel.[25]

I am reminded of a Jewish story about the two great rabbis, both experts on Maimonides, who die and go to heaven, where they continue to argue about an inconsistency between one Maimonidian text and another. Each rabbi proposes brilliant arguments and counterarguments, seeking to reconcile the apparent conflict. God, observing their marvelous debate, brings in Maimonides himself to resolve the conflict. Maimonides looks at the conflicting texts, smiles, and declares that one of them is a simple transcription error. There is no actual inconsistency! The rabbis dismiss Maimonides, complaining that *his* solution is far less interesting than their own.

It is in the argumentative tradition of these rabbis that I approach the text of Genesis. I am certain that some of the conflicts within the text of Genesis—for example, Abraham's willingness to argue with God on behalf of the mostly guilty Sodomites as contrasted with his unwillingness to argue with God on behalf of his own entirely innocent son—could be resolved by pointing to evidence that one of these texts was written by the "J author," while the other was written by the "E author."[26] That is a less interesting answer, however, than some of those provided by the traditional commentators. Because I want to engage the commentators and the text on the terms accepted by their readers over the millennia, I have not written a book about *who* wrote the Bible, but rather about *how* we should understand its often conflicting messages about justice.

The open-textured, often ambiguous nature of the Jewish Bible has fostered a rich oral tradition and thousands of commentaries on the biblical text. Within the Jewish tradition there are different kinds of biblical commentary: *pshat*, literal translation; *drash*, rabbinic explication; *remez*, symbolic interpretation; and *sod*, secret or mystical meaning. Jews love acronyms, and the acronym for these different kinds of biblical commentary is *pardes (pshat, remez, drash, and sod)*, which means "orchard." The orchard of interpretation is supposed to contain the many faces of the Torah.[27] Perhaps the most popular form of biblical commentary has been the midrashic Aggadah, which are stories, sometimes farfetched, elaborating on the biblical narrative and going beyond more text-centered *drash*. I will provide examples of such stories throughout this book.[28] One commentator went so far as to elevate the Aggadic stories to the status of Holy Writ: "If thou wishest to know Him, . . . learn Aggadah."[29]

To complicate matters even further, some contemporary commentators—most notably Abraham Joshua Heschel—argue that the Bible itself is midrash. Heschel regards the central event of biblical theology—the revelation at Sinai—as a midrash about how the law was given to the people of Israel. To take the narrative literally and believe that God actually spoke and handed over tablets is, Heschel argues, to confuse metaphor with fact. According to this view, there is *only* midrash, followed by midrash upon midrash. The stories of the Bible translate God's unknowable actions into familiar human terms that a reader can understand.[30] Maimonides also viewed some of the words of the Bible as "metaphorical," using "the language of man" and "adapted to the mental capacity of the majority of mankind. . . ."[31] Focusing on phrases such as "the hand of God" and His "glittering sword," Maimonides explains that these words are directed at people who have "a clear perception of physical bodies only."

The New Testament and the Koran were also subject to midrashic elaboration. Jesus excelled in the use of the midrashic technique, and the Gospels have been characterized as a "masterpiece of the Aggadah."[32] Mo-

17

hammed also used the midrash for the legendary material he incorporated into the Koran.

In this book I will focus primarily on the text of Genesis. When relevant, I will make references to various commentators and midrashim. I do not feel bound by any particular interpretation, nor do I regard any as authoritative or dispositive. Once a text is published, it belongs to us all and we may interpret it according to our own lights. The marketplace of ideas is the sole judge of the validity or usefulness of a given interpretation. Tradition certainly has "a vote but not a veto."[33] I surely reject the anti-intellectual approach of those contemporary Haredi (fervently Orthodox) rabbis who argue that "the mind of a man in our generation" is "forbidden" to contain "ideas and thoughts which he devises from his own mind, which were not handed down from earlier generations."[34] I have fought against this sort of anti-intellectual fundamentalism since I was a child studying in the yeshiva, and I continue to reject it as an adult teaching at Harvard. I am inspired far more by the approach suggested by the great sixteenth-century Bible commentator Rabbi Eliezer Ashkenazi, who insisted that "each and every one of us, our children and grandchildren until the conclusion of all generations," is "duty bound to examine the secrets of the Torah" by "accepting the truth from whoever says it":

> Neither ought we be concerned about the logic of others—even if they preceded us—preventing our own individual investigation. Much to the contrary, just as [our forebears] did not wish to indiscriminately accept the truth from those

who preceded them, and that which they did not choose [to accept] they rejected, so is it fitting for us to do. Only on the basis of gathering many different opinions will the truth be tested. . . . Do not be dismayed by the names of the great personalities when you find them in disagreement with your belief; you must investigate and interpret, because for this purpose were you created, and wisdom was granted you from Above, and this will benefit you. . . ."[35]

While my own ideas certainly owe an enormous debt to those of earlier generations, it is hoped that I can provide some new insights that derive from my unique experiences as a lawyer and teacher. Employing one's own experiences to expand knowledge is, after all, a central message of Genesis, in which the characters make mistakes, challenge, and are challenged by God.

Several of my students and colleagues have wondered why I have chosen to focus on the Book of Genesis, which contains many stories but few laws, rather than on the "law books" of the Bible. I have chosen to write about Genesis quite deliberately. I believe that the broad narratives of justice and injustice are more enduring than the often narrow, time-bound, and sometimes derivative rules of the Bible. Although their influence—especially that of the Ten Commandments and the principle of the talion—has been enormous, not all have stood the test of time. Some rules are no longer relevant. For example, much of the Book of Leviticus deals with animal sacrifices. Even the law books, which cover relationships among human beings, contain some proscriptions that few find binding today. The child who rebels against his father and mother is no longer stoned to death—if he ever was[36]—nor are witches summarily executed. These rules and others like them reflect anachronistic practices that almost certainly predate the Bible. The biblical narratives, especially in Genesis, are as fresh, as relevant, as provocative, and as difficult as they were in ancient times. They also provide context and give life to the rules that derive from them. The vignettes, short stories, and novellas that make up the early biblical narratives have few peers in the history of provocative texts on the human condition. As long as human beings ask questions about justice and injustice, they will continue to be interpreted and discussed. Many readers of this book will surely have their own interpretations—midrashim—of the biblical stories. I urge you to read this book in the questioning, argumentative spirit in which it was written and invite you to continue the dialogue by e-mailing your own interpretations to *alder@law.harvard.edu.** I will distribute interesting comments to my students and include you in the dialogue among generations.

*For those without e-mail, my address is:
  Harvard Law School
  Cambridge, Massachusetts 02138

---

1. See, for example, the parable of the wedding banquet at Matthew 22.

2. The disciples do not come off as well in several of the Gospels. See generally, Mark's gospel.

3. 7:20. Traditional commentators point to three biblical exceptions: Benjamin, Amram, and Yishai are without fault.

4. The Greek gods were also imperfect—as might be expected in a situation in which there are numerous gods, each with limited jurisdiction. More is to be expected of a single god with unlimited jurisdiction.

5. I offer an explanation for this intriguing fact in Chapter 11.

6. Midrash Rabbah Vol. 1, p. 68.

7. See *The Book of Women* (New Haven, Conn.: Yale, 1972), p. 87.

8. Bava Batra, 23b. Even this story is seen to convey a positive lesson. Professor Moshe Silberg interprets it as a "veiled criticism against [the] tendency to formalism." Moshe Silberg, *Talmudic Law and the Modern State* (New York: The Burning Bush Press, 1973), pp. 86–90.

9. Excerpts from my d'var *Torah* on June 16, 1956: "These three words—*chok* (divine decree), *mishpat* (a rule based on justice), and *g'zaira* (a despotic human decree)—have played a major role in the political evolution of many nations. The concept of *g'zaira* has been the basis of the absolute monarchy of the past and the totalitarianism of the present, while *mishpat* has been the essence of democracy and liberty throughout the ages. But *g'zaira*, the despotic decree, could not exist for long without help. The people as far back as the fifteenth century realized that the proclaiming of decrees without apparent reason is the sole privilege of G-d and not of mortal kings, and so in order to rationalize their despotic actions the monarchs utilize the concept of *chok*, the G-dly decree, and so there came to be the divine rights theory of monarchies, which claim that the law of the land was actually the *chok* of the Almighty, but that the king as the direct messenger of G-d could execute his desires without question as *chok* rather than *g'zaira*. As time progressed communism came into focus and sought also to rationalize its totalitarianistic principles by *chok* rather than *g'zaira*, and so they invented their own pseudo-gods, their Lenin or Stalin, who then acting as G-d of the Russian people could execute his own *chukim* so to speak without being questioned concerning them.

In our own United States, however, with the help of G-d, political evolution has always been based on the concept of the *mishpat*, justice, or, as we prefer to call it, democracy. We refuse to recognize any concept of *g'zaira*, and we demand that all law be opened to the checks and balances of *mishpat*. However, in a democracy such as ours all is neither black nor white when viewed under a practical light. There are times when our system seems to be approaching slowly but surely the method of *g'zaira*, and then just as slowly it advances and approaches *mishpat*. In a country such as this, a minority seeking to be heard must exert its greatest influence when the country approaches the period closest to *mishpat* and furthest from *g'zaira*. This period in practical American politics is known as the election year, the year a democracy is most vulnerable. The foreign as well as domestic policies of the administration, which are treated as unquestionable *chok* during the years 1953 to 1955 suddenly become open to as much question and criticism as any other manmade *mishpat* when 1956 rolls around."

10. Maimonides, ever the man of reason, rejected this distinction and struggled mightily to come up with reasons—often farfetched—for all the rules. He argued that many of the *chukkim* grew out of God's efforts to deal with the reality of idol worship and astrology particularly by the Sabians of the time the Torah was given. See Stern, Josef, *Problems and Parables of Law* (Albany SUNY, 1998).

11. p. 15. Although Ibn Ezra may have intended this statement as something of a put-down to those nonliteralists who allow their imaginations and interpretations to wander too far from the text, I will take his invitation literally, thereby remaining true to Ibn Ezra's own canon of interpretation.

12. One rabbinic source put the number at ninety-eight (Riskin at nine, citing the Vilna Gaen). Nahama Leibowitz, a contemporary commentator, goes even further, pointing to a tradition that the facets of the Torah are infinite (*New Studies in Bereshith* 19 [Genesis]; [Ehiner, Jerusalem] xxxii). Ibn Ezra concluded, "The end of the matter is, there is no limit to Midrashic interpretation" (Ibn Ezra at p. 17). Ibn Ezra

did state, however, "The literal meaning of a verse is never negated by Midrashic interpretations," at p. 18.

13. *Midrash Rabbah*, Foreword by Rabbi Dr. I. Epstein, vol. 1, p. xi.

14. Twersky, Isadore, *A Maimonides Reader* (Behtman, 1972), p. 28.

15. Lamm, Norman, *Faith and Doubt* (New York: Ktav Publishing House, Inc., 1971), pp. 124–25.

16. Epstein, I. "The Midrash" (Foreword), in Freedman, H., *Midrash Rabbah* (Soncino: London, 1983), pp. xxi–xxii.

17. Idem at p. xxii. See also Halivni, David, *Revelation Restored* (New York: Harper & Row, 1987).

18. In the final editing phases of this book, someone brought to my attention a 1905 book by a Philadelphia lawyer named David Werner Amram, entitled *Leading Cases in the Bible* (Philadelphia: J. H. Grennstone, 1905). He makes the point that

> The Bible has been studied almost exclusively by theologians and rarely by lawyers. The fact that lawyers, or men with legal training, have not found the Bible an object worthy of their serious attention has contributed not a little to its misinterpretation and to the misconceptions that have arisen out of it. The long continued misinterpretation of the biblical records in the interest of theological dogma, falsely called religion, or of race prejudice falsely based on the science of comparative sociology, has helped to bring the Bible and biblical study into disrepute. Men of modern times who love freedom in thought and in expression—and among this class lawyers are by training and professional practice easily among the first—have revolted from the influence of dogmatic religion and its superstructure of vanity and vexation of the spirit. With this revolt has come a concomitant loss of all interest in the Bible for its own sake, as a valuable record of history, custom and law. Thus the Bible has suffered for the sins of the churches and of the official expounders of the word of God. The pages of history are overburdened with testimony showing how every villainy practiced by officialdom and hierarchy, every intolerant edict of king or prelate, every special plea for vested rights founded on class privilege, every oppression of the many by the few, has been ably defended by the official mouthpiece of many a church. And even in our own day and time we see so-called ministers of religion encouraging and supporting similar wickedness and like their forerunners appealing to the Bible has become an object of contempt, but to its adherents it has remained an object of veneration. The former class do not read it at all; the latter read it in the light of official exposition, which is quite as bad, if not worse than not reading it at all.

While much of Amram's approach is an anticlerical polemic, some of his insights on particular stories, especially Job, are interesting. See also Cover, Robert, "Nomos and Narrative," 97 *Harvard Law Review* (November 1983), who takes an entirely different view of the uses of biblical narrative in jurisprudence.

19. *Midrash Rabbah*, vol. 1, p. 60.

20. See Kellner, Menachem, *Must a Jew Believe Anything?* (London: Littman, 1999).

21. See Laytner, Anson, *Arguing with God* (Northvale, NJ: Aronson, 1990), pp. 179–96.

22. Ibn Ezra also cites a verse in Genesis that has Abraham naming a place and the Bible saying "as it is said to this day" (22:14). Rashi interprets the verse as referring to the future. Deuteronomy 3:11 also alludes to future knowledge.

23. See Richard Elliot Friedman, *Who Wrote the Bible?* (New York: Harper & Row, 1987).

24. p. 10.

25. Pope John Paul II, *The Interpretation of the Bible in the Church* (Rome: Libreria Editrice Vaticana, 1993), pp. 71–72.

26. See Friedman, *Who Wrote the Bible?* p. 247.

27. See Riskin, Shlomo, *Confessions of a Biblical Commentator* at p. 3. The Jewish scholar Emmanuel Levinas's deconstruction of talmudic texts helped pave the way for Jacques Derrida and other deconstructionists. As one scholar has written: "Levinas is . . . one of the thinkers who made Derrida and deconstruction possible" (Susan A. Handelman, *Fragments of Redemption* [Bloomington: Indiana University Press, 1991], p. 179). Derrida wrote an entire essay on Emmanuel Levinas, "Violence and Metaphysics: An Essay on the Thought of Emmanuel Levinas," in *Writing and Difference,* trans. Alan Bass (Chicago: University of Chicago Press, 1978).

28. After the completion of the Hebrew Scriptures, midrashic creation in Aggadah obtained a dominating position in the spiritual life of Jewry. For a long period it was the vehicle for Jewish ideas, thoughts, feelings, and knowledge. Among the oldest Aggadic midrashim is undoubtedly The Aggadah recited on Passover evening, which according to one authority (Finkelstein, L., *The Oldest Midrash, The Harvard Theological Review,* 1938, pp. 291 ff.) was compiled between the second half of the third century and the first half of the second century B.C.E." (Epstein at p. xii).

29. Quoted in Epstein at p. xix. The more formalized midrashic process continued "in an unbroken line from the days of Ezra [around 400 B.C.] to the 11th century" (Epstein at p. xviii). There are also the Responsa, which are recorded rabbinic answers to legal (halakic) questions over time. For a remarkable example of such literature, see Oshry, Ephraim, *Responsa from the Holocaust* (Judaica Press, 1983).

30. See Gillman, Neil, *The Death of Death* (Woodstock, Vt.: Jewish Lights, 1997), pp. 32–33.

31. Twersky at p. 44.

32. Renan, E., *Histoire du Peuple d'Israel* (1893) v, p. 321, quoted in Epstein at p. xx, n. 1. The "Church fathers fully understood the importance of the midrashic method employed with telling effect by contemporary Jewish preachers . . . , and resolved to resort to the same spiritual weapon in order to place the dogmatic system of the Church on a firm basis."

33. Kaplan, Mordechai, *Not So Random Thoughts* (New York: Reconstructionist Press, 1966), introduction.

34. Rabbi Eliexer Shakh, criticizing Rabbi Joseph Soloveitchik, as quoted in Riskin, Shlomo, *Confessions of a Biblical Commentator,* at p. 25. Riskin points out that Maimonides explicitly introduced "novel ideas" (*hidushim*) in the textual meaning of the Bible. Idem at p. 4. Most modern Orthodox authorities accept the concept of *hidushim,* at least in a limited way.

35. Quoted in Riskin at pp. 9–10. Rabbi Ashkenazi believed that such an exploration would necessarily "straighten out our faith," but he appeared willing to risk the possibility that it might lead to apostasy. See p. 10.

36. The Talmud suggests that rebellious sons are not actually executed. Rabbi Jonathan said "he had once seen such a one and sat on his grave" (Sanhedrin 71a). The Talmud itself made it virtually impossible to execute a rebellious son, since he must be thirteen years of age to bear criminal responsibility, but still young enough to be a "son" and not a man. Professor Menachem Elon views the biblical rule as "intended to limit the powers of the *paterfamilias:* the head of the household could no longer punish the defiant son himself, according to his own whim, but had to bring him before the elders (i.e., judges) for punishment. In earlier laws (e.g., Hammurapi Code nos. 168, 169) only the father had to be defied; in biblical law, it must be both father and mother." See generally, Elon, Menachem, *The Principles of Jewish Law* (Jerusalem: Encyclopaedia Judaica, 1974), p. 491.

PART II

THE
TEN STORIES

CHAPTER 1

God Threatens—and
Backs Down

YHWH, God, commanded concerning the human [Adam],
*   saying:*
From every [other] tree of the garden you may eat, yes, eat,
but from the Tree of the Knowing of Good and Evil—
you are not to eat from it
for on that day you eat from it, you must die, yes, die. . . .

GENESIS 2:16–17

Now the snake was more shrewd than all the living-things of
*   the field that YHWH, God, had made.*
It said to the woman [Eve]:
Even though God said: You are not to eat from any of the
*   trees in the garden . . . !*
The woman said to the snake:
From the fruit of the [other] trees in the garden may we eat,
but from the fruit of the tree that is in the midst of the garden,
God has said:
You are not to eat from it and you are not to touch it,
lest you die.
The snake said to the woman:

Die, you will not die!
Rather, God knows
that on the day that you eat from it, your eyes will be opened
and you will become like gods, knowing good and evil.
The woman saw that the tree was good for eating
and that it was a delight to the eyes,
and the tree was desirable to contemplate.
She took from its fruit and ate
and gave also to her husband beside her,
and he ate.
The eyes of the two of them were opened
and they knew then
that they were nude.
They sewed fig leaves together and made themselves loincloths.

Now they heard the sound of YHWH, God, [who was]
    walking about in the garden at the breezy-time of the day.
And the human and his wife hid themselves from the face of
    YHWH, God, amid the trees of the garden.
YHWH, God, called to the human and said to him:
Where are you?
He said:
I heard the sound of you in the garden and I was afraid,
    because I am nude,
and so I hid myself.
He said:
Who told you that you are nude?
From the tree about which I command you not to eat,
have you eaten?
The human said:
The woman whom you gave to be beside me, she gave me from
    the tree.
And so I ate.
YHWH, God, said to the woman:

What is this that you have done?
The woman said:
The snake enticed me,
and so I ate.
YHWH, God, said to the snake:
Because you have done this, damned be you from all the
    animals and from all the living-things of the field;
upon your belly shall you walk and dust shall you eat, all the
    days of your life.
I put enmity between you and the woman, between your seed
    and her seed:
they will bruise you on the head, you will bruise them in the
    heel.
To the woman he said:
I will multiply your pain [from] your pregnancy,
with pains shall you bear children.
Toward your husband will be your lust, yet he will rule over
    you.
To Adam he said:
Because you have hearkened to the voice of your wife
and have eaten from the tree about which I commanded you,
    saying:
You are not to eat from it!
Damned be the soil on your account,
with painstaking-labor shall you eat from it, all the days of
    your life.
Thorn and sting-shrub let it spring up for you,
when you [seek to] eat the plants of the field!
By the sweat of your brow shall you eat bread, until you
    return to the soil,
for from it you were taken.
For you are dust, and to dust shall you return. . . .

YHWH, God, said:

Here, the human has become like one of us, in knowing good
   and evil.
So now, lest he send forth his hand
and take also from the Tree of Life
and eat
and live throughout the ages . . . !
So YHWH, God, sent him away from the garden of Eden, to
   work the soil from which he had been taken.
He drove the human out
and caused to dwell, eastward of the garden of Eden,
the winged-sphinxes and the flashing, ever-turning sword
to watch over the way to the Tree of Life.[1]

GENESIS 3:1–24

It is quite remarkable that a holy book, which purports to be a guide to conduct, begins with a clear rule that is immediately disobeyed, and a specific threat of punishment which is not imposed. God's first threat to humankind is unequivocal: He tells Adam, "From the Tree of the Knowing of Good and Evil, you are not to eat from it; for on that day that you eat from it, you must die, yes, die." The use of the Hebrew *mot tamut* repeats the words "die" so there is no mistaking the certainty of the threatened punishment.[2] "Doomed to die" is perhaps the best translation.[3] The certainty of the time frame for the punishment—"on the day"—is unique in biblical threats. Normally God simply says "you will die" or "you will surely die," but He never specifies the day.[4] Yet when Eve and Adam disobey God's first prohibition, God does not carry out his explicitly threatened punishment. Indeed, the Bible says that Adam lived 930 years. The disobedient couple and their progeny were punished, but in a way very different from what God had threatened.

What are we supposed to learn from a God who fails to carry out his very first threat? Generations of commentators have tried to answer this question. Some of the defense attorneys have sidestepped its troubling implications with creative wordplay. If God's days are one thousand years long, then Adam died seventy "years" short of one such "day."[5] This would render the threatened punishment trivial, at least in comparison with what God had threatened. Others argue that God didn't really mean that Adam would actually die on the day he ate of the tree, but rather that on that day he would be *sentenced* to an eventual death—in other words, he would become mortal.[6] That is not, however, what God said and—more important—that is certainly not what Adam or Eve understood God to say. God told Adam that he "must die, yes, die" on the "day that you eat from it," and Adam told Eve that God had commanded them not to eat or even "touch" it. It is clear from the story of the serpent that Eve interpreted God's threat as immediate death. A midrash says that the serpent pushed Eve against the tree and told her: "As you did not die from touching it, so you shall not die from eating thereof."[7] The serpent was right. Eve and Adam dined on forbidden fruit and both lived long lives. Taking the serpent's lesson to its logical conclusion, it would seem that God's commands can be disobeyed with impunity. God thus showed Himself to be a parent who makes idle threats—a rather ineffective model of discipline.

Although Adam and Eve's eventual punishment was considerably more lenient than the instant death

God had threatened, it was also imposed on their descendants. Hence the Christian concept of "original sin," which brought death into the world, increased "man's inclination to evil" and required the eventual redemption of a Savior.[8] The nature of God's punishments raises profound questions—for Christians, Jews, and Muslims alike—about His concept of justice. He punishes Eve by inflicting the pain of childbirth on *all* women and by making *all* women submissive to men. He punishes Adam by requiring *all* men to toil for their bread. Finally, God also banishes Adam and Eve from the Garden of Eden in order to assure that his wayward creations do not also eat of the tree of life and "live forever."[9] All for disobeying His command to refrain from eating the forbidden fruit of a tempting tree!

If we evaluate God by human standards, His first action as a lawgiver seems unfair. The essence of fairness in any system of threats and promises is adequate warning: Punishment should be threatened in unambiguous terms, so that the people to whom the threat is directed will understand; a punishment once threatened should be imposed, unless there are mitigating circumstances; and no additional punishments, not explicitly threatened, should be tacked on. Moreover, the punishment should be limited to the specific person or persons who violated the law, not to innocent descendants. Jewish law, as it eventually developed, recognized that "to punish one person for the transgression of another" is "inconsistent with the very idea of law."[10] Finally, punishment should be proportional to the harm caused.

God, of course, constantly violates these rules throughout the Bible—He kills without warning, punishes innocent children for the sins of their parents, and imposes disproportionate punishments[11]—so we should not be surprised that He begins His career as a lawgiver in this capricious manner. Commentators make heroic efforts to rationalize these apparent violations of human norms of fairness by reading ambiguity into God's clear words. For example, many later commentators interpret God's threat to Adam as punishment in the hereafter—a common explanation whenever God threatens punishment or promises reward but fails to carry it out. But the Jewish Bible never mentions the hereafter.* God tells Adam quite directly: "You are dust and to dust shall you return."[12] It is untrue to the text of Genesis to read into punishment threatened *here* and *now* an implicit postponement to a world to come. It is also—in the spirit of the Maimonidian debate described earlier—a far less interesting answer, which obviates the need to struggle with the text. Accepting an invisible afterlife in which threatened punishments and promised rewards are meted out, as some commentators do, provides a tautological answer to all questions about injustice in this world.[13] It is far more interesting to search for enduring interpretations based on what was believed at *the time*, not centuries *later*. In the end, it is the plain meaning of a threat that is most important. No one can deny that God plainly threatened Adam with one punishment and then inflicted a quite different one on Adam, Eve, and their descendants.

Moreover, the nature of the punishment God inflicted on all women raises the most profound issues of fairness. God directly commanded Adam, not Eve,

*I will deal with these issues in some detail in Chapter 13.

33

to refrain from eating of the Tree of Knowledge. Yet it was Eve, and all future Eves, who were punished most severely, not only in absolute terms, but also relative to Adam and future Adams: "Toward your husband will be your lust, yet he will rule over you." Here we find the origin of the infamous double standard regarding sex: Women must be monogamous toward their husbands, but husbands are free to direct their lust at other unmarried women—that is, women who do not "belong" to other men. In the command that wives must be submissive to husbands, we also see the origins of misogyny.

An anthropological explanation of Eve's punishment might take the form of a "just so" story.[14] These mythological tales begin with observable phenomena—for instance, a leopard's spots or an elephant's long ears—and weave narratives that purport to "explain" them. Just as leopards always had spots and elephants long ears, so too the double standard and the submissiveness of women had long been observable realities. The punishment of Eve could be viewed as a "just so" story explaining these observable phenomena. Yet there is an obvious difference: Spots and ears are biological facts with no moral connotation, whereas the double standard and the submissiveness of wives is anything but biologically determined and morally neutral. It is prescriptive as well as descriptive of past practices that are capable of changing—unless, of course, they are deemed to be divinely ordained.

The inequality of women—a characteristic of most traditional religions and cultures—violates modern sensibilities. For that reason, contemporary religious law struggles mightily to interpret the punishment of

Eve as the decision by God to assign to women a different, but not unequal, role in the life of the family. These efforts cannot help but invoke analogies to the "separate but equal" doctrine under which blacks were segregated from whites during the Jim Crow era of American history. Just as blacks were surely separate but never equal, so too wives were assigned different roles but were never the equals of their husbands. God's own words prove this inequality beyond dispute: Your husband "will rule over you." There is nothing ambiguous—either in the original Hebrew word *yimshol* or in the English translation "rule"—about the relative status of husband and wife. He is the ruler, she the ruled. All because Eve was persuaded by the serpent to eat the forbidden fruit and then invited Adam to do likewise.

Based on this sequence of events, it is neither logical nor moral that husbands should rule over wives. Eve had a far more compelling defense than Adam. She was never told directly by God about the prohibition, and she was misinformed about its scope by Adam, who told her that God's prohibition extended beyond eating and included even *touching* the fruit. This misinformation allowed the serpent—who was "more shrewd than all the living beings of the field"— to entice Eve into sin. Indeed, a midrash cautions: "You must not make the fence [around the law] more than the principled thing, lest it fall and destroy the plants."[15] In other words, if you make prohibitions so broad they will not be enforced, the law may lose its credibility, as it did to Eve. Meanwhile, Adam—the direct recipient of God's commandment—did not need to be enticed. He was simply offered the fruit and accepted it. Eve did not compel or order Adam to eat it. She did not act as a ruler and Adam as a subject. Why then does Adam and do all future Adams get to rule over Eve and all future Eves? We are not given a good answer. By any standard of law, justice, or equity, the punishment inflicted on all women on account of Eve's sin is unfair. Nor did the punishment rationally "fit the crime." What do labor pains, lust, and subordination have to do with Eve's sin?

It is interesting to speculate what God's punishments would have been had Eve eaten the fruit but never offered it to Adam or if Adam had rejected it. (In an effort to mitigate Adam's sin, a midrash speculates that "he had engaged in his natural functions [in other words, intercourse] and then fallen asleep," so that he was not present during the serpent's conversation with Eve and presumably was unaware that the fruit given to him by Eve came from the forbidden tree.[16]) If Eve alone had eaten, she would have knowledge of good and evil, and Adam would have remained happily ignorant and immortal. Who would have ruled over whom? We will never know.

Until the twentieth century, women were legally subordinate to men in nearly all countries. Historically a wife would not sue her husband or act independently of him. As recently as 1998, the Southern Baptist Convention, the largest Protestant group in the United States, declared that a wife should "submit herself graciously" to her husband's leadership.[17] There were also some advantages growing out of such subordination. Until the nineteenth century, a wife who committed certain crimes in the presence of her husband was deemed by the common law to be acting on his behalf and at his direction. The husband, not the wife, was held responsible. God, however, did

36

not grant Eve this advantage. Clearly he regarded her as the more culpable: She was punished before Adam and more severely.[18] Even Adam's defense showed less remorse. He blamed Eve *and God* for his own sin by saying: "The woman *whom you gave to be beside me*, she gave me from the tree" (emphasis added).

Throughout the Bible we see numerous instances of women regarded as legally subordinate but psychologically dominant and manipulative, especially when such a perspective serves the interests of the patriarchal society. Nor is this inconsistency limited to biblical times. As recently as the early 1950s, Ethel Rosenberg—who played a minor role in her husband Julius's espionage—was executed because she was deemed to be the stronger of the couple emotionally. When it comes to the role of women, male-dominated societies—from biblical times to the recent past and in some places to the present—want to have it both ways. They can point to the story of Adam and Eve as support for any number of double standards. By imposing misogynistic punishments on innocent future generations—instead of carrying out the punishment He had threatened—God paved the way for an inequality that would endure for millennia.

Even had God followed through precisely on his threat to Adam, there would still be questions about God's justice. If Adam and Eve did not know the difference between good and evil *before* eating of the tree, how could they fairly be punished for being deceived by the serpent into violating God's prohibition? In most societies committed to the rule of law, the basic test of responsibility is the capacity to distinguish right from wrong. If a paranoid schizophrenic shoots a man he honestly, but mistakenly, believes is about to shoot him, he cannot be held responsible for his conduct. As Maimonides posed the question in the language of his time: "By what right or justice could God punish" if humans lacked free will?[19]

Since sin is impossible without some understanding of the difference between right and wrong—animals can't sin—eating the forbidden fruit was the *prerequisite* for all *future* sins. This may explain the word "original," as it relates to the eating of the fruit, but it still doesn't explain "sin," since before eating the fruit Adam and Eve lacked the requisite knowledge to distinguish right from wrong. They were more like intelligent dogs disobeying a trainer's command than sentient human beings making a deliberate decision to do wrong.

Maimonides addressed this conundrum directly. He believed that Adam and Eve had been endowed with basic intelligence even before God commanded them not to eat of the tree: "A command is not given to ... one lacking intelligence."[20] Maimonides believed that they lacked knowledge relating only to matters of sexuality and shame. Yet if, as Maimonides argues, they did have sufficient judgment to understand commands, were they not right to eat from the Tree of Knowledge—even in the face of God's threat? Knowledge inevitably creates the desire for greater knowledge. That is the history and destiny of humankind. The quest for knowledge can never be satisfied. Curiosity may have killed the cat, but it has been the engine of human progress. The legendary official who at the end of the nineteenth century suggested closing the patent office because everything that could be invented already had been did not understand how innovations create the need for additional innovations ad infinitum. As Ecclesiastes observed: "God made man upright, but they have sought out many inventions" (7:29). Could an omniscient God really have expected humans created in His image to be satisfied with less knowledge than they were capable of obtaining? Were Adam and Eve not justified in engaging in religious disobedience of God's command? Is not greater knowledge with mortality more valuable then ignorant immortality? Would not most intelligent beings choose what Socrates called an "examined life" with mortality over an unexamined life without end?

At a more fundamental level, it can be argued that it is the knowledge of mortality itself that is essential to understanding, in any real sense, the difference between good and evil. An immortal being, knowing that he or she will never die, does not have to make difficult choices. Everything can be made right over time. It is the knowledge of mortality—the realization that life could end at any moment—that requires constant choices. A Buddhist maxim says, "Death is the best teacher," while to Kafka, "The meaning of life is that it ends." In this respect, God's threat can be seen as self-enforcing—a prediction rather than a threat: By eating of the Tree of Knowledge, Adam and Eve *learned* that they were mortal, something animals do not comprehend. *That* was the knowledge they obtained by eating the forbidden fruit. Realizing that they could die compelled them to make choices about good and evil. As rabbis, ministers, and priests remind us at funerals—particularly those of young people who die suddenly—we must always have our moral ledgers balanced, since death may strike at any time. In the absence of death, moral choices may be postponed forever. Thus, with a single bold act of defiance, human beings learned of their mortality and realized that they faced brief and painful lives, filled with difficult choices.

Knowledge brings with it the realization that life is not Eden, that it entails pain and toil, which will continue beyond your own life to that of your children and your children's children. Nothing worth having— children, sustenance, wisdom—will come without a heavy price. These are the burdens of knowledge. How much simpler is the innocence of Eden, where ignorance is indeed bliss. As Ecclesiastes recognized: "Because I increased my knowledge, I increased my sorrow." The mid–twentieth century theologian Martin Buber takes this observation one step further. He regards God's decision to inflict mortality on human beings as an act of compassion. "Now that human beings have discovered the tensions inherent in human life, God acts to prevent 'the eons of suffering' that would result from eating of the tree of life. Hence, death."[21]

My own favorite interpretation of God's failure to carry out His first threat is that God Himself was still learning about justice and injustice. The text of Genesis supports the view of an imperfect, learning God. When He creates, He stands back in wonderment and, like a human artist looking at a canvas, observes that His creations are "good," thus implying it might have turned out otherwise. An omniscient and omnipotent God would have no need to look back at what He knows will always be perfect. Later He repents the creation of man, in effect conceding that this particular creation was not so good.[22] As we will see in subsequent narratives, this is a God capable not only of "repenting," but also of being persuaded by humans and of learning from His own divine mistakes. Perhaps He realized that He was wrong to threaten immediate death as a consequence for the desire to obtain knowledge. God should have realized that His test of Adam and Eve was really a "catch-22." Had the humans remained obedient, they would have been barely distinguishable from the beasts—hardly a fitting status for those created in God's image. By disobeying God's unfair prohibition, however, they became the original sinners whose punishment would be transmitted from generation to generation. God's first command is an example of law without reason—*chok*. God never sought to explain to Adam why he had to refrain from eating the fruit of knowledge. On the contrary, His command defies reason, since it is entirely natural for humans to seek knowledge, especially when it is so pleasant to taste and easy to secure. It is not surprising, therefore, that God's first command is disobeyed. Perhaps God learns an important lesson from His initial failure as a lawgiver: Humans are more likely to obey reasoned rules consistent with their nature than arbitrary dictates that fly in the face of everything human beings are about. Perhaps God's initial command necessarily had to be a *chok*, since humans lacked the knowledge presumed by reasoned orders. Once Adam and Eve ate of the fruit of knowledge they became subject to rule by human reason. Similarly with young children who lack reason, a parent's earliest commands must necessarily be *chukim*, which gradually evolve into *mishpatim* as children develop their ability to understand rather than simply obey. Parents are sometimes slow to recognize that reasoned orders, when age appropriate, tend to be more effective than authoritarian commands. In-

41

stead some become too comfortable with the power to issue unreasoned dictates. Martinet judges never seem to understand this reality of human nature: They become furious when people disobey their commands, even if the command itself is not substantively important. "Because *I* said so," is the common refrain. Contempt of court is the sanction for disobeying even a trivial order of a judge. I have seen judges impose harsh punishments for minor violations of their orders, citing the "majesty of the law" or "the dignity of the court." A wise judge often backs away from his initial threat, realizing that the violation does not really warrant the threatened punishment.

If God Himself realized He was wrong to threaten the harsh punishment of immediate death, then perhaps He became more understanding of the sin of Adam and Eve. I offer a contemporary midrash on this issue. A friend of mine who is a federal judge had to sentence a woman to prison on a Monday. He was bound by the sentencing guidelines that mandated imprisonment, despite the fact that she was a first-time offender whose boyfriend had enticed her to transport his drugs. On Sunday the judge was home taking care of his toddler. The judge inadvertently forgot to lock his front door and the child wandered into the street, where a truck barely missed running him over. The judge realized that he had made a terrible mistake and that he had been given a second chance. The next day he refused to sentence the woman to prison, saying that she too had made a mistake and was entitled to a second chance. Perhaps I ought not to analogize a federal judge to God, although lawyers have long joked that when God has

42

delusions of grandeur, he sometimes acts as if He were a federal judge.

God, like some parents and judges, finds it less difficult to threaten than to carry out His threats, especially one that would destroy what He created. Moreover, in the case of Adam and Eve, there was a mitigating circumstance: The serpent did, after all, beguile Eve, who in turn enticed Adam. We see here the first excuse in the Bible. There are many more to come.

Finally, maybe God realized that He was acting out of self-interest in denying to those He had created in His own image the most important aspect of that divine image, namely the continuing quest for greater knowledge. A midrash states that the serpent told Eve that God Himself "ate of this tree" and "hates to have a rival in His craft."[23] The God who threatened Adam is Himself an ever-learning God, not a statically omniscient Being Who knows everything there is to know from the very beginning. Perhaps the command to forbear from eating the forbidden fruit was a test of Adam and Eve's willingness to obtain knowledge even if it required transgression. Recall that God gave Adam and Eve an opportunity to explain their actions before imposing punishment: "What is this that you have done?" Some commentators point to this to support the idea that every person has the right to a defense. A midrash, however, notes that the serpent was given no opportunity to defend his actions and from this concludes that the wicked deserve no defense. Since "the wicked are good debaters," the serpent would have argued: "Thou didst give them a command, and I did contradict it. Why did they obey me, and not Thee? Therefore God did not enter into argument

43

with the serpent."[24] Not a particularly compelling point, since the midrash seems to assume that God would lose the argument to a snake! I guess even the writers of this midrash had some doubts about God's omniscience.

In any event, if Adam and Eve had explained that they believed themselves entitled to knowledge, even at the risk of disobeying their Creator, God might have responded differently—perhaps more leniently, perhaps more harshly—to a principled act of disobedience. I recall a case at Harvard where a student altered his transcript in order to be admitted, claiming that he wanted to obtain the knowledge that comes with a Harvard education. The administration board was not sympathetic to his argument.

The novelist Philip Roth wrote that "without transgression there is no knowledge"—suggesting that all true knowledge requires rule breaking.[25] Perhaps God was simply warning human beings of the double-edged nature of knowledge and of its potential—if misused—to destroy humankind. Maybe God decided to wait and see what Adam and Eve—and their descendants—*did* with that knowledge: whether they used it for good or for evil. Only then could God decide whether or not Adam and Eve did the right thing or—if they did the wrong thing—how serious their crime was and whether His initial punishments were sufficient. We know from contemporary experiences that knowledge itself is neutral, whether it be knowledge of nuclear physics, genetic engineering, computer science, or anything else. It is how we use this knowledge that really matters.

The subsequent story of the Tower of Babel supports this interpretation. God saw nothing wrong with all people speaking the same language—and thus increasing their knowledge by communication—until they misused this important tool by working together to build a tower that reached the heavens. The midrash says that "the enterprise [of building the tower] was neither more nor less than rebellion against God."[26] It was only then that God confounded their language, thus reducing their ability to share knowledge.

As the builders of Babel learned, humans must not use their knowledge to break down the barriers between man and God. Adam and Eve were expelled from Eden to prevent them from becoming like God—knowledgeable *and* immortal. In building the Tower of Babel, their descendants were once again seeking to use their knowledge to close the distance between the human and the divine by ascending to the heavens. They were trying to circumvent God's decision to deny humans access both to the Tree of Knowledge and the Tree of Eternal Life. God responded by making the sharing of information more difficult. From now on human beings would speak different languages, not only making the gathering of knowledge a slower process, but allowing wisdom—which takes longer to acquire—to accompany knowledge.

The story of the Tower of Babel can be seen therefore as a parallel to the story of the forbidden fruit. Both involve the inherent human need to increase knowledge. In both instances humans push the envelope beyond the boundaries acceptable to God. The consequences in each case can be viewed as self-fulfilling prophecy: Now that Adam and Eve have eaten from the Tree of Knowledge, humans have the intelligence necessary to improve or destroy the world.

So too with the tower builders and their descendants: If they use their collective intelligence without foresight, wisdom, and moral constraint, they may well succeed in producing apocalypse, thus merging our earthly world with God's heavenly domain.

For whatever reasons God decided not to punish Adam and Eve with the instant death He had expressly threatened, He conveyed a confusing message to future sinners. One of the insights Adam and Eve gained from eating of the tree is that God does not always carry out His threats—that sin (and crime) is not always followed by the threatened punishment. Such knowledge can be quite dangerous.[27] The serpent told them God was bluffing, they called God's bluff, and God backed down—at least to the degree that He did not kill them immediately. No wonder God did not want them to gain this knowledge. He would henceforth have a hard time enforcing His commandments. In fact, God's mixed message about the wages of sin may well have contributed to the Bible's first murder.

---

1. This and all quotations from Genesis are taken from *The Five Books of Moses*, trans. Everett Fox (New York: Schocken Books, 1995).

Genesis 2:16–17. The Bible begins with creation, and man appears only on the sixth day. Many midrashim have been written about the first five days, but there is a tradition prohibiting speculation on what came before "the beginning." "You may speculate from the day that days were created, but you may not speculate on what was before that" (*Midrash Rabbah*, vol. 1, p. 9). In support of this view, it is observed that the first letter of the Bible is a *beth*—the Hebrew equivalent of "b" or "beta"—whose shape is open in the front and closed at the back, thereby signifying open inquiry about what happens after creation but a closing of all inquiry as to what took place before. Notwithstanding this tradition, there has always been speculation as to the universe *b'terem kol*—before everything.

2. A midrash interprets the repetition of "die" to mean that not only would Adam die, but his descendants would also die (*Midrash Rabbah*, vol. 1, p. 131).

3. *"surely eat . . . doomed to die.* The form of the Hebrew in both instances is what grammarians call the infinitive absolute: the infinitive immediately followed by a conjugated form of the same verb. The general effect of this repetition is to add emphasis to the verb, but because in the case of the verb 'to die' it is the pattern regularly used in the Bible, for the issuing of death sentences, 'doomed to die' is an appropriate equivalent" (Robert Alter, *Genesis,* p. 8, notes 16–17).

4. In I Kings 2:42 Solomon says to Shimei that "on the day thou goest out [of Jerusalem] thou shalt surely die."

5. *Midrash Rabbah,* vol. 1, p. 154.

6. See Kugel, James, *The Bible As It Was* (Cambridge: Harvard University Press, 1997), pp. 67–71; and Ramban, *Commentary on the Torah, Genesis* (New York: Shilo, 1971), p. 74. Rashi avoids the issue.

7. See Rashi and also *Midrash Rabbah,* vol. 1, p. 150. Ginzberg, p. 72, A Midrash asks where Adam was during this conversation. It answers: "He had engaged in intercourse and fallen asleep."

8. *The New Catholic Encyclopedia,* p. 779; *The New Schaff-Herzog Encyclopedia of Religious Knowledge,* p. 443.

9. This banishment also seems to contradict the notion that Adam and Eve were originally created to be immortal and that God carried out his threat of death by denying them eternal life as a punishment for disobeying his prohibition against eating of the Tree of Knowledge.

10. Elon, Menachem, *Jewish Law* (New York: Matthew Bender, 1999) at pp. 175–76.

11. He kills Nadav and Avihu without fair warning. He punishes Moses without fair warning. Moreover, in the Ten Commandments He is explicit that His punishments will be imposed on the innocent children, grandchildren, great-grandchildren, and even great-great-grandchildren of sinners (Exodus 20:5).

12. Rabbi Simon ben Yochai manages to find a "hint" of the hereafter even in this verse, interpreting "return" to mean "thou shalt go to the dust, yet thou shalt return—at the resurrection" (*Midrash Rabbah,* vol. 1, p. 169).

13. See Chapter 13. p. tk

14. See Amram at p. 21.

15. *Midrash Rabbah,* vol. 1, p. 150.

16. *Midrash Rabbah* (Bereshith, p. 149).

17. *New York Times,* June 10, 1998, p. 1.

18. See Amram at pp. 28–29.

19. Twersky at p. 78.

20. See Twersky at p. 250. A midrash speculates that Eve was Adam's second wife. His first, Lilith, "remained with him only a short time because she insisted upon enjoying full equality with her husband" (Ginzberg at p. 65). Recently a fundamentalist Christian publication, published by Jerry Falwell, condemned the use of the name *Lilith* by a concert organizer, arguing that Lilith was a "demon." See *Boston Globe,* June 25, 1999, p. A23.

21. Quoted in Gillman at p. 44.

22. 6:6.

23. Bialik and Ravnitsky, *The Book of Legends,* p. 20.

24. Ginzberg, p. 77.

25. Roth, Philip, *American Pastoral.*

26. Ginzberg at p. 179.

27. The knowledge that sin is not always followed by punishment can also be uplifting, allowing people to refrain from sinful acts simply because they are wrong. See pp. 108–9.

CHAPTER 2

Cain Murders—and Walks

It was, after the passing of days
that Kayin [Hebrew for Cain] brought, from the fruit of the
* soil, a gift to YHWH [Hebrew for God],*
and as for Hevel [Hebrew for Abel], he too brought—from the
* firstborn of his flock, from their fat-parts.*
YHWH had regard for Hevel and his gift,
for Kayin and his gift he had no regard.
Kayin became exceedingly upset and his face fell.
YHWH said to Kayin:
Why are you so upset? Why has your face fallen?
It is not thus:
If you intend good, bear-it-aloft,
but if you do not intend good,
at the entrance is sin, a crouching demon,
toward you his lust—
but you can rule over him.

But then it was, when they were out in the field
that Kayin rose up against Hevel his brother
and he killed him.
YHWH said to Kayin:
Where is Hevel your brother?
He said:

I do not know. Am I the watcher of my brother?
Now he said:
What have you done!
A sound—your brother's blood cries out to me from the soil!
And now,
damned be you from the soil,
which opened up its mouth to receive your brother's blood from
*   your hand.*
When you wish to work the soil
it will not henceforth give its strength to you;
wavering and wandering must you be on earth!
Kayin said to YHWH:
My iniquity is too great to be borne!
Here, you drive me away today from the face of the soil,
and from your face must I conceal myself,
I must be wavering and wandering the earth—
now it will be
that whoever comes upon me will kill me!
YHWH said to him:
No, therefore,
whoever kills Kayin, sevenfold will it be avenged!
So YHWH set a sign for Kayin,
so that whoever came upon him would not strike him down.
Kayin went out from the face of YHWH
and settled in the land of Nod/Wandering, east of Eden.

Kayin knew his wife;
She became pregnant and bore Hanokh.
Now he became the builder of a city
and called the city's name according to his son's name,
*   Hanokh.*

GENESIS 4:3–17

49

The Bible's first sin seems trivial to the secular mind, especially in light of the threatened punishment. Eating forbidden fruit is, at worst, a sacred misdemeanor, much like a Jew eating unkosher food or a Catholic eating meat on Friday—when that prohibition was still on the books. I am reminded of a *New Yorker* cartoon following the Catholic Church's change of position on this issue. An assistant devil asks Satan: "Now what do we do with all the people who are here for eating meat on Friday?" The essence of the crime of eating forbidden food is disobeying God's command, not the inherent nature of the substantive violation. A midrash characterizes the first sin as "violating a light command,"[1] though Christianity regards it as original sin.

The second sin, however, was an aggravated felony by any standard. Cain murdered his younger brother and then tried to cover it up. His motive was petty jealousy over God's unexplained preference for Abel's offering. Yet despite the severity of his crime, God is relatively soft on Cain. God does not impose proportional punishment. Instead He makes him a fugitive and a wanderer. Being excluded from the clan could, of course, carry serious consequences in primitive society, since it returned the excluded person to the state of nature and exposed him to the elements as well as the animals. (This may explain Rashi's interpretation of "the mark of Cain" as restoring the fear of Cain in animals.) Even in early England, being denied the protection of the "king's peace" was dangerous. But at least there was a chance of survival by the resourceful outsider. It was not capital punishment.

Like most criminal defendants, Cain whines about his sentence: "My iniquity is too great to be borne!"

(The Hebrew word is *avoni,* which has been variously translated as "my sin," "my punishment," and "my iniquity.") Cain expresses fear that he in turn will be murdered. God further softens his punishment by setting a sign on him, warning all that Cain is in God's witness protection program, and if anyone kills him, "vengeance shall be taken on him sevenfold." Yet another unjust threat of disproportionate punishment! Hasn't God learned anything from the failure of his first threat? Interestingly, the commentators generally reject the plain meaning of the threatened punishment against anyone inclined to kill Cain: "The verse does not mean that God will punish him seven times as much as he deserves, for God is just and does not punish unfairly." This is a remarkable view for several reasons. First, how can anyone say that God never imposes more punishment than an individual deserves? The Bible is full of examples of excessive and unjust punishment—at least by human standards. In this case, the wrongdoer would at least have been warned of the sevenfold punishment—whatever sevenfold might mean in the context of killing another![2] In other instances God punishes with no warning.

Why then is God so much more sympathetic to Cain—who knew the difference between right and wrong, who killed for a trivial reason, and who then tried to cover up his murder—than he was to Adam and Eve—who did not know right from wrong, who were tricked into committing a victimless crime, and who admitted their violation (though blamed it on others)?

Some commentators have observed that God Himself may have been partly to blame for Cain's crime. By denigrating Cain's offering, God provoked the young man's anger. Simeon ben Yochai translated God's words to Cain as "the voice of thy brother's blood cries out *against me* from the ground." This "seems to regard Cain and Abel as two gladiators, wrestling in the King's presence [and] if the King desires it, he may separate them," or he may allow one to kill the other by ignoring his plea. According to this interpretation, God heard Abel's cry and did not intercede. Thus He is partially responsible for the resulting tragedy.[3] A rabbinic Aggadah has Cain saying to God, "There is neither justice nor judge" in the world.[4] In effect, Cain is accusing God of having provoked him into fratricide. A contemporary observer makes a similar point: "In this story, God behaves like the most inept of parents."[5]

If God's action and inaction provoked Cain into killing Abel, then it becomes understandable why God would mitigate Cain's punishment. Provocation has traditionally been recognized as a mitigating consideration, though the victim is generally the provocateur.

Other commentators have argued that the sin of Adam and Eve was worse than the crime of Cain, because they violated a direct command from God, while Cain's murder preceded any commandment against killing. As a midrash put it: "Cain slew, but had none from whom to learn [the enormity of his crime]."[6] Another midrash elaborates on this excuse, suggesting that Cain offered the following defense: I had never seen a man killed, so how was I to know that the stones I threw at Abel would take his life?[7] This defense is an early variant on what eventually became the McNaughton rule of legal insanity, which exculpates a person who does not understand "the nature and quality" of his act or know that it is "wrong." A mentally retarded man who squeezes a child in order to show affection is not held responsible for murder if the child dies.

There are several problems with this argument. First, the legacy left to Cain by his parents included knowledge of right and wrong, and anyone with such knowledge understands it is wrong to murder. We refer to crimes such as murder as *malum in se*—wrong in themselves, inherently wrong. No criminal statute is required to tell a civilized person that it is wrong to kill. Eating a prohibited fruit, on the other hand, is the kind of crime we call *malum prohibitum*—a crime only because it is prohibited by law. Second, anyone who has had experience with animals understands death, and Cain knew that his brother had sacrificed animals. Third, recall Cain's famous answer to God—"Am I my brother's keeper?" (or in the translation we are using: "Am I the watcher of my brother?"). In addition to originating the great tradition of answering a question with another question, its substance suggests that Cain realized he had done something so terrible that he would deny it even to God. Fourth, Abel's blood cried out "from the soil," suggesting that Cain buried his brother after killing him—an act that indicates he both understood the finality of death and attempted to conceal the evidence. Fifth, the Bible uses the plural of blood, *d'mai*, in describing what was crying out. This led some commentators to conclude that Cain had inflicted multiple wounds on Abel to assure he would die. Finally, God did warn Abel, though not specifically about murder. After rejecting Cain's offering, but before the killing, He asked the disgruntled young man, "Why are you so upset? Why has your face fallen?" Then He admonished Cain, "If you intend good, bear-it-aloft, but if you do not intend good, at the entrance is sin, a crouching demon, toward you his lust—but you can rule over him."

This phrase has been interpreted as God's warning to human beings that despite *His* omniscience, *we* have free will. We can rule over our evil inclinations. A midrash relates the following story to illustrate free will: A man encounters a hunter holding a bird in his hand. The hunter asks the man to guess—at the peril of his own life—whether the bird is alive or dead. The bird is alive, but if the man says it is alive, the hunter will suffocate it by simply keeping it cupped in his hand for a moment. If the man guesses it is dead, he will open his hand and allow it to fly away. The man answers the hunter by saying, "Its life and death are in your hands."[8]

Like the hunter, Cain had free will as to whether his brother would live or die. God had cautioned him to rule over his demons, but Cain succumbed to sin and murdered his brother. Rashi interprets God's reference to "the entrance" as meaning "the entrance of your grave." Yet he does not ask why God spared Cain the punishment of death. Rashi does raise the intriguing question of why Cain was afraid of being slain, since there were not yet people in the world, other than Adam and Eve—and he certainly did not fear that his own mother and father would kill him. This begs the even larger question concerning the absence of other people who would make procreation possible. The Bible says, "And Cain knew his wife, and she conceived." Most of the traditional commentators simply avoid this inconvenient question, as I painfully learned in my days at the yeshiva. This has led skeptics—such as the lawyer Clarence Darrow in the famous Scopes "monkey" trial—to mock the Bible for its inconsistency. I remember feeling somewhat vindicated when I saw the play *Inherit the Wind* and watched Clarence Darrow cross-examine William Jennings Bryan about "where Cain got his wife."[9] Some traditional commentators note that the text of the Bible does not purport to render a complete history; the oral tradition amplifies the text and provides answers to such questions.

We are still left wondering why God is so soft on Cain's murder of Abel. Does He not value human life more than the fruit of a tree—or even compliance with His unexplained prohibitions? This seems unlikely, since biblical and midrashic tradition tend to value human life greatly, recognizing that when a person, especially one still capable of having children, is killed, so too are all of his or her potential descendants. According to a midrash, God says to Cain, "The voice of thy brother's blood . . . cries out . . . , and likewise the blood of all the pious who might have sprung from the loins of Abel."[10] The talmudic principle "He who kills a single human being, it is as if he has destroyed the entire world" grows directly out of the Cain and Abel narrative.[11] Those who engage in genocide do so with the goal of preventing future generations. It is impossible to comprehend what was lost in the Holocaust or any other mass murder—how many of those killed might have saved the lives of countless others by, for example, discovering cures for diseases? Even the cost of one killing is incalculable.

One resolution of the apparent conflict between God's soft punishment of Cain and the Bible's high regard for life is the possibility that the murder by Cain of Abel was the punishment inflicted *on* Adam and Eve for their sin. For a parent, there is no greater tragedy than having one child murder another. An intriguing midrash elaborates on the impact of the son's actions on their parents. The text says that Cain "rose up" (*va'yyakom*) against Abel, thus implying that Cain "lay beneath" Abel and was forced to defend himself against his stronger brother. A midrash infers that the brothers were engaged in a "legal argument" and that Cain saved himself from Abel's anger by importuning his brother to spare him on account of their parents: "We two only are in the world: what will you go and tell our father [if you kill me]?" Abel was "filled with pity" and let him go, whereupon the ungrateful Cain "rose up and killed" Abel. Rabbi Yochanan derives from this midrash the proverb: "Do not do good to an evil man, then evil will not befall you."[12]

Some commentators expressed concern that Cain's lenient punishment would fail to deter potential killers from acting on their own evil impulses, especially since Cain eventually becomes "the builder of a city." Crime seems to pay in the early biblical world. Consequently some commentators saw the need to create fantastic midrashim describing the horrible, if delayed, punishment visited upon Cain and his descendants. The most extreme is the following tale of divine retribution:

> The end of Cain overtook him in the seventh generation of men, and it was inflicted upon him by the hand of his great-grandson Lamech. This Lamech was blind, and when he went a-hunting, he was led by his young son, who would apprise his father when game came in sight, and Lamech would then shoot at it with his bow and arrow. Once upon a time he and

his son went on the chase, and the lad discerned something horned in the distance. He
naturally took it to be a beast of one kind or
another, and he told the blind Lamech to let
his arrow fly. The air was good, and the quarry
dropped to the ground. When they came close
to the victim, the lad exclaimed: "Father, thou
hast killed something that resembles a human
being in all respects, except it carries a horn on
its forehead!" Lamech knew at once what had
happened—he had killed his ancestor Cain,
who had been marked by God with a horn. In
despair he smote his hands together, inadvertently killing his son as he clasped them. Misfortune still followed upon misfortune. The
earth opened her mouth and swallowed up the
four generations sprung from Cain—Enoch,
Irad, Mehujael, and Methushael. Lamech,
sightless as he was, could not go home; he had
to remain by the side of Cain's corpse and his
son's. Toward evening, his wives, seeking him,
found him there. When they heard what he had
done, they wanted to separate from him, all the
more as they knew that whoever was descended
from Cain was doomed to annihilation. But
Lamech argued, "If Cain, who committed of
malice aforethought, was punished only in the
seventh generation, then I, who had no intention of killing a human being, may hope that
retribution will be averted for seventy and
seven generation." With his wives, Lamech re-
paired to Adam, who heard both parties, and
decided the case [for separation brought by the
wives] in favor of Lamech."[13]

This midrash reminds me of the old Hays Office, which used to censor any motion picture that failed to show crime followed by appropriate punishment.[14] Life, however, is often more like modern films, such as *Primal Fear* and *Sleepers*, in which the criminal gets away with it. Woody Allen's 1989 masterpiece *Crimes and Misdemeanors* wonderfully captures the frequent asymmetry between crime and punishment—a reality that Genesis recognizes but the midrashic commentators often seek to deny.

Soon after Cain killed his brother, God "repented" over His creation of human beings because they were so awful. No wonder! God was not doing a very good job deterring crime. He was sending conflicting messages about the consequences of sin. He was allowing humans to get away with murder! It is not surprising, therefore, that "the Lord saw that the wickedness of man was great in the earth." The system of divine rewards and punishment was not working. The crime rate was skyrocketing. It was time for God to get tough.

---

1. Ginzberg, vol. 2, p. 49.
2. *The Torah with Rashi*, Sapirstein edition (Art Scroll, Mesorah, 1995), p. 45, fn 5. Quoting Gur Aryeh; Leket Bahir.
3. *Midrash Rabbah* (Bereshith), p. 189.
4. Quoted in Armstrong, Karen, *In the Beginning* (New York: Ballantine, 1996), p. 36. Ironically, these are the same words attributed to Rabbi Elisha; see p. 235.
5. Armstrong at p. 36.
6. *Midrash Rabbah*, vol. 1, p. 191.
7. Ginzberg at p. 110.
8. A shorter variant of this story can be found in *Midrash Rabbah*, vol. 1, p. 157.
9. *The Scopes Trial*, Notable Trials Library (1990), p. 302.
10. Ginzberg at p. 110.
11. The Mishnah derives this principle directly from the language of the Cain and Abel narrative:

[I]n capital cases, his [the executed person's] blood and the blood of his [eventual] posterity lie at his door until the end of the world, for thus have we found in the case of Cain who slew his brother, as it is said, "thy brother's blood [Hebrew word *damin*] crieth"—it does not say "thy brother's blood [*dam*—singular]" but "thy brother's bloods [*damin*—plural]," thus indicating both his blood and the blood of his succeeding generations. . . . Therefore was a single man only created to teach you that if anyone destroy a single soul from the children of man, Scripture charges him as though he had destroyed a whole world. . . . (Mishna Sanhedrin 4:5)

12. *Midrash Rabbah*, vol. 1, p. 187. If the fight began as a legal argument and then escalated into a murderous brawl, the legal consequences might be complex. A litigant who takes the law into his own hands by starting a fight may still be able to raise a self-defense claim if his opponent's response is disproportionate. Perhaps the complexity of the matter, which is barely hinted at in the text, explains God's relative leniency toward Cain.

13. Ginzberg, pp. 116–17.

14. The Hays Office, which was created in 1922 by movie industry moguls to help prevent government censorship of motion pictures, imposed a self-regulating "Production Code." The code's specific rules included

I. CRIMES AGAINST THE LAW

These shall never be presented in such a way as to throw sympathy with the crime as against law and justice or to inspire others with a desire for imitation.

1. Murder

a. The technique of murder must be presented in a way that will not inspire imitation. . . .

c. Revenge in modern times shall not be justified.

The code was accompanied by an official list of "Reasons," which explained:

The treatment of crimes against the law must not . . .

2. *Inspire potential criminals* with a desire for imitation.

3. *Make criminals seem heroic* and justified.

Revenge in modern times shall not be justified. In lands and ages of less developed civilization and moral principles, revenge may sometimes be presented. This would be the case especially in places where no law exists to cover the crime because of which revenge is committed.

See Moley, Raymond, *The Hays Office* (New York: The Bobbs-Merrill Company, 1945), at pp. 241–48 (emphasis in original).

CHAPTER 3

———

God Overreacts—and
Floods the World

Now it was when humans first became many on the face of the
*   soil*
and women were born to them,
that the divine beings saw how beautiful the human women
*   were,*
so they took themselves wives, whomever they chose.

YHWH said:
My rushing-spirit shall not remain in humankind for ages, for
*   they too are flesh;*
let their days be then a hundred and twenty years!
The giants were on earth in those days,
and afterward as well,
when the divine beings came in to the human women
and they bore them [children]—
they were the heroes who were of former ages, the men of name.

Now YHWH saw
that great was humankind's evildoing on earth
and every form of their heart's planning was only evil all the
*   day.*

God Overreacts—and Floods the World

Then YHWH was sorry
that he had made humankind on earth,
and it pained his heart.
YHWH said:
I will blot out humankind, whom I have created, from the face
*   of the soil,*
from man to beast, to crawling thing and to the fowl of the
*   heavens,*
for I am sorry that I made them.
But Noah found favor in the eyes of YHWH.
[God then flooded the world for forty days]

GENESIS 6:1–8

Now God blessed Noah and his sons and said to them:
Bear fruit and be many and fill the earth!
Fear-of-you, dread-of-you shall be upon all the wildlife of the
*   earth and upon all the fowl of the heavens,*
all that crawls on the soil and all the fish of the sea—
into your hands they are given.
All things crawling about that live, for you shall they be, for
*   eating,*
as with the green plants, I now give you all.
However: flesh with its life, its blood, you are not to eat!
However, too: for your blood, of your own lives, I will
*   demand-satisfaction—*
from all wild-animals I will demand it,
and from humankind, from every man regarding his brother,
demand-satisfaction for human life.

Whoever now sheds human blood,
for that human shall his blood be shed,
for in God's image he made humankind.

61

*As for you—bear fruit and be many, swarm on earth and be-
come many on it!*
God said to Noah and to his sons with him, saying:
*As for me—here, I am about to establish my covenant with
you and with your seed after you,*
*and with all living beings that are with you: fowl, herd-ani-
mals, and all the wildlife of the earth with you;*
*all those going out of the Ark, of all the living-things of the
earth.*
I will establish my covenant with you:
All flesh shall never be cut off again by waters of the Deluge,
Never again shall there be Deluge, to bring earth to ruin!

GENESIS 9:1–11

Like most rulers who are soft on crime and unhappy
with the results, God overreacted and swung the pendulum in the opposite direction. We have seen this
happen repeatedly in our own world: In the 1960s enforcement of drug laws was lax; the death penalty
seemed a relic of the past; prison terms for violent
crimes were shrinking. Then the public and politicians began to rail against rising crime rates. The response was draconian drug laws, dramatic increases in
capital punishment, and an exploding prison popula-
tion. In the early days of humankind God too saw
"evildoing." His response was to be "sorry" that He
made human beings—in the words of our translation—
and to kill everyone in the world, except for one family, that of the righteous Noah.

Before we get to the injustice of such mass murder, we should pause to consider the concept of a God
who is "sorry" about or "repents" His own creation,
because He is surprised at what those He created are

62

doing. The midrash describes God declaring that the creation of humans out of earthly elements was "a regrettable error on My part."[1] Quite an admission for a God! Can such a God be omniscient?[2] If so, He should have known what He was doing when He created man whose "every form of their heart's planning was only evil all the day." A midrash compares God to a baker who has made bad dough: "How wretched must be the dough when the baker himself testifies it to be poor." Another analogizes God to a planter of trees who knows that someday, he will have to cut them down. But God is not a fallible baker. Nor are people trees. God is supposed to be omnipotent and omniscient. Yet even He was surprised by the human capacity for evil and thus decided to destroy not only all the people He created, but also all the animals, birds, and fish.[3] God's fit of pique seems more characteristic of an adolescent in a schoolyard who not only quits a basketball game when he's losing, but takes the ball home as well. In this case, however, God was playing with more than a basketball, and creators do not simply have the right to destroy the human life they have created. Parents may not kill their children just because they turn out bad. A just being can't destroy and start from scratch, even if He is God. Saving one family doesn't solve the moral problem. God would seem to have been obligated to work with what He had created. Yet the Bible makes no reference to any ameliorative steps God might have taken in an effort to improve human beings before killing them all. Maybe a code of laws. Perhaps a few examples of proportional public punishment. God could at least have tried something more humane before He lashed out so promiscuously at all living beings. But no. God moved directly from inconsistent and infrequent punishment to total destruction, thus setting a terrible example for lawmakers that has, unfortunately, been followed throughout history.

What is the message we are supposed to take from this display of naked, uncalibrated power? We know that God is capable of bringing floods—any second-rate God can do *that!* But why is this God incapable of a rational, proportional, and individual response to evil? Why must He destroy with so broad a brush? There are few satisfying responses to this question among the commentators.

Again, there is the "just so" story explanation: There may actually have been a flood in the Near East that wiped out much of human and animal life in the region. Many ancient cultures include accounts of a huge and destructive flood.[4] This terrible event became part of the consciousness and tradition of the biblical writers. A religious explanation was necessary; hence the story of Noah's Ark. As anthropological history, this sort of folktale is understandable. As part of a narrative of divine justice, it cries out for further normative explication.

The traditional commentators focused on several possible justifications: first, the flood was delayed punishment for Cain's murder of Abel. If so, such a punishment would truly be unjust, for the guilty murderer himself becomes a builder of cities and is allowed to live a long, successful life, while his descendants—the innocent along with the guilty—are killed en masse several generations later. Second, there was what can best be characterized as the "eugenics" argument, namely that "the divine beings"—whoever they were—had taken "the human women" as wives and procreated with them. There is also a reference to "the giants" (*nephilim*) who were on the earth in these days. Some have speculated—despite any scientific support—that this bizarre reference may represent a deep, past, collective memory of a time when early *Homo sapiens* roamed the earth alongside late Neanderthal man or other primitive beings. In any event, God needed to "cleanse" the earth of such overpowering hybrids, if humanity was to thrive. Any such eugenic solution obviously required the destruction of innocent babies along with guilty adults, but it sounds indefensible to the contemporary ear.

A midrash analogizes the flood to a natural "epidemic [which] visits the world [and] which slays both good and bad."[5] But the flood was not an epidemic; it was a deliberate punishment inflicted by God.[6] Some commentators claim that God did, in fact, give the people a warning and an opportunity to repent. According to this interpretation, God's reference to the days of man being 120 years is a veiled threat: Humans have 120 years to shape up or God will destroy them. A variation on this argument holds that Noah tried to get his fellow humans to stop their violence. Only when he failed did God carry through with His threat to "blot out humankind."

The defense lawyer commentators reject the possibility that God's destruction of the entire world was unjust. God's justice is a constant with these commentators; everything else is variable.[7] But the God of the Jewish Bible is a *learning* God as well as a *teaching* God, and perhaps He was wrong in flooding the world. He seemed to have acknowledged His error by "repenting" his decision to destroy the world just as He had earlier "repented" His decision to create man.

When God made His covenant with Noah after the flood, He promised never again to bring any floods to destroy the world. Yet He knew that people would turn bad again. Indeed, He expressly promises never to "curse the soil again on humankind's account, since what the human heart forms is evil from its youth" (8:21). Nevertheless, He absolutely precluded Himself from bringing another flood. This certainty suggests that God may have realized He made a mistake, one He did not want to repeat. When God saw how evil man could be, He had a shock of self-realization: He had created this evil creature in His very own image, so maybe *He too* has the capacity to do evil—a capacity He must learn to control. Like a person who understands that he needs to make a public promise in order to control his destructive instinct, God bound Himself never to flood the earth again. Even God needs rules.

After the flood God did what He should have done *before* He killed everybody: He enacted a code of laws that explicitly punished murder by death. "Whoever now sheds blood, for that human shall his blood be shed." By doing so, God recognized that the evil inclinations of human beings can be controlled, or at least in part by law. From now on God would deal with evil in a more calibrated and individualized manner, rather than by indiscriminate destruction. Moreover, His laws would grow out of the experiences of both man and God, rather than mere fiat. Man would now understand the need for law, as a result of seeing the consequences of lawlessness.

The image of a God who teaches not only by His successes but also by His failures is an appealing one. Every good teacher knows that acknowledging mistakes

66

and learning from them is an excellent pedagogical technique—better in many respects than pretending to be all-knowing or perfect. In my initial year as an assistant professor, I asked a first-semester student a question about a judge's instructions to the jury in a case we were studying. He gave me a perplexed look and stammered unresponsively. I then realized that I had made a mistake in framing the question—I had assumed the case had been tried to a jury, when in reality it had been tried to a judge. I immediately acknowledged my faux pas. From that point on, the class was much more relaxed and open. Students were more willing to risk being wrong now that their professor had acknowledged making a mistake. For several years thereafter I deliberately repeated my mistake.

An important part of the wonder of the Jewish Bible, and especially of Genesis, is the imperfection of every character in the drama, including the One who plays the leading role. The Jewish God is great and powerful, but even He is not perfect—at least not in the beginning.

For those who believe that God must be perfect, there is a religiously correct variation on this argument: The perfect God understands that in order to be a good teacher, He must *appear* to humans to be an imperfect, learning God, open to mistake, argument, persuasion, and repentance. So He speaks in the language of man, "repenting" His creation.[8] We will soon see that He is willing to argue with a mere mortal and even be bested in debate with His creatures. A God who can admit that His mind has been changed by mere humans is a truly great teacher. Those of us who try to be good teachers can learn a great deal about pedagogy from the ever-learning God of Genesis.

The story of the flood, therefore, is the story of God's overreaction to evil; His failure to deal with it in a just manner; His eventual realization that He did wrong; His promise not to make the same mistake twice; and His enactment of a legal code to punish individual wrongdoing. Indeed, God's learning—and teaching—process continues in the next episode of the Bible, when God seems to backslide and Abraham teaches Him an important lesson about the individualization of justice. The teacher becomes the student and the student the teacher. After all, somebody had to straighten God out about justice before matters really got out of hand.

---

1. *Midrash Rabbah*, vol. 1, p. 221.

2. This question is raised in the midrash by a Gentile and answered evasively. *Midrash Rabbah*, vol. 1, p. 222.

3. The midrash justifies even the killing of the animals on the ground that they too had engaged in copulation with different species. *Midrash Rabbah*, vol. 1, p. 228.

4. The Akkadian and Babylonian civilizations also depict a great flood in their respective histories. *Oxford Dictionary of World Religions* (New York: Oxford University Press, 1997), p. 349.

5. *Midrash Rabbah*, vol. 1, p. 214.

6. A divine punishment can, of course, take the form of an epidemic or plague, as it did in Pharaoh's day. But if it were punishment, as distinguished from a natural phenomenon, it would raise the same moral questions. The flood, as deliberate punishment, is indistinguishable from the fire and brimstone threatened against Sodom and Gomorrah that Abraham protested. God did not make any analogy to an epidemic in that instance. He acknowledged that it would be unjust to sweep away the innocent along with the guilty.

7. Compare Rabbi Levi Isaac of Berditchev. There is also a tradition suggesting that Noah was wrong for not arguing with God—as Abraham subsequently did—about his plans to destroy the world. Bodoff, Lippman, "The Real Test of the Akedah: Blind Obedience Versus Moral Choice," *Judaism* 42 (winter 1993): 74–75.

8. In the Book of Job, God says that Satan "incited Him against Job." Maimonides interprets this divine variation on "The Devil made me do it" excuse—as another example of God speaking in the language of man. See Job 2:3–5, Art Scroll edition, Miesorah Publications (New York, 1994), pp. 22–23.

CHAPTER 4

Abraham Defends the Guilty— and Loses

Now YHWH had said to himself:
Shall I cover up from Avraham [Hebrew for Abraham] what
I am about to do? For
Avraham is to become, yes, become a great nation and
mighty [in number],
and all the nations of the earth will find blessing through him.
Indeed, I have known him,
in order that he may charge his sons and his household after
him:
they shall keep the way of YHWH,
to do what is right and just,
in order that YHWH may bring upon Avraham what he spoke
concerning him.
So YHWH said:
The outcry in Sedom and Amora—how great it is!
And their sin—how exceedingly heavily it weighs!
Now let me go down and see:
if they have done according to its cry that has come to me—
destruction!
And if not—
I wish to know.

The men turned from there and went toward Sedom,
but Avraham still stood in the presence of YHWH.
Avraham came close and said:
Will you really sweep away the innocent along with the guilty?
Perhaps there are fifty innocent within the city,
will you really sweep it away?
Will you not bear with the place because of the fifty innocent
    that are in its midst?
Heaven forbid for you to do a thing like this,
to deal death to the innocent along with the guilty,
that it should come about: like the innocent, like the guilty,
Heaven forbid for you!
The judge of all the earth—will he not do what is just?
YHWH said:
If I find in Sedom fifty innocent within the city,
I will bear with the whole place for their sake.
Avraham spoke up, and said:
Now pray, I have ventured to speak to my Lord,
and I am but earth and ashes:
Perhaps of the fifty innocent, five will be lacking—will you
    bring ruin upon the whole city because of the five?
He said:
I will not bring ruin, if I find there forty-five.
But he continued to speak to him and said:
Perhaps there will be found there only forty!
He said:
I will not do it, for the sake of the forty.
But he said:
Pray let not my Lord be upset that I speak further:
Perhaps there will be found there only thirty!
He said:
I will not do it, if I find there thirty.
But he said:
Now pray, I have ventured to speak to my Lord:

70

Perhaps there will be found there only twenty!
He said:
I will not bring ruin, for the sake of the twenty.
But he said:
Pray let my Lord not be upset that I speak further just this
*   one time:*
Perhaps there will be found there only ten!
He said:
I will not bring ruin, for the sake of the ten.
YHWH went, as soon as he had finished speaking to Avraham,
*   and Avraham returned to his place.*

GENESIS 18:17–33

Several generations after promising Noah that he would never again destroy the world by flood, God reneged on His promise. He decided to destroy the cities of Sodom and Gomorrah by hail and brimstone. To be sure, these two cities are not exactly the whole world, and hail and brimstone is not quite a flood. But God didn't seem to get the *principle* behind his promise to Noah. He was relying on a technical distinction that undercut the policy against mass destruction. Rabbinic commentary recognizes this with a midrash elaborating on Abraham's argument: "You swore that You would not bring a flood upon the world again. . . . A flood of water You won't bring, but a deluge of fire You would bring? Would you with subtlety evade Your oath?"[1] Abraham challenges God, and politely but firmly he tries to set His creator straight. Hence the powerful story of Abraham's argument with God.

What gives Abraham the "right" to argue with God and question his intentions? The answer must lie in the unique relationship between God and His peo-

71

ple. The relationship between God and the Jewish people is covenantal—that is, in the nature of a legally binding contract. As one commentator has put it: "God is transformed from an 'absolute' into a 'constitutional' monarch. He is bound, as man is bound, to the conditions of the constitution."[2] There are certainly examples in contemporary life of parents making contracts with their children: allowance in exchange for tasks; rewards for good grades. There are even instances in history of slaveholders contracting with slaves: freedom after x number of years of servitude. But a contract between the Creator and those He created? What a remarkable notion! This theme of mutually obligatory contract resonates through much of Jewish history, prayer, literature, and even song.

God makes a covenant first with Noah, then with Abraham, and then again with Jacob. Noah never invokes it. Abraham does, reminding Him of His promise to do justly.[3] Abraham's grandson Jacob goes even further in a subsequent story, explicitly making his acceptance of God conditional upon God satisfying His end of the deal: "*If* God be with me, *if* He protects me on this journey that I am making, and gives me bread to eat and clothing to wear, and *if* I return safely to my father's house—*then* God shall be my God."[4] (An earlier variation on my youthful "deal" with God to be more religious in exchange for a Dodger world championship.) Some commentators (such as Rabbi Abahu) tried to deny the conditional nature of Jacob's promise. But others (such as Rabbi Yochanan) interpreted it as it was written: "If all the conditions that God promised me . . . are fulfilled, then I will keep my vow."[5] The conditions are, in fact, met and Jacob keeps his vow. A model of contractual compliance—at least for a time.

A contract bestows rights on *both* contracting parties. The Jewish people have the right to insist that God keep His side of the bargain forever—or at least explain why He has not done so. Throughout Jewish history—from the destruction of the Temples, to the Crusades, to the Inquisition, to the pogroms, and especially to the Holocaust—Jews have been demanding an answer from their contracting partner. It has rarely been forthcoming, but we persist.

The very word "chutzpah"—which I took as the title for one of my books and which means "boldness," "assertiveness," a "willingness to challenge authority"—was first used in the context of demanding that God keep His side of the covenant. It appears in the Talmud[6] as part of the Aramaic expression *chutzpah k'lapei shemaya*—chutzpah even against heaven. Abraham was the first to demonstrate such chutzpah, but surely not the last. The most famous postbiblical exemplar of chutzpah against heaven was the eighteenth-century Hasidic master Rabbi Levi Yitzchak of Berditchev, who repeatedly invoked God's contract in challenging God's injustice toward his covenantal partners. On one occasion he threatened to expose God's promises as "false." On another he sued God and threatened to refuse to cooperate with plans to keep the Jewish people in exile. On one Yom Kippur, a simple tailor sought forgiveness from the great rabbi for having talked disrespectfully to God. The rabbi asked him what he had said, and the tailor told him:

> I declared to God: You wish me to repent of
> my sins, but I have committed only minor of-

fenses: I may have kept leftover cloth, or I may have eaten in a non-Jewish home, where I worked, without washing my hands.

But you, O Lord, have committed grievous sins: You have taken away babies from their mothers, and mothers from their babies. Let us be quits: May You forgive me, and I will forgive You.

The great rabbi looked at the tailor and replied: "Why did you let God off so easily?"[7] It is this argumentative tradition that Abraham initiated when he challenged God's justice toward the Sodomites.

Abraham's argument with God raises one of the most troubling and recurring issues of theology: Can God's justice be judged by human beings according to standards of human justice? If not, by whom and by what standards can God's justice be evaluated? The alternative is to assume—tautologically—that whatever God does, regardless of how unjust it may seem to us, is by definition just. Whatever God commands must be done without question or challenge. This would imply that humans should learn about justice from God's actions—even if we don't understand or agree with them. But what are we to learn from the flood, the binding of Isaac, the Job story, and the Holocaust? We cannot abdicate our own human responsibility to define justice in human terms. Such an approach is the first step on the road to fundamentalism. The Sodom narrative appears to reject the fundamentalist approach and to suggest that God has submitted Himself to at least some human judgment through the covenant.

The story begins with a soliloquy in which God explains why He is going to tell Abraham about His plans to destroy the sinning cities. Abraham's destiny is to teach the world to "keep the way of God, to do what is right and just." Abraham understands his role, but when God announces His plans, Abraham immediately sees a conflict: If he "keeps the way of God," he will not "do what is right and just," because God is Himself planning to do something terribly unjust. So Abraham challenges God in the terms of His mandate: "The judge of the earth—will He not do what is just?" Abraham's idea of what is just must necessarily reflect his own human standards of justice, under which only the guilty are punished. God could easily have responded by saying: "How dare you challenge My concept of justice? You cannot understand My ways. You cannot judge divine justice by human standards."

The God of the Book of Job responds in precisely that manner when Job refuses to accept the injustice that God inflicts on him and his children. It is instructive to contrast the learning God of Abraham with the more certain God of Job. Job's God rebukes His challenger, asking rhetorically:

> Where were you when I laid the foundations for the earth? . . . Do you understand the laws which govern the heavens? . . . Would you go so far as to undermine My judgment, put Me in the wrong so that you might be right? Do you have strength comparable to that of God? Can you, like He, produce the thunder's clap?

In other words, the God of Job pulls rank on His human challenger. His answer is simply a function of

His power. To borrow a wonderful line from a Ring Lardner story: " 'Shut up,' he explained." And Job does more than merely shut up. He submits to God's bullying tactics: "I can understand nothing," he apologizes. "It is beyond me. I shall never know." In bending to God's one-upmanship, Job gives up his own ideas of justice, which—on their own merits—are far more persuasive than God's. Job, after all, is absolutely innocent, yet God allows Satan to inflict on him and his family the worst sorts of punishment. What kind of a God would test a just person by deliberately killing his ten children? Even the traditional commentators recognize the killings were unjust. Accordingly, one of them comes up with an ingenious interpretation under which God did not authorize the actual killing of Job's children. He simply authorized Satan to hide them during the test so that Job would believe that they were dead; God then returned them (and more) after Job passed the test. Others argue that Job was not an actual historical person, merely a literary construction. After all, he did live in the land of Oz!*

But Job—whether actual or fictional—*believed* that God had killed his innocent children and quite properly challenged God's justice. Job's arguments are compelling, but he surrenders them when God appears from out of the whirlwind and invokes His superior power. Job loses the argument not on the merits, but rather by default. It is not a debate; it is an arm-wrestling contest. Job responds to God's show of force by denying his own intellect—"I can understand nothing. It is beyond me. I shall never know." Job the dis-

---

*The broader question arises, of course, if Job is a fictional character, why not Adam, Eve, Abraham, etc.? Abraham Joshua Heschel's view of the Bible as midrashic metaphor would accept an affirmative response to this question.

sident[8] thus becomes Job the fundamentalist. By invoking His power instead of His reason to respond to Job's entirely legitimate question, the God of justice becomes the God of power.

It is difficult to imagine a greater injustice than seeing an all-powerful being kill your innocent children and then having Him rebuke you for questioning the morality of His actions. If the classic definition of chutzpah is to murder your own parents and then demand mercy because you're an orphan, then the classic definition of tyranny is to kill a person's children and demand that he humbly accept this injustice as fair. The Book of Job endures as a great work despite, not because of, God's response in the final chapters. It is the deep human arguments of Job and his friends about the suffering of good people that have resonated for centuries with those who have witnessed and experienced injustice, and not God's muscle-flexing and unsatisfying response. Ultimately God wins the argument with Job not because He is right, but because He is God. This is reminiscent of what lawyers often say about Supreme Court justices: Their judgments are binding not because they are right; they are right only because their judgments are binding. We, the readers, learn absolutely nothing about the nature of justice from God's peremptory response to Job's probing questions. The God of Job is about as informative as a drill sergeant who barks, "Do it because I say so," or a parent who replies, "Because I'm your parent, that's why!"

In my view, the God with whom Abraham argues is far more interesting and a much better teacher. He accepts Abraham's challenge in Abraham's own human terms. In doing so, God understands that pulling rank—invoking naked power—is not an effective pedagogical device. God's invitation to "reason together"[9] is a far better technique, designed to foster a human process for achieving justice, rather than a knee-jerk acceptance of superior orders. The God who invites Abraham to argue with Him about justice is a God who encourages rational discourse. The God who rebukes Job for trying to understand an obvious injustice is a God who promotes unthinking fundamentalism. One of the beauties of the Bible is that even its God speaks in different voices over time.

Biblical commentators have sought to reconcile the reasoning God of Abraham with the peremptory God of Job. One distinction is that Abraham was party to a covenant with God. Job was not. Job is not identified as a Jew in the Bible. He was, of course, subject to the Noachide laws, but he was not a beneficiary of the same sort of broadly binding mutual covenant as the one between God and Abraham. It did not include the right to argue back. Abraham's covenant bestows a unique bundle of obligations and rights, including the right to challenge the other Party to keep His promise. Job had no such right. His relationship with God was that of subject to autocrat. Job must know his place—as a subordinate who dares not question his master's justice. Job is rebuked precisely for purporting to argue with God as an equal:

> "Should the King be accused of wantonness . . . ?" "It is sacrilege to ascribe injustice to the Almighty. . . ."[10] "Would you undertake to declare the Most Righteous at fault?"[11] "Who has ever said to Him, 'You have acted unjustly'?"[12]

Job, who remains silent in the face of these rebukes, could easily have appealed to precedent, reminding God of what Abraham had said. Why then
did Job not invoke the precedent of Abraham in response to God's pointed question "Who has ever said
to Him, You have acted unjustly?"[13] Perhaps Job took
the question to be rhetorical, or maybe he realized
that because he did not have a covenant with God,
his relationship to the Almighty was not one of citi-
zen to constitutional monarch; it was of subject to absolute ruler. God engages in dialogue only with those
who are His covenantal partners. With others, like Job,
He simply acts, orders, and expects complete sub-
servience, obedience, and acceptance.

In most religions, the autocratic God of Job prevails
over the dialogic God of Abraham, for the simple reason that the endemic injustice of the real world can
never be explained in human terms. I do not think
that the awful injustices that have afflicted innocent
human beings over the millennia—from the flood to
the Crusades to the plagues to the Holocaust—can be
justified even in divine terms, but that is a claim that
can never be substantiated, since we, as humans, are
capable of thinking only in human terms. If the
tragedies and cataclysms of the world can never be explained by God in ways understandable to humans,
what's the use of dialogue with the divine? In the end
God will have to say, as He did to Job, You cannot understand my ways. In other words, God did not answer Job's question about why the righteous suffer and
the unrighteous prosper because there is no adequate
answer. God simply points to the marvels of creation
and remains silent about the inadequacy of His justice. It is easier to create a physical universe than to

assure justice. If there were a world to come, He could have referred to reward and punishment after death. Instead He leaves it to others—particularly Elihu—to make the case for the justice of His actions. Since God Himself cannot defend the injustice of the world, He must leave that task to others—who *can* argue, as God cannot, that only God understands the apparent injustice of the world. Yet even if we cannot fully understand apparent injustice, we have an obligation to argue against it, as Abraham, Job, and their intellectual progeny have tried to do.

To accept the conclusion of the Book of Job that God's justice is not subject to human understanding is to abdicate all human judgment about God's actions and to accept the injustices of our world (as Ecclesiastes seems to do). Anything that God does is by definition just, even if it is something as awful as the Holocaust. Taken to its logical conclusion, this would mean that everything that happens is just, leading inexorably to the naturalistic fallacy that confuses what is with what ought to be. I cannot imagine a possible meaning of "justice" that could include the Holocaust, and it is not surprising that this inexplicable catastrophe shook the faith of so many erstwhile believers.[14] In the wake of the Holocaust, it is more difficult to shrug one's shoulders and sigh that God works in mysterious ways. Nor can plausible explanations be offered that do not unfairly demean the victims. When an ultra-Orthodox rabbi blamed the Holocaust on Jews who ate pork, he was roundly and appropriately condemned.

The Holocaust simply cannot be explained away as an example of God's justice that we, as humans, cannot understand.[15] Many victims want no part of a God who would regard the Holocaust as just—even in His own terms. Jacob was prepared to cancel his grandfather's covenant if God did not deliver him safely to his father's house; surely a believer who saw his entire family murdered by the Nazis has the right—indeed, the obligation—to wonder if the God he believed in is a God of justice.

Abraham's defense of Sodom and Gomorrah teaches us that silence in the face of injustice—even God's injustice—is a sin. This view would later be made explicit in the verse "Thou shalt not stand idly by the blood of thy neighbor."[16] It takes courage to rail against injustice; it takes great courage to rail against a king's injustice; it takes the greatest courage to rail against God's injustice—especially if you believe in God's omnipotence. If people are to preserve their faith in God, they need a God with whom they can argue and remonstrate, as Abraham did in the Sodom narrative—in the strongest of terms and without pulling any punches.[17] Maybe that is why the Jews, who have suffered so much, have chosen (or been chosen by) a God with whom they can at least argue, rather than the more peremptory God who reprimands Job. The God who is sued by Rabbi Levi Yitzchak of Berditchev is Abraham's God, not Job's. The God who endowed kings and emperors with the divine authority never to be wrong is closer to Job's God.

Now, back to Abraham's legal argument with God. The standard translations do not do justice to Abraham's rebuke of the God with whom he had just made a covenant. Here is what Abraham says:

> Will you really sweep away the innocent along
> with the guilty?

Perhaps there are fifty innocent within the city,
will you really sweep it away?
Will you not bear with the place because of the
fifty innocent that are in its midst?
Heaven forbid for you to do a thing like this,
to deal death to the innocent along with the
guilty,
that it should come about: like the innocent,
like the guilty,
Heaven forbid for you!
The judge of all the earth—will He not do what
is just?

Abraham's powerful language and his use of the term "sweep" would seem as much directed toward the past flood as toward His intended destruction of the two cities. A midrash worries that some might say that it is God's "trade to destroy the generations of men in a cruel manner," pointing to the flood along with other destructions.[18] Rashi explicitly refers to the parallel of the flood:

> It would be a "profanation" (*chullin*) of Thee,
> in that men would say, "It is His wont to destroy the righteous and the wicked without discrimination. He did so to the generation of the Flood, and to the generation of the dispersal of races, and now He does so again?"[19]

It is interesting that the text of the narrative never explicitly says that God told Abraham that He definitely intended to destroy the cities. It simply says that the sin of these cities is "exceedingly grievous" and that God was going to "descend and see" and perhaps destroy (*calah*). Rashi interprets God's personal visit as a means of teaching that a judge must not give a verdict in a criminal case based on hearsay evidence. He must see for himself. It is also another hint that the God of Genesis is not necessarily omniscient: He must actually observe before He can know for sure. God then asks Himself: "Shall I hide from Abraham that which I am doing?" Abraham quickly figures out what God is up to. He remembers what God did to the sinners of Noah's generation. So he assumes—correctly, it turns out—that God is at it again. He's going to destroy the innocent along with the guilty, just as He did in the flood. Will He never learn?

Abraham realizes that the only way to get God's attention is to upbraid Him in the strongest terms. So he uses the Hebrew term *"chalila Lekha,"* which the translators render as "heaven forbid" or "far be it from you." But the word *"chalila"* is not nearly so polite. It comes from the Hebrew root for "profane." It would be profane of you—cursed of you, unkosher of you[20]— to kill the righteous along with the wicked. (Ironically, Elihu—God's defender in Job—uses the same word, *"chalilah,"* in rebuking Job: "It is sacrilegious to ascribe injustice to the Almighty" [34:10]. Yet that is precisely what Abraham did—at least in hypothetical terms.) Remarkably, God agrees with Abraham's argument, in effect acknowledging the profanity of His bringing the flood, which did "sweep" away many righteous along with the wicked. He accepts Abraham's argument and agrees to save the entire city, provided a certain number of righteous people can be found in it.

There is an obvious logical inconsistency in Abraham's argument. God could simply destroy the city and save the fifty righteous people. That would satisfy the premise of Abraham's rebuke about killing the righteous along with the wicked. But Abraham asks God to save the entire city—including the vast majority of wicked—for the sake of the fifty righteous. Illogical as it is, God goes along with this demand. This leads Abraham to engage in a typical lawyer's argument: Having convinced his adversary to accept the *principle*, Abraham nudges Him down the slippery slope. He asks God: What if there are only forty-five righteous people, would you destroy the whole city for the lack of five? Pretty clever. Then he asks the same question of forty, thirty, twenty, and ten.[21] This kind of argument is reminiscent of the quip attributed to George Bernard Shaw, who once asked a beautiful actress if she would sleep with him for a million pounds. When she said that of course she would sleep with him for one million pounds, Shaw replied, "Now that we've established the principle, we can haggle over the price."

God surely saw the flaw in Abraham's advocacy. He could have responded, "Look, Abraham. You accuse me of overgeneralizing—of sweeping along the righteous with the unrighteous. And you have a point. But you're guilty of the same thing: You are sweeping the wicked along with the righteous, and giving them a free ride. If I find fifty—or forty or even ten—righteous, I will spare *them*. You've convinced me of *that*. But why should I spare the wicked just because there happen to be fifty righteous people in their city?"

Instead God accepted Abraham's *moral* argument but eventually rejected its *empirical* underpinnings. God did not find a sufficient number of righteous people to spare the city, so He simply spared the handful of good people He did find, namely Lot's

84

family—which was in many ways akin to Noah's family.[22] They were certainly not perfect, as it turned out,[23] but they were far better than their contemporaries and townsfolk. The important point is that God permitted Abraham to argue with Him on moral grounds, and although He eventually went through with the plan to destroy the city, He was persuaded by Abraham's moral argument.[24] It was more than a Pyrrhic victory, since it established an enduring principle of justice.

The question remains, if Abraham's moral argument was illogical, why did God accept it? Permit me to offer the following interpretation, building on the idea of a God who is teaching as well as learning in His interactions with His human creations.

The text is clear as to why God decided to tell Abraham about His intentions in regard to Sodom and Gommorah: because God had selected Abraham as His messenger to "instruct" his descendants "to keep the way of the Lord in order to do justice and righteousness" (*tzdakah umishpat*). In other words, God's encounter was to be a lesson for Abraham in the ways of *human* justice and righteousness. An omniscient God is, of course, capable of distinguishing the guilty from the innocent (though He hasn't always acted on this distinction). Humans, however, cannot simply *discern* who are guilty and who innocent. We need a *process*—a legal *system*—to distinguish the innocent from the guilty. Nor is this a simple task. Inevitably human beings will make mistakes. We will sometimes convict the innocent and acquit the guilty. That is in the nature of any human fact-finding process.

It is easy to assure that no innocent will ever be convicted, if that is the *sole* object: Simply acquit everyone about whom there is the slightest doubt as to their guilt, no matter how unreasonable. It is also easy to assure that no guilty person is ever acquitted, if that is the *only* goal: Simply convict everyone against whom there is even the slightest suspicion of guilt, no matter how farfetched. No system in history has ever managed to convict all of the guilty without also "sweeping along" some innocents. Every rule of evidence or procedure that makes it easier to acquit the innocent—for example, the "two witnesses" rule of the Bible—also makes it easier for some guilty people to escape justice.[25] Likewise, every rule that makes it easier to convict the guilty—for example, current reforms that no longer require "corroboration" of rape accusations—also makes it easier to convict some innocents. The difficult task is to strike the proper balance.

In the end, every system of justice must decide which is worse: convicting some innocents or acquitting some guilty. Tyrannical regimes always opt for the former: It is far better that many innocents be convicted than that *any* guilty be acquitted. Most just regimes tend to opt for the latter: It is far better that some guilty go free than that innocents be wrongly convicted. This is the approach ultimately accepted in the Bible, with its generally rigorous safeguards for those accused of wrongdoing.

In addition to deciding on this basic preference, every system of justice must also quantify—at least implicitly. The Anglo-American system, for example, has proclaimed that "it is better that ten guilty persons escape than one innocent suffer."[26] That is surely an approximation, but it sends an important message: Our preference for not convicting the innocent is a very strong one, but it is not absolute; we acknowledge that in order to convict large numbers of guilty, we will sometimes have to convict an innocent. We will try our best to prevent such an injustice, but we will not simply acquit everyone in order to avoid it. This is the way a mature and just system operates.

Although it appears from the language of the narrative that Abraham is teaching God a lesson about justice, it may well be that it is really God—the great pedagogue—who is teaching Abraham a lesson about the inherent limitations on human justice, so that Abraham could instruct his descendants to do justice in a mature and balanced fashion—rejecting both extremes of acquitting everyone about whose guilt there is any doubt and convicting everyone against whom there is any suspicion. By accepting Abraham's moral principle—that a sufficient number of innocent people in a group requires the sparing of the entire group, including the guilty—God was teaching Abraham how to strike the appropriate balance. Since human beings are never capable of distinguishing precisely between the guilty and the innocent, it would be unjust to destroy a group that might contain as many as fifty innocents. The same would be true of forty-five, forty, thirty, twenty, and even ten. It would not be true of only one or two. It is significant that Abraham ends his argument at the number ten. Why did he not continue to try to bargain God down even further? After all, Abraham knew that there was at least *one* righteous person in Sodom—his own relative Lot. Yet he stopped at ten, thus achieving a moral victory but losing the case. Why? Some commentators suggest that Abraham *knew* that any number less than ten would not convince God, since Noah and his family numbered eight, and they were not enough to spare the entire world from the flood.[27] But God had promised not to repeat the destruction He had wrought on Noah's contemporaries, so this argument seems to lack persuasiveness. Others argue that since ten is the requirement for a minyan—a congregation—any less than that number is insufficient. But the traditional requirement for a minyan is ten *men,* and it cannot be justly argued that righteous women do not count when it comes to saving a community. A more rational and less sexist variation on this is that without a core number of righteous people, it will not be possible to influence the multitudes of wicked, as evidenced by Noah's inability to change his generation of sinners.

My own interpretation is simple. Ten, although an arbitrary number, suggests an approximate balance between convicting the innocent and acquitting the guilty. Without knowing the number of wicked people in Sodom, it is impossible, of course, to come up with a precise ratio. But the number ten, even standing alone, is neither trivial nor daunting. Since it is always possible that *any* substantial group of guilty people could include one or two innocents, selecting so low a number would make it impossible to construct a realistic system for convicting the guilty. But tolerating the conviction of as many as ten innocents would make any system of convicting the guilty unjust, or at least suspect. When the number of people on Illinois' death row who were freed because of their possible innocence recently reached double figures, the public began to express concern. Seemingly, the execution of one or two possibly innocent people was not sufficient to stimulate reconsideration of the death penalty, but once the number climbed beyond ten, even many death penalty advocates began to question whether the system was working fairly. The Anglo-American ratio—better ten guilty go free than even one innocent be wrongly convicted—is also somewhat arbitrary, but it too uses the number ten in attempting to strike the proper balance.

What we see, perhaps, is an extraordinary example of interactive teaching and learning. God is willing to accept Abraham's rebuke—illogical as it may seem—in order to teach Abraham that he, a mere mortal, will need to construct a just and effective system for distinguishing between the innocent and the guilty. In the process God too may have learned that He has been insufficiently sensitive to the plight of the innocent who are swept along with the guilty.

The story of Abraham's argument with God has been particularly salient to me as a criminal defense lawyer.[28] I know that most of my clients are guilty of the crimes with which they are charged. I know this not because they tell me—very few confess to their lawyers (only one has ever confessed to me). I know it as a statistical matter, since the vast majority of people charged with crime in America, and in other democratic countries, are guilty. Thank goodness for that! Imagine living in a country where the majority of people charged with crime were innocent. That might be the case in Iraq, Iran, or China, but certainly not in any country with a relatively fair and nonrepressive legal system. So I can safely assume that my clients are no different from the statistical norm—a majority of them are guilty. If anything, my appellate clients are *more* likely to be guilty than those of a typical trial lawyer, since my clients have already passed through the most significant check on prosecutorial error or abuse—the trial. They have already been found guilty by a jury. Some of my clients have been innocent, but they were almost certainly in the minority.

When I decide to take a case, I rarely know whether any particular client is among the guilty majority, the innocent minority, or somewhere in between. Were I to take the position—urged on me by many, including my mother—that I should represent only the innocent, I would probably have taken fewer than a handful of cases over my thirty-five-year career. It is extremely rare that I know for certain that a prospective client is innocent. I have my suspicions (which sometimes have turned out to be mistaken—both ways). I can never, however, be certain. This is even more true at the beginning of my representation, when I know relatively little about the case. As time passes and I learn more, I often reach a more informed view. Even if I come to believe that my client is guilty, I cannot leave a case once I have undertaken the responsibility for completing it (unless the client violates certain rules), any more than a surgeon could abandon a half-completed operation upon learning that his patient was sicker than originally assumed, or a priest could walk out of a confession upon being told of sins he did not anticipate.

I represent the probably guilty for several important reasons of principle. The first is that I, like all human beings, cannot always distinguish between the guilty and the innocent. If only those who were obviously innocent could get decent lawyers to represent them, many innocent clients would remain unrepresented by competent lawyers. I represent the probably guilty, therefore, in order to prevent injustice to the possibly innocent. This is in the tradition of the Sodom narrative, at least as I interpret it. I represent the probably guilty for the sake of the possibly innocent.

Second, I represent the probably guilty to assure that the government is always challenged, that it never gets sloppy, lazy, or corrupt. If our legal system were ever permitted to act on the statistical assumption that the vast majority of defendants are guilty, then prosecutors would grow less careful about whom they charged with crime, and the statistics might become reversed, as it has in some autocratic regimes. Abraham understood how important it was to challenge authority, even divine authority. Although God was eventually able to carry out His plan against the sinners of Sodom, Abraham made it tougher for God. In the end many of my clients go to prison—thankfully none have ever been executed—but I try hard to challenge the government at every turn. In doing so, I'm following in the tradition of advocacy originated by Abraham.

Third, I am a teacher, and I must teach by example. I cannot tell my students that *they* should represent defendants who may be guilty, but that *I* am too good for such dirty work. If our legal system requires that all defendants be represented by zealous lawyers, then I must be willing to serve in that role, no matter how personally unpleasant it may sometimes be. Abraham too was a teacher, and he has taught generations of human rights advocates never to remain silent in the face of a perceived injustice—even if it means standing up for the guilty.

It is always distressing when the guilty go free. But it is a price we must be willing to pay for assuring that the innocent are only rarely convicted. The occasional acquittal of the guilty to preserve the rights of all is a difficult concept that continues to confound and engender controversy, but it lies at the core of any civilized concept of justice. In the Sodom narrative, we see God as a great teacher and Abraham as a challenging student. Both learn from the exchange: God learns that might alone does not make right, and that it is unjust to sweep the innocent along with the guilty. Abraham learns that right alone cannot save the wicked, and that perfect justice is too much to expect of any legal system. Both learn that the essence of justice is striking the right balance. Soon thereafter God gives Abraham a test of justice that teacher and student both appear to fail. But before we get to the *akaida*—God's command to Abraham that he sacrifice his son—let us consider what God ultimately did to the sinners of Sodom and what happened to the one righteous family. It turns out that even the most innocent among the citizens of Sodom were not so righteous after all. They remind me of some of my innocent clients.

---

1. Laytner at p. 46, quoting Leviticus Rabbah and Genesis Rabbah.

2. Fromm, Eric, quoted in Laytner at p. xvii.

3. Abraham also questions whether God will satisfy His part of the deal. Genesis 15:8.

4. Genesis 28:20–21.

5. Laytner, Anson, *Arguing with God, A Jewish Tradition* (New Jersey: Aronson, 1900), pp. xiii–xiv.

6. Sanhedrin 10:5.

7. Laytner at p. 184.

8. Safire, William. *The First Dissident: The Book of Job in Today's Politics*, 1st ed. (New York: Random House, 1992).

9. Book of Isaiah 1:18.

10. Job 34:10.

11. Job 34:17.

12. Job 36:23.

13. Technically, Abraham did not tell God He *had* acted unjustly, but rather that He *would* act unjustly if He swept away the innocent with the guilty. This suggests

that it is more appropriate to be critical in order to *prevent* a future injustice than to criticize a past one. But the distinction based on tense is a bit reminiscent of President Clinton's famous distinction based on what "the meaning of 'is' is."

14. The Job story, as well as the Holocaust, raises the general issue of theosophy, which has been popularized by the book *When Bad Things Happen to Good People* by Rabbi Harold S. Kushner, who lost a son to illness. Theologians, philosophers, and victims have struggled with this issue since the beginning of time. See Chapter 13.

15. There are, of course, important differences among the flood story, the Sodom story, the *akeida* story, the Job story, and the Holocaust. God himself brought the flood; no one else is responsible (though some commentators fault Noah for not arguing on behalf of the innocent, as Abraham did). God also destroyed Sodom, but only after a "trial" and eyewitness observation. God told Abraham to sacrifice his son, thus requiring active complicity by Abraham. God authorized Satan to kill Job's children and expected Job to accept this injustice. The Nazis perpetrated the Holocaust, as God stood idly by. Of course, for those who believe that God is responsible for everything, there are no differences. Some try to have it both ways by arguing that God get credit for all good things but no blame for bad things. A variation on this reductionistic theme is that God does no bad things, only good things that mere humans do not comprehend.

16. Leviticus 19:16.

17. See Wiesel, Elie, "A Prayer for the Days of Awe," *New York Times*, Oct. 2, 1997, p. A19.

18. Ginzberg at p. 251.

19. Soncino Bible, p. 91.

20. One translation uses the phrase "it would be sacrilege" (Sapperstein edition).

21. Commentators speculate on why the number 45 is included among the others, which are all multiples of 10.

22. God does not seem to count babies and children among the innocent or righteous, and the commentators are generally silent about this problem.

23. Both engaged in questionable sexual behavior after being singled out for rescue by God.

24. Some commentators argue that God knew all along that there were fewer than ten righteous people and simply allowed Abraham to make his futile argument. But the text supports the view that God did not know the extent of the evil and had to go down and find out for Himself.

25. The Talmud recognizes this by prescribing, "If one murdered a human being and there were no witnesses, they put him in a prison cell and feed him sparing bread and scant water." Mishnah Sandhedrin 9:5. Commentators suggest that this shrinks the abdomen, and he is then fed barley "to cause rupture of the stomach." This would completely undercut the command of the Torah that in the absence of two witnesses "he shall not be put to death" (Deuteronomy 17:6).

26. Sir William Blackstone in Bartlett, John, *Familiar Quotations* (Boston: Little, Brown and Company, 1955). p. 325.

27. Various commentators try to explain why nine would also not be strong enough.

28. I was shocked to find almost no discussion of Abraham's argument in the Midrash Rabbah. Even Ginzberg in his *Legends of the Jews* has only a brief elaboration (pp. 250–53).

CHAPTER 5

Lot's Daughters Rape Their Father — and Save the World

[T]he men of the city, the men of Sedom, encircled the house,
from young lad to old man, all the people [even] from the
*   outskirts.*
They called out to Lot and said to him:
Where are the men who came to you tonight?
Bring them out to us, we want to know them!
Lot went out to them, to the entrance, shutting the door behind
*   him,*
and said:
Pray, brothers, do not be so wicked!
Now pray, I have two daughters who have never known a
*   man,*
pray let me bring them out to you, and you may deal with
*   them however seems good in your eyes;*
only to these men do nothing,
for they have after all, come under the shadow of my roof-
*   beam!*
The messengers pushed Lot on, saying:
Up, take your wife and your two daughters who are here,
lest you be swept away in the iniquity of the city!
When he lingered,

Lot's Daughters Rape Their Father—and Save the World

*the men seized his hand, his wife's hand, and the hand of his
    two daughters
—because YHWH's pity was upon him—
and, bringing him out, they left him outside the city.
It was, when they had brought him outside, that [one of them]
    said:
Escape for your life, do not gaze behind you, do not stand
    still anywhere in the plain:
to the hill-country escape, lest you be swept away! . . .*

*But YHWH rained down brimstone and fire upon Sedom and
Amora, coming from YHWH, from the heavens,
he overturned those cities and all of the plain, all those settled
    in
the cities and the vegetation of the soil.
Now his wife gazed behind him, and she became a pillar of
    salt. . . .*

*Lot went up from Tzo'ar and settled in the hill-country, his
    two daughters with him, for he was afraid to settle in
    Tzo'ar.
So he settled in a cave, he and his two daughters.
Now the firstborn said to the younger:
Our father is old,
and there is no man in the land to come in to us as befits the
    way of all the earth!
Come, let us have our father drink wine and lie with him
so that we may keep seed alive by our father.
So they had their father drink wine that night,
then the firstborn went in and lay with her father—
but he knew nothing of her lying down or her rising up.
It was on the morrow that the firstborn said to the younger:
Here, yesternight I lay with Father.
Let us have him drink wine tonight as well,*

then you go in and lie with him,
so that we may keep seed alive by our father.
They had their father drink wine that night as well,
then the younger arose and lay with him,
but he knew nothing of her lying down or her rising up.
And Lot's two daughters became pregnant by their father.

GENESIS 19:4–36

After agreeing with Abraham that he would not destroy Sodom if he could find ten righteous people, God sends two messengers (or angels in disguise) to the city. They encounter Lot, who invites them to his home, which the men of the city then surround, demanding that Lot give his guests to them for their sexual pleasure. Lot responds in a remarkable manner: He offers his two virgin daughters to the crowd in place of his guests. But the crowd rejects Lot's substitution and presses against the door in quest of the men. Lot's guests protect their host and warn him to remove his family from the city, which is about to be destroyed. Lot, his wife, and his two daughters are told not to look back at the devastation, but his wife disobeys: She is turned into a pillar of salt. Then, after escaping the fire and brimstone, Lot is made drunk by his daughters and seduced by each of them so that they may become pregnant and keep their seed alive.

The story of Lot is really the story of the three women in his life—none of whom is named—and tells much about the Bible's attitude toward the female sex.

Lot is saved because God "remembered Abraham."[1] This suggests that he remembered Abraham's argument about not sweeping away the righteous with

96

the unrighteous, and Lot was more righteous than the other Sodomites. But was he really a righteous man? By offering his daughters to the crowd, did he demonstrate righteousness? By the standards of his time and place, the answer is yes. After all, the patriarch Abraham, who is regarded as a paragon of virtue, twice offered up his own wife for the sexual pleasure of those who might threaten him, in order to protect himself. The first instance took place when Abram and Sarai (their names were later changed to incorporate God's presence) journeyed to Egypt. Abram had his wife pose as his sister—subjecting her to sexual conquest but saving his own life. She was eventually returned to her husband after God afflicted Pharaoh with plagues.[2] The second instance took place after the destruction of Sodom, when Abraham and Sarah were journeying to the south and encountered Abimelech, the king of Gerar. Again Abraham subjected his wife to possible adultery, saying she was his sister.[3] Again she was saved, this time after God came to Abimelech in a dream and threatened him with death. Abimelech, who had not yet touched Sarah, made a brilliant argument to God in his own defense: "Will you slay even a righteous nation?" These words are reminiscent of Abraham's own plea to God on behalf of the possibly innocent people of Sodom. It also introduces the legal principle that an honest and reasonable mistake of fact, which negates culpability, will generally be defense to a criminal act. By thus invoking Abraham's own argument in the Sodom case, Abimelech persuaded God to spare him. God replied that if Abimelech returned Sarah, then Abraham would pray for him, and since Abraham is a prophet, his prayers would be answered. Nachmanides boldly states that Abraham "sinned a great sin" by exposing Sarah in the way he did, but he inexplicably characterizes the sin as "unwitting."[4] It was anything but, since Abraham calculated the risks to his wife's virtue and weighed them against the risks to his own life. This sort of cost-benefit thinking seems to run in the family: Isaac later did the same thing to his wife. It has been argued in defense of Abraham and Isaac that since they had prophetic powers, perhaps they knew that God would rescue their wives from the would-be seducers. Although Lot lacked such powers, maybe he realized that the sexual preferences of those demanding his male guests would cause them to turn down his daughters. His offer was simply a ruse to gain time. Even if these ploys could somehow be justified, they still used women as sexual commodities. It is fair to conclude, therefore, that righteousness was not measured in the Bible by how a man treated *his* women—wives, daughters, sisters—even if he bartered them to others for their sexual satisfaction.

There is another, less sexist and more universal interpretation, which is suggested by the bizarre episode that ends the Lot story. His daughters, believing that the entire world (at least the entire world to which they had access) had been destroyed, feel it necessary to seduce their father in order to bear children. They are not punished for their incest. Perhaps the message is that the perpetuation of life is more important than the rules of sexual propriety. In the case of Lot's daughters, they may have believed that the continuation of humanity depended on their breaking the taboo against incest and even rape. After all, the act of getting a sexual target drunk and then having sex with him when he's unconscious is rape. Thus the first example of "acquaincance rape"—really intra-familial sexual abuse—in the Bible is by women against a man. Why am I not surprised!

At a more general level, the message may be to favor a kind of situational ethic—at least when sex is involved—over a more categorical imperative. Some rules of conduct are relative, while life is absolute. Jewish law eventually adopts this approach for most rules, permitting them to be broken in order to save life (*pikuach nefesh*). Deuteronomy mandates us to "choose life." During the Holocaust many women had to choose between their sexual virtue or their life. Those who chose life were not condemned by rabbinic authorities.[5] They had followed the examples of Abraham's wife and Lot's daughters.

In the case of Abraham, the patriarch placed his own life above the sexual virtue of his wife and acted without her consent. In Lot's case, the women acted without the consent of the man. (Lot also acted without the consent of his daughters in offering them as substitutes for his guests.) In these instances, life was perpetuated.[6]

It is interesting to contrast the actions of Lot's daughters with those of Noah's sons. Noah—also a virtuous man in his generation—became drunk and "uncovered" himself within his tent. His son Ham saw his father's nakedness and told his other two brothers, who, "walking backward" so as to avoid seeing their father's nakedness, covered him. When Noah awoke from his drunken stupor and learned what Ham had done, he cursed his progeny, the Canaanites.[7] Commentators interpret Ham's actions as more than mere voyeurism. An imaginative midrash says that Ham attempted to "perform an operation upon his father designed to prevent procreation."[8] Rashi suggests that Ham "indulged a perverted lust upon him." But whatever Ham did, it was not for a procreational or lifesaving purpose; thus Ham's descendants were cursed and Lot's daughters forgiven. The children born to Lot's daughters became the leaders of the Moabites and the Ammonites. Sforno observed: "Because the intention of Lot's daughters had been good, their descendants inherited the land."[9]

What about Lot's wife, whose only crime was to look back after an angel dressed as a man told her not to? Does her entirely understandable need to glance backward at the family she left behind warrant so severe a punishment? Even the midrash acknowledges that "her mother love made her look behind to see if her married daughters were following." Is that a crime? What does her death tell us about the value placed on the life of a woman? Commentators have struggled mightily to justify the death of Lot's wife. Rashi speculates that her real sin had been to refuse "salt"—that is, hospitality—to Lot's angelic guests. Well, I guess that deserves death instead of a rebuke from Emily Post! Others come up with equally implausible justifications. The pillar of salt was a visible symbol of the wages of turning your back on God. Augustine says that Lot's wife "serves as a solemn and sacred warning that no one who starts out on the path of salvation should ever yearn for the things that he has left behind."[10] But if "the things" left behind are family members, such a command defies human nature. During the Inquisition many Jews who converted to Christianity looked back in distress as their own flesh and blood were murdered. Josephus, the Jewish historian who abandoned Judaism but repeatedly turned back to write about the Jews, wrote that Lot's wife was "overly curious" about Sodom and was changed into a pillar of salt. Ironically, Josephus was accused by some of his Roman contemporaries of being "overly curious" about his own heritage.[11] Josephus demonstrated his own ambivalence about his rejection of Judaism by testifying: "I have seen this pillar, which remains to this day." Contemporary Israeli tour guides also point to a salt pillar near the Dead Sea—a natural part of the Niegev landscape—claiming that it bears a resemblance to a woman looking over her shoulder.

The narrative of Lot and his wife and daughters continues the theme of woman as seducer, entrapper, disobeyer, sinner, sexual commodity, and—ultimately—procreator. She may be bad, but she is never as bad as the worst of men. For example, when Lot's house is surrounded by sexual predators, they are all men. But she is rarely as good as the best of men. A midrash does praise Sarah as ranking "higher than her husband" in prophecy. "She was sometimes called Iscah 'the seer' on that account," but this is an exception.[12] Biblical woman may be more crafty and conniving than her male counterpart, but she is not generally as morally elevated (though there are exceptions). God does not usually speak to her directly, but He punishes her for disobeying the commands issued to men. This subordinate yet blameworthy role of women in the Book of Genesis will recur in several subsequent stories. Indeed, in the very next story—the binding of Isaac—the silence of Sarah is deafening, as her only child is led by his father to the slaughter.

1. Several commentators interpret this verse as saying that Lot was saved on account of Abraham, because he was the patriarch's nephew or because he moved to Sodom at Abraham's behest. Yet another early example of virtue-by-status.

2. Genesis 12:10–20.

3. Genesis 20:1–18.

4. Quoted in Riskin at p. 11.

5. See at Oshry, Efroim, *Responsae from the Holocaust*, pp. 183–94.

6. Ginzberg at p. 255.

7. 9:21–25.

8. Ginzberg at p. 165.

9. Soncino at p. 99. Some commentators criticize Lot's older daughter for naming her child Moab, which identifies the child as her own father's. The younger child, whose name did not explicitly identify its father, was rewarded by being a forebearer of David and the Messiah.

10. Kugel at p. 192.

11. Jewish tradition forbids criticizing non-Jews in the presence of converts, recognizing that the convert will retain a natural affinity for his non-Jewish heritage and family.

12. Ginzberg at p. 203.

CHAPTER 6

Abraham Commits Attempted Murder—and Is Praised

Now after these events it was
that God tested Avraham
and said to him:
Avraham!
He said:
Here I am.
He said:
Pray take your son,
your only-one
whom you love,
Yitzhak [Isaac in English],
and go-you-forth to the land of Moriyya/Seeing,
and offer him up there as an offering-up
upon one of the mountains
that I will tell you of.
Avraham started-early in the morning,
he saddled his donkey,
he took his two serving-lads with him and Yitzhak his son,
he split wood for the offering-up
and arose and went to the place that God had told him of.
On the third day Abraham lifted up his eyes

and saw the place from afar.
Avraham said to his lads:
You stay here with the donkey,
and I and the lad will go yonder,
we will bow down and then return to you.
Avraham took the wood for the offering-up,
he placed them upon Yitzhak his son,
in his hand he took the fire and the knife.
Thus the two of them went together.
Yitzhak said to Avraham his father, he said:
Father!
He said:
Here I am, my son.
He said:
Here are the fire and the wood,
but where is the lamb for the offering-up?
Avraham said:
God will see for himself to the lamb for the offering-up,
my son.
Thus the two of them went together.
They came to the place that God had told him of;
there Avraham built the slaughter-site
and arranged the wood
and bound Yitzhak his son
and placed him on the slaughter-site atop the wood.
And Avraham stretched out his hand,
he took the knife to slay his son.
But YHWH's messenger called to him from heaven
and said:
Avraham! Avraham!
He said:
Here I am.
He said:
Do not stretch out your hand against the lad,

do not do anything to him!
For now I know
that you are in awe of God—
you have not withheld your son, your only-one, from me.

GENESIS 22:1–12

No biblical narrative is more dramatic, more poignant, and more confusing than God's command to Abraham that he sacrifice his son Isaac. What kind of a God would ask such a thing of a father? What kind of a father would accede to such a request, even from a God? Why did Abraham, the man who argued so effectively with God over the fate of strangers, suddenly become silent in the face of so great an injustice toward his own beloved son? Why did God praise Abraham for his willingness to engage in an act of ritual murder? And what are we to learn from a patriarch who follows, without question, immoral superior orders to murder an innocent child?

These, and other questions, have been debated by Jews, Christians, and Muslims for generations. Again, there are the trivial answers, designed to justify everything God and Abraham did. Some of the defense lawyer commentators argue that Abraham knew that God was merely testing him and that He would never let him actually kill his son. A variation on this interpretation comes from the fact that God never explicitly commanded Abraham to sacrifice Isaac, but rather to "offer" him. These commentators argue that Abraham realized God would not accept his offer and would stay his hand, pointing to Abraham's assurance to his servants that both he and Isaac will return: "You stay here with the donkey, and I and the lad will go yonder, we will bow down and then return to you."[1] As one midrash put it: "God informed Abraham by making him unintentionally prophesy"—a divinely inspired slip of the tongue.[2]

The problem with this "defense" is that if Abraham knew the outcome, then it wasn't really a test—or at least a fair test. One who knows the answer to a test in advance is a cheat. Moreover, based on God's past behavior, why would Abraham trust that his son would survive? After all, this is the same God who destroyed the world in the flood and was prepared to sweep away the innocent along with the guilty in Sodom. Why would such a God not also expect one of His followers to kill a single child?

On the face of it, it seems that Abraham believed that God wanted him to kill his son and that the patriarch was willing to do just that. Why would the man who argued with God over strangers be prepared to murder his own son without protest?

There is, of course, the possibility that Abraham went along with God's command for entirely self-serving reasons: He believed that if he disobeyed God's direct order, God would kill him as he killed Lot's wife. By killing his own son, Abraham would be saving himself. Remember that this is the same Abraham who twice sacrificed Sarah's virtue to save his own neck. Remember too that God *invited* Abraham to argue with Him over the condemned of Sodom, but he *commanded* Abraham to sacrifice Isaac. Failure to comply with a direct command from God carried a divine punishment. To suggest a slightly less selfish motive, perhaps Abraham decided that if he refused God's command, both he and Isaac would be killed by God, but if he complied, God might spare at least one of them. We do not know, of course, what was going through Abraham's mind as he lifted the knife to slay his son, but in light of his prior history—especially with Sarah—a self-serving motive cannot be entirely excluded. A midrash suggests a different spin on Abraham's self-interest.

> It shows that out forefathers presupposed the existence of another world beyond this one. If not for Avraham's belief in *olam haba* [the world to come], he certainly would not have agreed to sacrifice his only son and continue living a life without hope and without a future. He was ready to listen to God's commandment, knowing that for his sacrifice in this world, God would repay him well in *olam haba*.[3]

This turns Abraham's great test into a simple cost-benefit decision. Indeed, the very word "repay" connotes a crass balancing of benefits. Neat as the equation may seem, there is no textual support that the patriarch believed in a world to come. Absent any guarantee of eternal reward for following God's command, Abraham's decision to kill Isaac is especially dramatic precisely because it would have left him with "a life without hope and without a future." He was willing to accept such a life for one reason alone: because God commanded it.

Maimonides refuses to attribute Abraham's compliance to simple fear of consequences: "For Abraham did not hasten to kill Isaac out of fear that God would slay him or make him poor, but solely because it is man's duty to love and to fear God, even without hope of reward or fear of punishment."[4] But why then is

Judaism (as well as other religions) so premised on reward and punishment, both in this world and in the
world to come? I believe that true morality can best
be judged in the absence of threats or promises.[5] The
atheist who throws himself in front of a car to save a
child is performing a truly moral act, because he expects no divine reward. The religious person who
strongly believes that he will be rewarded for his moral
acts and punished for his immoral ones in the hereafter may simply be making a long-term cost-benefit
analysis. Blaise Pascal, a seventeenth-century French
philosopher and mathematician, argued that faith is a
worthwhile gamble, since we lose nothing if we believe and God does not exist, but we risk spending
eternity in hell if we do not believe and God turns
out to be real. The fallacy is that God may despise
those who engage in such self-serving wagers and prefer those who honestly doubt or even disbelieve. Maimonides argued strongly against the midrashic
variation of "Pascal's wager":

> Let not a man say, "I will observe the precepts
> of the Torah and occupy myself with its wis-
> dom in order that I may obtain all the bless-
> ings written in the Torah, or to attain life in
> the world to come; I will abstain from trans-
> gressions against which the Torah warns, so that
> I may be saved from the curses written in the
> Torah, or that I may not be cut off from life in
> the world to come." It is not right to serve God
> after this fashion, for whoever does so, serves
> Him out of fear. This is not the standard set
> by the prophets and sages. Those who may
> serve God in this way are illiterate, women, or
> children whom one trains to serve out of fear,

till their knowledge shall have increased, when they will serve out of love.[6]

According to other commentators, Abraham was not aware of the world to come—of reward and punishment after death.[7] If so, the stakes were even higher. The death of Isaac would be forever, not simply a transition from this life to the next.

Even the noble motive attributed to Abraham by Maimonides and other commentators is somewhat self-serving. Abraham placed his allegiance to the all-powerful God above his obligation as a parent and a husband. He never even consulted with his wife about his decision to sacrifice *their* son. Of course, Sarah was not entirely blameless, either. After all, she was prepared to sacrifice Abraham's other son, Ishmael, to her own ambitions for Isaac—a deed for which she was called a "sinner" by Maimonides. It was only God's intervention that saved Ishmael from certain death.[8]

What then is the nature of God's test of Abraham? The best evidence of that comes from God's own mouth when He declares that Abraham passed the test: ". . . now I know that you are in awe of God." The actual Hebrew word is *y'rei*, which literally means "afraid" or "in fear of" God. But what kind of a moral test is that? Acceding to an immoral command out of fear does not show much courage or virtue. What if a powerful human king had presented Abraham with a similar, terrible choice: "Either kill your child or I will kill you"? Would we *praise* a father for being "afraid" of the king, or being "in awe" of the king and killing the child? Of course not. At most we might *understand* why the father, like those parents during the Holocaust who abandoned or even sacrificed their crying children, might have made such a decision.[9] We might even feel uncomfortable condemning them. But praise them? Never. Why then do we praise Abraham? He may have passed *God's* test of justice, but he failed his *own* test of justice, as he articulated it during his argument over the condemned of Sodom—namely that it is always wrong to kill the innocent, even if God commands it.

In addition to failing his own test of justice, Abraham also fails every contemporary test of justice. No one today would justify killing a child because God commanded it. A contemporary Abraham would be convicted of attempted murder, and his defense—"I was just following superior orders"—would be rightly rejected. Of course, today we believe that people who hear commands from God are insane, but even if we were to entertain such a claim, we would condemn anyone who acted on it by killing a child. Indeed, there are religious cults that cite the Bible in support of abusing disrespectful children, but we correctly reject their claim that the Bible supersedes their legal obligation, especially when it comes to children.[10]

My Harvard colleague Professor Jon Levenson of the Divinity School makes a powerful argument against viewing Abraham's actions through the prism of contemporary abhorrence to the murder of children. In the days of the patriarch, child murder was distinguished from child sacrifice. The former was almost universally condemned, the latter widely accepted as a show of gratitude toward the gods. (As recently as five hundred years ago, Incas in South America were still sacrificing children to their gods, as preserved mummies prove.)[11] God did not order Abraham to "murder" his son; such a command would have violated the Noachide laws against shedding innocent blood. God ordered Abraham to "sacrifice" his son, and sacrifice is different from murder, as evidenced by the inclusion of "whom you love" in the description of the sacrificed object. You murder those you hate; you sacrifice what you love most.

Professor Levenson makes an interesting argument against judging *historical* figures by the moral standards of a later age. Kierkegaard anticipated and answered Levenson's argument:

> Perhaps in the context of his times, what [Abraham] did was something quite different. Then let's forget him, for why bother remembering a past that cannot be made into a present?[12]

Abraham is not seen as a mere historical figure whose actions are simply described; he is a *biblical* patriarch whose actions are supposed to be eternal, not timebound. Abraham is supposed to be more than a man for all seasons. He is seen as a man to be emulated forever. Levenson acknowledges that Abraham, by being willing to sacrifice his son, violated the Torah's explicit prohibition against child sacrifice,[13] but, like other traditional commentators, he argues that Abraham's actions took place before the Torah was given at Sinai[14] and that "any attempt to derive practical norms for ourselves immediately and directly from Abraham's experience . . . is thus a denial of the Torah, rather than an implementation of it." This argument, clever as it is, proves too much. If accepted, it would make all of Abraham's actions—from his rejection of idol worship to his argument on behalf of the sinners of Sodom—irrelevant to current life. Yet we do derive "practical norms" from Abraham's pre-Sinaic actions. Indeed, Levenson himself derives a very important norm from the *akeidah*, praising Abraham as "a man who scrupulously observes God's commandments" and who "fears" the Lord. How are we to decide which norms are universal and which time-bound?

At an even more fundamental level, why should sacrifice be so highly valued at the expense of other—even other biblical—norms? Abraham may have been entitled to sacrifice "what is most precious" to *him*—as long as it was *his* to sacrifice. His life, his fortune, his health—yes. But his son? No! His wife's son? Certainly not! Where did Abraham get the right to sacrifice Sarah's only and last child, especially since he could, as a man, have more children with other wives? Indeed, he had six more children with his next wife. Levenson might argue that judged by the standards of his day, Abraham owned his son—just as he owned his wife. Isaac was *his*, to do with as he wanted. By sacrificing Isaac, Abraham *was* giving up something that was *his*—not Sarah's. But this argument takes moral relativism beyond all meaning. By *any* moral, as distinguished from descriptive, standard that Levenson or others could articulate, it would have been wrong for Abraham to sacrifice Isaac. It is significant that Levenson proposes no standard—other than the immoral practices of the time—by which Abraham's sacrifice of Isaac could be justified.[15] Abraham's critics may be wrong for failing to consider the historical conditions that allowed for human sacrifices. But the fact that some of Abraham's contemporaries may have been willing to sacrifice their children does not make Abraham's actions praiseworthy. Surely there were some, even in those days, who refused to sacrifice their children. Perhaps they lost their own lives for their refusal. Why should we judge Abraham by the common—or lowest—standard of his era; should we not expect more of a man who is presented as a paragon of virtue for all times and places? The closest Levenson comes to his own standard of judgment is to praise Abraham for his "radical obedience to the divine commandments"[16] and for his "complete trust" in God.[17]

"Trust" in this context can have multiple meanings. It can mean that Abraham trusted that God was right in ordering him to sacrifice his son and was prepared to do the terrible deed. This is *moral* trust. It could also mean that he trusted that God would never actually permit the slaughter of an innocent child. This is *empirical* trust. Trust, in the latter sense, can be illustrated by the experiment in which you ask a loved one to fall backward into your arms. If they trust you *to catch them*, they will willingly fall. That is empirical trust. Moral trust would be a willingness to fall backward even if they knew you would not catch them, because they trusted your judgment that a broken back is not such a bad thing! It is not clear in which sense trust is used in the context of the *akeidah*.

Kierkegaard, in his famous essay on the *akeidah*— "Fear and Trembling"—focuses on Abraham's "faith" and argues that he suspended his own ethical principles in demonstrating his faith. Kierkegaard too is unclear whether he means faith that God would not require Abraham actually to sacrifice Isaac (empirical faith) or faith that if He did, it would be the right thing (moral faith).[18] If the latter, then Kierkegaard fails to provide a persuasive argument for why we should praise faith over parental responsibility.

How then do the traditional commentators explain God's command, Abraham's actions, and the praise we are supposed to heap on both of them? What lessons about justice are we supposed to derive from this extraordinary tale of injustice?

First there is God's command. How are we to assess it? The "defense lawyer" commentators have a simple-minded, reductionist justification of God's command. One writes, "The nature of this trial calls for an explanation, since there is no doubt that the Almighty does not try a person in order to prove to Himself whether he is capable of withstanding the trial, since God is all-knowing and has no doubt about anything."[19] But the text itself is richer than this tautological answer, since the angel of God says, "For *now* I know that you are in awe of God" (or that you "fear" God). This suggests that the trial was not fixed, as some commentators argue—that neither God nor the angels knew what its outcome would be. Just as God believed and hoped that Job would pass the diabolical test concocted by Satan, God probably also believed and hoped that Abraham would pass the test that God contrived for him. (Some commentators argue that Satan provoked God into testing Abraham just as he did with regard to Job.) But God could not be certain, because since the day Adam and Eve ate from the Tree of Knowledge and learned right from wrong, man had the capacity to choose freely. Perhaps if the test had been a simple one—between good and evil—God could be confident that Abraham would choose good over bad. But which is "good" and which "bad" in the context of a divine command to kill one's own son? Even God and His angels could not be certain of Abraham's answer. They had to wait for Abraham to act, and only then could the angel declare, "For now I know. . . ." This idea of God's uncertainty is supported by some contemporary commentators,[20] who argue that Abraham's "decision could not be known—even by God—until he actually made it by bringing down the knife on his son's body."[21]

Other commentators try to have it both ways. Of course God knew what Abraham would do, even though Abraham had complete free will.[22] The purpose of the test, therefore, was "to translate into action the potentialities of [Abraham's] character and give him the reward of a good deed, in addition to the reward of a good heart."[23] In other words, God rewards good actions more than good intentions. But this begs the important question Would it have been good if Abraham had actually carried out God's command and sacrificed his son? Would the killing of Isaac have given Abraham "the reward of a good deed"? As it was, Abraham got to have his cake and eat it, too. He got brownie points for following God's command, *and* he got his son back. But for purposes of evaluating the morality of Abraham's actions, we should judge him as if he actually plunged the knife into Isaac's throat. Would *that* story have appeared in the Bible? If not, why does this story appear—since *Abraham's* mens rea (state of mind) and actus reas (actions) are essentially the same as they would have been had he actually killed his son?

Some midrashic commentators go so far as to suggest that Abraham did actually kill Isaac and that God then brought him back to life. Isaac then "stood on his feet and spoke the benediction 'Blessed are Thou,

O Lord, who quickenest the dead.'"[24] These commentators do not take this suggestion to its logical conclusion by asking whether Abraham deserves praise for actually killing Isaac—if that's what he did.

A twentieth-century rabbinic commentator, Avraham Yitzhak Kook, contrasts the Abraham story with "the absolute self-surrender characteristic of idolatry." According to Rabbi Kook, primitive idolatry required its followers to ignore "parental pity" if the gods so commanded "and made cruelty towards sons and daughters the keynote of Molech worship. . . ."[25] Molech was the Canaanite God of fire who demanded the sacrifice of children. I must admit I do not understand the distinction Rabbi Kook seems to make between Abraham's actions and those of his Molech-worshiping contemporaries. Abraham too allowed his "self-surrender" to God's unjust command to triumph over his pity and obligation to his son. And the importance accorded Abraham's willingness to sacrifice his son can be said to have made "cruelty towards sons"—or at least a willingness to be cruel—a "keynote" of Jewish worship. Abraham's *God* is surely to be contrasted with the Canaanite *God*, since the former stays Abraham's hand, whereas the latter allows the sacrifices to go forward. But Abraham's *own* conduct cannot be contrasted favorably with that of Canaanite parents who willingly sacrificed their children to Molech, unless Abraham never really intended to carry out God's commands, in which case he loses points on the faith scale.

In an effort to escape this harsh conclusion, another modern commentator offers a radical interpretation of the Abraham story. Lippman Bodoff, a Jew working within the Orthodox tradition, proposes that in testing Abraham, God hoped that Abraham would *refuse*

His command to murder Isaac. The object lesson of the story, according to Bodoff, is to send a message "that God does not want even his God-fearing adherents to go so far as to murder in God's name or even at God's command."[26] God was "testing Abraham to see if he would remain loyal to God's revealed moral law"—namely the prohibition against murder—"even if ordered to abandon it."[27] According to Bodoff, Abraham would pass the test only if he stood up to God and said: "'I can't do it; it is contrary to Your moral law.'"

How might he have managed such an act of defiance? Abraham could have reminded God of His covenant with Noah, which made explicit what had been implicit at least since Cain killed Abel—namely that killing is wrong. Even a heavenly voice cannot make the killing of an innocent child right. The Talmud recounts a wonderful legend that makes the point that once God gives humans His law, He may not interfere with the human process for interpreting and applying it. The legend tells of a rabbinic dispute between Rabbi Eliezer ben Hyrcanus (a brilliant but somewhat arrogant rabbi who lived at the beginning of the second century A.D.) and the other members of the yeshiva over a rather arcane issue concerning an oven:

> On that day R. Eliezer brought forward every imaginable argument, but they did not accept them. Said he to them: "If the halakah [oral law] agrees with me, let this carob-tree prove it." Thereupon the carob-tree was torn a hundred cubits out of place. . . . "No proof can be brought from a carob-tree," they retorted. Again

he said to them: "If the halakah agrees with me, let the stream of water prove it!" Whereupon the stream of water flowed backward. "No proof can be brought from a stream of water," they rejoined. [Finally] he said to them: "If the halakah agrees with me, let it be proved from heaven!" Whereupon a Heavenly Voice cried out: "Why do ye dispute with R. Eliezer, seeing that in all matters the halakah agrees with him!" But R. Joshua arose and explained: "It is not in heaven!" What did he mean by this?— Said R. Jeremiah: That the Torah had already been given at Mount Sinai; we pay no attention to Heavenly Voice, because Thou hast long since written the Torah at Mount Sinai.[28]

The Talmud then relates how a rabbi asked the prophet Elijah what God did next. According to the story, God laughed with joy and said, "My sons have defeated me [in argument]." If God's voice is not enough to change the law regarding an issue of ritual, why should it be enough to overrule the most fundamental law of humanity: Thou shalt not murder?[29] At the very least, Abraham could have pointed to God's covenant with Noah and asked God to resolve the conflict between His written and oral command before agreeing to slaughter his son.[30] It shows no disrespect to point to conflicting authority and seek guidance. When Abraham argued with God over the sinners of Sodom, he had no contrary authority—other than his own sense of justice—to which to refer.

There is a wonderful midrash that elaborates on the conflict between God's general prohibition against murder and His specific command to murder in this case. As Isaac questioned his father about the absence of a lamb for the burnt offering, a wicked angel named Samael upbraided Abraham, saying: "What means this, old man! Hast thou lost thy wits? Thou goest to slay a son granted to thee at age of hundred!" Abraham was resolute: "Even this I do." Then the angel prophesied that after Abraham sacrificed Isaac, God would condemn him: "Tomorrow He will say to thee, 'Thou art a murderer, and art guilty.'" Still, Abraham responded, "I am content."[31] Abraham, according to this interpretation, was willing not only to sacrifice his son, but also to break God's law against murder and be rebuked as a murderer, as long as God personally ordered him to do so. Immanuel Kant would have had Abraham respond more directly to God's command with a reference to the categorical imperative against murder: "That I ought not to kill my son is certain beyond a shadow of a doubt; that you, as you appear to be, are God, I am not convinced...."[32] Or as Bob Dylan put it:

God said to Abraham, go kill me a son. Abe said, man, you must be puttin' me on.

But Kant and Dylan beg the critical question: What if Abraham believed it really was God and that He was not putting him on?

Bodoff goes so far as to say that if Abraham had actually killed Isaac and received praise for that act, we would have had "a religion to which few and perhaps none of us could subscribe...." But this raises the disturbing question of why so many *can* subscribe to a religion in which Abraham is praised for his *willingness* to obey God's immoral command. Here is where Bodoff's interpretation is truly radical. He claims that

119

Abraham never intended to carry out God's unjust command. He expected God to countermand it at the last minute—he had *empirical*, not *moral* trust. He was willing to fall backward, confident that God would catch him before he hit the ground. He was not willing to accept God's moral assurance that killing Isaac was the right thing to do. Bodoff argues that Abraham was resolved to violate God's command if, at the last minute, God did not countermand it. In other words, as much as God was testing Abraham, "Abraham was testing the Almighty." And the reason for the test is understandable: This is a God who swept many innocent along with the guilty in the flood but who acceded to Abraham's moral argument over the innocents of Sodom. Which God was He, really? Had He learned the lesson of not condemning the innocent? This test would answer that question for Abraham. Had God failed the test—had he not stayed Abraham's hand—Abraham would have broken the covenant and said, "If the God I have found demands the same kind of immorality that I saw in my father's pagan society, I must be mistaken [in accepting Him and] I must look further."

Bodoff tells us that God passed the test by sending an angel to stay Abraham's hand and in doing so told Abraham and the rest of the world that He does not demand blind obedience to immoral superior orders. His is a code of justice that eventually develops a process for deciding what is right and wrong. That process includes codification, as in the Noachide code, and argumentation, as in the Sodom narrative. But it does not include uncritical acceptance of the immoral commands of heavenly voices.

This is a brilliant and positive interpretation that

makes both God and Abraham appear just, but it is difficult to reconcile with the text. After all, God's angel—purporting to speak for God—praises Abraham for his willingness to sacrifice Isaac. If God had really wanted Abraham to refuse His command, why does He have His messenger praise him for his willingness to comply? Here Bodoff is at his weakest, claiming that the angel—being only a messenger of God and not himself omniscient—was unaware of the true intention of God's test as well as Abraham's true intention to refuse God's order. The following midrash is more faithful to the text:

> When God commanded the father to desist from sacrificing Isaac, Abraham said: "One man tempts another, because he knoweth not what is in the heart of his neighbor. But Thou surely didst know that I was ready to sacrifice my son!"
>
> God: "It was manifest to Me, and I foreknew it, that thou wouldst withhold not even thy soul from Me."
>
> Abraham: "And why, then, didst Thou afflict me thus?"
>
> God: "It was My wish that the world should become acquainted with thee, and should know that it is not without good reason that I have chosen thee from all the nations. Now it hath been witnessed unto men that thou fearest God."[33]

As this midrash points out, there is an even more fundamental problem with Bodoff's fascinating interpretation. How does he know that Abraham intended to stay his own hand if God had not sent the angel?

Abraham surely behaves as if he is ready to slay Isaac. Why should we not assume that he intended the natural consequences of his actions, which ended with him stretching out his hand and taking the knife to kill his son? Here an analogy to the law of attempted murder may be helpful.

The law of attempts deals directly with the problem of ascertaining a person's true intentions when he has *not* completed the crime but appears to have intended it. A vast literature has developed around this issue.[34] I recently argued a case that was similar, in certain respects, to the Abraham story. My client was accused of attempted murder after the police found him on top of another man, holding a knife over the other man's body. The police drew their guns and ordered my client to drop the knife, which he did. My client claimed that he did not intend to kill the other man, merely to frighten him into submission. Even if the police had not intervened, he said, he would never have plunged the knife into the other man's body. According to Bodoff, this was roughly the mind-set of Abraham at the moment the angel intervened.

How should the law go about assessing a claim of this kind? We can never know for certain what my client would or would not have done had the police not intervened. The facts of the case were consistent with either possibility. The man my client was accused of attacking had been dating my client's sister. Their relationship had been a troubled one, and someone burned down the sister's house, injuring her severely. The prosecution argued that my client believed that his sister's boyfriend had caused the fire and was trying to kill him in revenge. My client maintained that he had gone to see the other man to complain that he had not even bothered to visit the sister. A fight broke out, and my client was either holding the man at bay until the police arrived or trying to kill him. The jury believed the prosecution and convicted my client. Although we eventually won the appeal on an unrelated ground, the law of attempts supported the prosecution's case.

The law, in simplified terms, says that if a person changes his mind *without the intervention* of an outside force—the police or the angel—he is entitled to the benefit of the doubt. The law will presume that his change of mind was *internally* generated.[35] But if he withholds his hand as the result of an outside source—the police or the angel—the law will presume that he would have completed the crime *but for* the intervention of that outside source. It is, of course, possible that even in a case where the police stopped him, he would have stopped himself if the police had not been there. But we presume the opposite, because it appears—from the external evidence—that he had made the decision to proceed. We can never know for sure, since we are incapable of entering into his mind, but the degree of likelihood is deemed sufficient to overcome the general presumption of innocence and the requirement of proof beyond a reasonable doubt. (My ten-year-old daughter believes that Abraham was conflicted and that the angel represents his "better instinct" [*yetzer ha-tov*], which eventually prevailed. If so, the "angel" was an internal, rather than an external, source.)

Applying these principles to the Abraham narrative, one finds it difficult to accept Bodoff's interpretation. Both the text and general principles of law make it more likely that Abraham intended to kill his son.

That is certainly the *apparent* message of the test, as even Bodoff concedes. Indeed, he characterizes his interpretation as "a coded countermessage." And he has the right to his interpretation, since one of the glories of the Bible is its Rorschach test quality: its seventy faces and its amenability to multiple midrashim—interpretations.

Bodoff's analysis also suggests a somewhat darker interpretation—namely that Abraham *failed* God's test. He would have killed his son had God not sent the angel, and God was upset at Abraham for his willingness to kill on command. There is textual support for this interpretation as well. After all, it is *God* who commands Abraham directly at the beginning of the story. If Abraham had passed God's test with flying colors, we might expect *God Himself* to come down and praise Abraham. Instead God sends a mere messenger. In addition, when God first commands Abraham to offer up his son, He refers to Isaac as Abraham's "only son, whom thou lovest."[36] But after Abraham fails the test, the angel refers to Isaac twice as "thine only son,"[37] eliminating the description "whom thou lovest." This suggests that the angel does not believe that a father who was willing to sacrifice his son can be said to love him.[38] Moreover, God Himself never speaks to Abraham again.[39] Sarah dies soon thereafter. Isaac emerges from the experience a shattered person, who rarely speaks until his deathbed (where he is tricked by his son). One can only imagine the trauma a son would go through upon learning that his father was prepared to kill him. I would have loved to overhear the conversation between Isaac and his father on the way down from the sacrificial mountain: "You were preparing to do *what*?" To be sure, Abraham is rewarded with long life, wealth, a new wife, more children, and patriarchy, but in some respects all this seems like a consolation prize for doing his best, but not quite enough in God's eyes.[40] His personal relationship with God ended, because he disappointed his covenantal Partner. According to this interpretation, God used Abraham as an object lesson for future generations. People in those days sacrificed their children when the gods commanded it. Abraham was willing to do the same. But God's angel stopped him, thus signaling that *this* God was different. Indeed, some modern commentators, noting Isaac's silence and victimization by his father and son, as well as the advanced age of his parents when he was born, have speculated that he may have been retarded or emotionally disturbed. Throughout history parents have sacrificed retarded and disturbed children. This may explain Abraham's willingness to accept God's command. The message of this story is not in what *Abraham* did in setting out to sacrifice his son. It is in what *God* did in refusing Abraham's sacrifice. Abraham passed the test of obedience but failed the test of moral self-determination. Like a good student who messes up one exam, Abraham learned a great deal from the experience and was able to teach future generations from his own mistake.

An even more disturbing conclusion is offered by the writer and Nobel Peace Laureate Elie Wiesel, who argues that not only did Abraham fail the test, but so did God. No God should ever ask a father to kill his child, and no father should ever agree to do so. God may have eventually saved Isaac *physically*, but He crippled him emotionally, killing his mother in the process. A midrash recites how "Abraham returned home alone, and when Sarah beheld him, she exclaimed, Satan spoke truth when he said that Isaac was sacrificed and so grieved was her soul that it fled from her body."[41]

Even Bodoff concedes that many wrong lessons have been gleaned from this story. Perhaps the most disastrous is the concept of "daat torah," prevalent among some Hasidim, whereby the individual sacrifices his intellect on the altar of blind obedience to the words of the sages or a charismatic rabbi. The murder of Yitzhak Rabin by a Jewish fundamentalist who believed he was following God's command may be the best known consequence of this know-nothing interpretation of the Abraham narrative.

A more uplifting metaphoric interpretation, similar to my daughter's, is offered by a contemporary Conservative rabbi named Harold Schulweis, who suggests that Abraham passed the test by refusing to kill Isaac. He sees "the angel who stays Abraham's hand [as] a symbol of Abraham's moral conscience"—an aspect of Abraham, rather than of God. "Abraham's acceptance of the voice of the Lord's angel over God's commanding voice expresses his faith in a moral God who could not will the death of an innocent."

My own favorite interpretation is that by commanding Abraham to sacrifice Isaac, God was telling Abraham that in accepting the covenant, he was not receiving any assurances that life would be perfect. Far from it. Through that terrible test, God was demonstrating—in a manner more powerful than words could ever convey—that being a Jew often requires sacrificing that which is most precious to you—even children. The history of the Jewish people has certainly borne that out. During the Crusades, the Inquisition, and especially the Holocaust, many "Abrahams" made the decision to kill their own "Isaacs," sometimes to prevent their forced conversion, other times to prevent their torture, rape, and eventual murder. The traditional view of the *akeidah* influenced the willingness of Jews "to turn the Biblical prohibition against murder into an act that became recognized as a legitimate form of *kiddush ha-shem* [honoring of God], when fathers killed their children and wives and then committed suicide rather than face forced Baptism during the crusades."[42] Perhaps this took religious zealotry too far, but during the Holocaust even baptism could not save "genetic" Jews. Parents had to kill or abandon crying babies in order to prevent Nazis from finding Jews in hiding. In one poignant episode during the Holocaust, ninety-three teenage girls—students of a Jewish seminary in Cracow—reportedly took their own lives after learning that they were going to be forced to serve as prostitutes for German soldiers. Before taking poison, they collaborated on a poem, which included the following lines: "Death does not terrify us; we go out to meet him. We served our God while we were alive; We shall know how to sanctify Him by our death. . . . We stood the test, the test of the binding of Isaac."[43] These have been the tragic realities of Jewish life, and God was warning Abraham that the covenant offered no assurances that such sacrifices would not be required.[44] Sometimes God would intervene. Sometimes He would not. That is the nature of a covenant. So if a Jew witnesses tragedy—even the worst of tragedies, as did Job and those who saw their children die in the Crusades and Holocaust—do not think that God has broken the covenant. Religion is not a panacea for all of life's tragedies.

An Israeli rabbi made a similar point in the context of his nation's daily struggle: "Every parent in Israel who sees his son off to the army hears the divine command: 'Take your son, your only son, whom you love. . . .'"

I also have a favorite interpretation of why Abraham argued with God about the Sodomites but not about his own son. Good people are sometimes reluctant to argue for self-serving ends. They demand justice for others but are silent in the face of injustice to them. I have seen fellow Jews march energetically for the civil rights of others but sit passively when their own rights are violated. Many Jews who marched for the rights of blacks in the 1960s did nothing during the Holocaust. There is something more noble in advocacy for others than in self-serving advocacy. To be sure, some Jews speak up only for Jewish causes, not for others, but a great many are active in the struggle for universal human rights. The Bible instructs us not to "stand idly by the blood of your neighbors"; Hillel interpreted this to mean "If I am not for myself, who will be for me, [but] if am for myself alone, what am I?" The two apparently conflicting Abraham stories teach us to seek an appropriate balance between advocating for strangers and advocating for our own families.

Even if one concludes that the two Abrahams are irreconcilable, this too makes an important point: Genesis speaks with multiple voices; it does not seek to convey a singular message. The Abraham who argues with God represents one voice, while the Abraham who places his complete faith in God represents another. The New Testament explicitly speaks in multiple voices—the Gospel according to Mark, Matthew, and so on, while the different voices of the Old Testament are implicit. Genesis—as contrasted, for example, with the Ten Commandments—is not written in the voice of God; the stories are not presented from His point of view; indeed, God is described as simply one of the actors. Multiple points of view assure multiple interpretations.

Whatever interpretation the reader ultimately finds meaningful, one conclusion is clear: No one can read the story of the *akeidah* literally and accept it as a clear guide for human action. It cries out for explication, for disagreement, for reflection, and for concern. It provides no answers, only eternally unanswerable questions, and in that respect it is the perfect tool for teaching the realities, limitations, and imperfections of both divine and human justice. The story of Abraham and Isaac is real life writ large, with all of its tragic choices, ambiguities, and uncertainties.

---

1. 22:5.
2. *Midrash Rabbah*, vol. 1, p. 492, n. 6.
3. Weissman, Moshe, *The Midrash Says* (Brooklyn, NY: Bnai Yakov, 1980), p. 205.
4. Quoted in Leibowitz, Nehama. *Studies in Bereshith (Genesis)*. 4th rev ed. (Jerusalem: World Zionist Organization, Department for Torah Education and Culture, 1985), p. 189.
5. See Dershowitz, Alan, "Good Character Without Threat or Promise," in *The Power of Character*, ed. Michael S. Josephson and Wes Hanson (San Francisco: Jossey-Bass, Inc., 1998), pp. 268–75.
6. Twersky at p. 83. It is interesting to contrast Maimonides' sexism in comparing women to children with his progressive attitude toward a husband's obligation to satisfy his wife sexually—except if he is a scholar!
7. *Midrash Rabbah*, vol. 1, p. 376.
8. This is one of the rare instances in which an angel of God appears to a woman, Hagar. A midrash draws interesting parallels between the Isaac and Ishmael stories:

and the Lord's messenger called out to him from the heavens. This is nearly identical with the calling-out to Hagar in 21:17. In fact, a whole configuration of parallels between the two stories is invoked. Each of Abraham's sons is threatened with death in the wilderness, one in the presence of his mother, the other in the presence (and by the hand) of his father. In each case the angel intervenes at the critical moment, referring to the son fondly as *na'ar,* "lad." At the center of the story, Abraham's hand holds the knife. Hagar is enjoined to "hold her hand" (the literal meaning of the Hebrew) on the lad. In the end, each of the sons is promised to become progenitor of a great people, the threat to Abraham's continuity having been averted. Alter, Robert, *Genesis* (New York: W. W. Norton & Company, 1996), p. 106.

9. See Finkelman in Dershowitz, Alan, "The Case of the Speluncean Explorers: A Fiftieth Anniversary Symposium," *Harvard Law Review,* vol. 112, no. 8, June 1999, p. 1906.

10. Dershowitz, Alan, *Taking Liberties* (New York: Contemporary Books, 1988), p. 119, 271.

11. *New York Times,* April 7, 1999, p. 1.

12. Kierkegaard, Soren, *Fear and Trembling* (New York: Penguin, 1985), p. 60.

13. Leviticus 20:2–6, Exodus 13:11–16, Numbers 3:44–51.

14. Some rabbinic commentators try to have their theological cake and eat it too in this regard. Sometimes they argue that the patriarchs knew the Torah (see B. Rabbah), and other times they argue that they did not.

15. Levenson, Jon D. "Abusing Abraham: Traditions, Religious Histories, and Modern Misinterpretations," *Judaism* 47 (Summer 1998): 259–77.

16. Levenson at p. 274.

17. Levenson at p. 268. This is Kierkegaard's concept, which Levenson also criticizes as an incomplete justification.

18. "All along he had faith, he believed that God would not demand Isaac of him, while still he was willing to offer him if that was indeed what was demanded." Ibid at p. 65.

19. See Rabbenu Nissim, quoted in Leibowitz, Nahama, at p. 188 and Maimonides, quoted in Leibowitz, pp. 188–89.

20. Bodoff at p. 80.

21. Ibid., quoting sources.

22. Maimonides.

23. Maimonides, quoted in Leibowitz at p. 191.

24. Ginzberg at p. 282.

25. Rabbi Kook, quoted in Leibowitz at p. 204.

26. Bodoff at p. 71.

27. Bodoff at p. 76.

28. Baba Metzia, 59b.

29. One traditional answer is that the rabbis refused to listen to God's interpretation after He had given them the Torah, while Abraham's encounter with God preceded the Torah and came at a time when God gave orders orally.

30. One midrash suggests that Abraham should have made a different argument to God: "When You commanded me to sacrifice Isaac, I should have replied: 'Yesterday You told me: "In Isaac shall thy seed be called..." Nevertheless, I restrained my impulse and did not reply....'" See also *Midrash Rabbah,* p. 498.

31. *Midrash Rabbah,* vol. 1, p. 494.

32. Schulweis, Harold, *For Those Who Can't Believe* (New York: HarperCollins, 1994), p. 81.

33. Ginzberg, pp. 283–84.
34. For an interesting parallel between the law of attempts and halakah, see Nachshoni, Y., *Studies in the Weekly Parashah* (New York: Mesotah, 1998), pp. 96–98.
35. Locus penitente is defined as:

> a place for repentance; an opportunity for changing one's mind; an opportunity to undo what one has done; a chance to withdraw from a contemplated bargain or contract before it results in a definite contractual liability; a right to withdraw from an incompleted transaction. *Morris* v. *Johnson*, 219 Ga. 81, 132 S.E. 2d 45, 51. Also, used of a chance afforded to a person, by the circumstances, of relinquishing the intention which he has formed to commit a crime, before the perpetration thereof. Black, Henry Campbell, *Black's Law Dictionary*, 6th ed. (St. Paul, Minn.: West Publishing Co., 1990), p. 941.

In the law of attempts, locus penitente refers to that point in time after an attempt has technically occurred when the defendant can undo that crime by changing his mind and removing the danger.
36. Genesis 22:2.
37. Genesis 22:12, 16.
38. My student Meron Hacohen suggested this interpretation.
39. Armstrong, p. 69.
40. Shlomo Riskin, a modern Orthodox rabbi, was criticized for suggesting that Abraham should have argued for the life of Isaac and that he may have failed the test. Riskin at p. 13.
41. Ginzberg, p. 286.
42. Bodoff, p. 86, note 4.—The mass suicide at Masada exemplifies this perspective.
43. *The Reconsructionist*, New York, March 5, 1943, pp. 23–24. See also Brownmiller, Susan, *Against Our Will: Men, Women and Rape* (New York: Simon & Schuster), p. 332. Some historians have wondered whether this incident occurred as described, though no one doubts that Jewish women were raped during the Holocaust or that references to the binding of Isaac were common during periods of Jewish victimization. See Baumel, Judith Tydor, *Double Jeopardy, Gender and the Holocaust* (London: Valentine Mitchell, 1998), pp. 117–38.
44. Riskin at p. 17.

CHAPTER 7

Jacob Deceives—and
Gets Deceived

*When her days were fulfilled for bearing, here: twins were in
   her body!*
The first one came out ruddy, like a hairy mantle all over,
so they called his name: Esav [Esau in English]/Rough-One.
After that his brother came out, his hand grasping Esav's heel,
*so they called his name: Yaakov [Jacob in English]/Heel-
   Holder. . . .*
The lads grew up:
Esav became a man who knew the hunt, a man of the field,
but Yaakov was a plain man, staying among the tents.
*Yitzhak grew to love Esav, for [he brought] hunted-game for
   his mouth,*
but Rivka [Rebecca in English] loved Yaakov.

Once Yaakov was boiling boiled-stew,
when Esav came in from the field, and he was weary.
Esav said to Yaakov:
Pray give me a gulp of the red-stuff, that red-stuff,
for I am so weary! . . .
Yaakov said:
Sell me your firstborn-right here-and-now.

Esav said:

*Here, I am on my way to dying, so what good to me is a
    firstborn-right?*

Yaakov said:

Swear to me here-and-now.

He swore to him and sold his firstborn-right to Yaakov.

Yaakov gave Esav bread and boiled lentils;

he ate and drank and arose and went off.

Thus did Esav despise the firstborn-right.

GENESIS 25: 24–34

*Now when Yitzhak was old and his eyes had become too dim
    for seeing,*

he called Esav, his elder son, and said to him:

My son!

He said to him:

Here I am.

He said:

*Now here, I have grown old, and do not know the day of my
    death.*

*So now, pray pick up your weapons—your hanging-quiver
    and your bow,*

go out into the field and hunt me down some hunted-game,

and make me a delicacy, such as I love;

bring it to me, and I will eat it,

that I may give you my own blessing before I die.

Now Rivka was listening as Yitzhak spoke to Esav his son,

*and so when Esav went off into the fields to hunt down
    hunted-game to bring [to him],*

Rivka said to Yaakov her son, saying: . . .

*Pray go to the flock and take me two fine goat kids from
    there,*

I will make them into a delicacy for your father, such as he
    loves;
you bring it to your father, and he will eat, so that he may
    give you blessing before his death.
Yaakov said to Rivka his mother:
Here, Esav my brother is a hairy man, and I am a smooth
    man,
perhaps my father will feel me—then I will be like a trickster
    in his eyes,
and I will bring a curse and not a blessing on myself!
His mother said to him:
Let your curse be on me, my son!
Only: listen to my voice and go, take them for me.
He went and took and brought them to his mother, and his
    mother made a delicacy, such as his father loved.
Rivka then took the garments of Esav, her elder son, the choic-
    est ones that were with her in the house,
and clothed Yaakov, her younger son;
and with the skins of the goat kids, she clothed his hands and
    the smooth-parts of his neck.
Then she placed the delicacy and the bread that she had made
    in the hand of Yaakov her son.
He came to his father and said:
Father!
He said:
Here I am. Which one are you, my son?
Yaakov said to his father:
I am Esav, your firstborn.
I have done as you spoke to me:
Pray arise, sit and eat from my hunted-game,
that you may give me your own blessing.
Yitzhak said to his son:
How did you find it so hastily, my son?
He said: indeed, YHWH your God made it happen for me.

Yitzhak said to Yaakov:
Pray come closer, that I may feel you, my son,
whether you are really my son Esav or not.
Yaakov moved closer to Yitzhak his father.
He felt him and said:
The voice is Yaakov's voice, the hands are Esav's hands—
but he did not recognize him, for his hands were like the
    hands of
Esav his brother, hairy.
Now he was about to bless him,
when he said:
Are you he, my son Esav?
He said:
I am.

GENESIS 27:1–24

Now Lavan had two daughters: the name of the elder was
    Lea, the name of the younger was Rahel [Rachel in
    English].
Lea's eyes were delicate, but Rahel was fair of form and fair
    to look at.
And Yaakov fell in love with Rahel.
He said:
I will serve you seven years for Rahel, your younger
    daughter. . . .
So Yaakov served seven years for Rahel,
yet they were in his eyes as but a few days, because of his love
    for her. . . .
Now . . .
he took Lea his daughter and brought her to him,
and he came in to her.
Lavan also gave her Zilpa his maid,
for Lea his daughter as a maid.

Now in the morning:
here, she was Lea!
He said to Lavan:
What is this that you have done to me!
Was it not for Rahel that I served you?
Why have you deceived me?
Lavan said:
Such is not done in our place, giving away the younger before
    the firstborn;
just fill out the bridal-week for this one, then we shall give you
    that one also,
for the service which you will serve me for yet another seven
    years.
Yaakov did so—he fulfilled the bridal-week for this one,
and then he gave him Rahel his daughter as a wife.
Lavan also gave Rahel his daughter Bilha his maid,
for her as a maid.
So he came in to Rahel also,
and he loved Rahel also,
more than Lea.
Then he served him for yet another seven years.
[Rachel eventually gives birth to Joseph, to whom Jacob gives
    a coat of many colors.]

GENESIS 29:16–30

So it was, when Yosef [Joseph in English] came to his
    brothers,
that they stripped Yosef of his coat,
the ornamented coat that he had on,
and took him and cast him into the pit. . . .

Meanwhile, some Midyanite men, merchants, passed by;
they hauled up Yosef from the pit

and sold Yosef to the Yishmaelites, for twenty pieces-of-silver.
They brought Yosef to Egypt.

But they took Yosef's coat,
they slew a hairy goat
and dipped the coat in the blood.
They had the ornamented coat sent out
and had it brought to their father and said:
We found this;
pray recognize
whether it is your son's coat or not!
He recognized it
and said:
My son's coat!
An ill-tempered beast has devoured him!
Yosef is torn, torn-to-pieces!

GENESIS 37:23–33

Jacob, one of the most complex and interesting of the patriarchs of Genesis, lived a life of greatness and devotion to God, but also one of deceit and guile. His children seemed to follow in his footsteps. Yet God blesses Jacob repeatedly, bestowing on his male children the honor of tribal leadership. Why is such checkered conduct so highly rewarded?

A passing glance into Jacob's personal history shows us a man who cheated his twin brother, Esau, twice. The first time, the young Jacob withheld food from his fainting brother until Esau "sold" him his birthright. The second time, the mature Jacob—at the behest of his calculating mother—tricked his blind, dying father into giving him the blessing reserved for his brother. According to a midrash, Jacob had even

137

tried to emerge first from the womb by grabbing hold of Esau's heel. The midrash justifies the actions of the patriarch-to-be by speculating that Jacob "had been conceived first."[1] The evidence offered in support of this speculation seems more metaphoric than scientific. "The first drop was Jacob's . . . for consider: if you place two diamonds in a tube, does not the one put in first, come out last?"[2]

Some commentators go to great lengths in their efforts to justify Jacob's trickery, arguing that since he was far more suited to the work of leadership, and since God had prophesied to their mother that "the elder shall be servant to the younger," he was carrying out God's will.[3] Church fathers, like the rabbis, excused the ruse. Jerome called it a laudable lie, and Aquinas and Augustine defended the deception.[4] Some commentators argue that Isaac was not actually deceived, since he suspected that it was Jacob who was obtaining the blessing. But even if all of that is true, it is also true that Jacob employed means—extortion and deception—that are unacceptable in a just society. What then are the lessons to be learned from Jacob's acts of deception?

Let me offer an interpretation from the perspective of a teacher of law. The entire Book of Genesis is about the early development of justice in human society. Jacob is born into a world with few rules and many inconsistent precedents regarding deception. His father and grandfather, Isaac and Abraham, pretended their wives were their sisters in order to save their own lives. Moreover, his God is inconsistent in carrying out threats and promises. The result is a violent and lawless world. Remember too that the world of Genesis is without a hereafter in which virtue on earth is rewarded in heaven and vice on earth is punished in hell. All reward and punishment, both divine and earthly, are given in this world, where all can see the workings of justice.[5] All too often the inhabitants of Jacob's world saw virtue punished and vice rewarded—at least in the short run.

Along comes Jacob, whose entire life appears to offer proof that in the long run people reap what they sow. He who lives by deceit shall himself be deceived. The biblical narrative goes out of its way to show that Jacob's deceptions against others are turned back against him—over and over again. Moreover the deceptions inflicted upon Jacob are strikingly symmetrical with those he inflicted upon his brother and father.

First he is deceived by his father-in-law, Lavan, who plays bait and switch with his daughters. After working seven years for the hand of Lavan's younger daughter, Rachel, Jacob wakes up to discover that he has married the older daughter, Leah. Lavan's explanation of the deception brings home the symmetry: "Such is not done in our place, giving away the younger before the firstborn." After learning of Jacob's prior deceptions, Lavan describes his son-in-law as "my bone and flesh," which some have interpreted as soul mates in deception. Jacob had to understand the not-so-subtle moral of the story: Just as Jacob deceived in order to undo the natural order of birth, he was deceived to restore it.[6] Just as Jacob deceived his dim-sighted father, so too was he deceived in the darkness of his wedding tent.[7]

A midrash elaborates on Jacob's poetic justice. When he awakes on the morning after his wedding night and sees that he has slept with Leah, he reproaches her, saying: "O thou deceiver, daughter of a deceiver, why didst thou answer me when I called Rachel's name?" Leah responds: "Is there a teacher without a pupil? I but profited by thy instruction. When thy father called thee Esau, didst thou not say, here am I?[8] So did you call me and I answered you."[9]

After marrying Lavan's daughters (and their hand-maids) and having children by them, Jacob deceives Lavan by sneaking away with his entire family and cattle, while his father-in-law was shearing sheep.[10] He persuades his wives to join him with "great rhetorical cunning."[11] His wife Rachel also deceives her own father by stealing his idols and then covering up her theft. (A midrash says that Rachel stole her father's idols so "that her father might not learn about their [Jacob and family] flight *from his Teraphim*" [emphasis added]. This suggests that Rachel actually believed the idols had power of communication!)[12]

Later in life Jacob is deceived by his own children. Considering their lineage and training, it should not be surprising that they seem deceptive by nature. In the Dina story, which we consider in the next chapter, "The sons of Jacob answered Shechem and Hamor his father with guile [*b'mirma*]." They tricked all the men of the clan of Hamor into circumcising themselves, and then, while the Hamorites were weak, Simeon and Levi slaughtered them all.

Jacob was also tricked into believing that his youngest son, Joseph, had been eaten by a wild beast. The means employed to *deceive* Jacob were strikingly similar to the means Jacob had employed to *deceive* his father. Just as Jacob masqueraded beneath the fur of a goatskin, Jacob's sons killed a "hairy goat" and dipped Joseph's coat in its blood. What goes around comes around.

I have repeatedly observed the consequences of deception in the cases I teach and work on. One striking example was a prosecution against a restaurant owner whose establishment was burned to the ground. An inspection of his books revealed that the restaurant was overinsured: It had been valued far in excess of its meager income. For that reason, the owner was indicted for insurance fraud and arson. Eventually he confided to his lawyer that he had been cheating on his taxes by keeping false books understating his income. In fact, the restaurant was making a fortune—in cash—and was underinsured. A rival, understanding the catch-22, torched the restaurant. The case was eventually plea-bargained. As Sir Walter Scott was to put it centuries earlier: "Oh, what a tangled web we weave, when first we practice to deceive!"

If we are to read Jacob's life as a cautionary tale warning against the wages of deception, why then did the wily Jacob find so much favor in God's eyes? Why did God select this family to lead His chosen people? To understand God's seemingly unwarranted fondness for both father and sons one must appreciate that they were acting in a state of nature. In such a state, guile and deception are valuable traits, especially as alternatives to violence. There is no recourse to a legal system in the world of Genesis—no lawsuits, no injunctions, no penal sanctions. In order to succeed and not be victimized, an individual must rely on either violence or guile. Another ambitious man who believed that he was entitled to his older brother's birthright might have killed his competitor, as so many siblings have done in history and literature. Jacob simply outsmarted Esau, thus following in the family tradition established by his father and grandfather, both of whom had outwitted kings, rather than his ancestor Cain, who had resorted to fratricide. Like Odysseus in Greek literature, Jacob is praised as a wily man, ready and able to employ guile and deception to navigate the dangerous waters of life. In his interactions with other humans, Jacob eschews the violence of his more physical twin, Esau, preferring brain to brawn.[13]

Guile is the great leveler between the physically unequal. Jacob understands that he is no match for his stronger brother in the arena of physical combat. Nor is his clan a match for the far more numerous and warlike tribes. Accordingly, he must rely on his wit. It is interesting to note that the one attribute that is equally characteristic of biblical man and woman is guile. Although women are presented as physically, spiritually, and economically weaker than their male counterparts, they are equally adept at using trickery to level the playing field. Eve, Lot's daughters, Sarah, Rebecca, Rachel, Leah, Tamar, and Potaphar's wife all rely on their feminine wiles. Jacob, by favoring guile over the brute force of his stronger brother, can be said to be reflecting the feminine as well as the Jewish aspect of Rebecca's twins. Jews as a people and the women of Genesis share a common need to resort to guile in order to achieve the equality denied them in physical strength.

Jacob's actions toward his fellow man are often more tactical than principled. In the Dina story discussed in the next chapter we will see Jacob condemn the violence of his sons Simeon and Levi not because it is wrong, but because it will make him look bad in the eyes of his neighbors and subject him to possible retaliation. It is noteworthy that he does not condemn their deceptiveness in misusing circumcision, only their violence. For Jacob, noble ends justify ignoble means, as long as the benefits outweigh the costs. Because his family is weak in number but strong in intellect, he prefers the weapon of wit over sword. He chooses the battlefield on which he can win. In a world without law, what better qualification for leadership could there be?

Jacob extorts and tricks his brother into surrendering the benefits of his primogeniture, because he knows that he will be a more suitable leader. He is right. His mother knows he is right. Even his blind father suspects he may be right. And God knows he is right. Perhaps having Jacob born after his stronger brother was a test of his leadership skills: Can a second-born child depose his older brother from his "natural" status as leader? He passes the test with flying colors, though not without paying a heavy moral and psychological price.

For all of his trickery, Jacob never tries to deceive God. He bargains with Him, even wrestles with Him, but he is always straight with God. The result is that God blesses Jacob with leadership, but makes him understand that the wages of deception are deception. He who lives by guile will suffer from guile. In a world where deception is often rewarded in the short run, the life of Jacob demonstrates that over time we reap what we sow. Viewed backward—as all history is viewed—we see that Jacob pays a high personal price for the qualities that make him a good leader in a world before formal law. He tells Pharaoh: "Fear and evil have been the days of the years of my life."[14] Clearly, although Jacob was a great leader who left a wonderful legacy, the constant deceptions took an enormous toll on his personal life. This is a trade-off that will be repeated throughout history, especially in the lives of great leaders.

A contemporary commentator sees a more powerful moral in the Jacob narrative: "God's memory is just; the punishment of evil is not escaped. Sooner or later we all eat at the table of consequence."[15] In support of this long-term view of symmetrical justice, he cites a traditional rabbinic interpretation of the Jacob story: "Whoever maintains that the Holy One is lax in dispensing justice is grievously mistaken. God is long suffering but ultimately collects His due. Jacob made Esau break out into a cry only once, but . . . the descendants of Jacob were punished" both in the near term and throughout Jewish history.[16]

As with Jacob, we do sometimes see long-term, symmetrical justice. When such justice occurs, it becomes a first-page news item, as with the case of Lamija Jaha, an Albanian Muslim whose parents had sheltered Jews during the Holocaust and whose family was rescued by Israel nearly sixty years later.[17] More often, life confirms the maudlin observation of Ecclesiastes:

> I have seen wrong-doers being carried with pomp to their graves, and, as men return from the sacred ground, the evil-doers are praised in the city where they had acted thus. Indeed, this is vanity!
>
> Because judgment upon an evil deed is not executed speedily, men's hearts are encouraged to do wrong, for a sinner commits a hundred crimes and God is patient with him, though I

know the answer that "it will be well in the end with those who revere God because they fear Him and it will be far from well with the sinner, who, like a shadow, will not long endure, because he does not fear God."

Here is a vanity that takes place on the earth—there are righteous men who receive the recompense due to the wicked, and wicked men who receive the recompense due to the righteous. I say, this is indeed vanity.

If the intended message of the Jacob narrative is that you (and your descendants) inevitably reap what you sow, it is a false and dangerous message. All too often the wages of sin are prosperity and happiness. It is precisely because justice is not the natural condition of mankind—or the inevitable workings of God—that we are obliged to pursue it actively and not take it for granted. As the subsequent Book of Deuteronomy will mandate: Justice, justice shall you *pursue*—actively. Nor will it be simple. As Abraham taught us, some guilty must go free to assure that the innocent are not wrongly convicted. For those who now believe in a hereafter, those guilty will eventually receive their just deserts. For those who believe that the only justice is here on earth, the occasional freeing of the guilty will be seen as a necessary cost of every fair process of justice. Perhaps the freed guilty person will suffer in his life as Jacob did. Perhaps not. The story of a Jacob is a lesson about the symmetry of justice even in the absence of formal law. Yet even the presence of formal law does not always assure perfect justice in the real world. However, as we will see in the next chapter, the absence of formal law often leads to vigilantism.

---

1. Soncino Chumash at p. 141, n. 26.
2. *Midrash Rabbah*, vol. 2, p. 563.
3. Genesis 25:23.
4. See Plant, W. Gunther, ed., *The Torah: A Modern Commentary* (New York: Union of American Hebrew Congregations, 1981), p. 190.
5. Some rewards and punishments are, however, postponed to future generations. This is similar, in some respects, to the hereafter. See Chapter 13 infra.
6. See Kass, Leon, *Commentary*, March 1999, p. 48.
7. Ibid. at p. 49.
8. Ginzberg at p. 361.
9. *Midrash Rabbah*, vol. 2, p. 650.
10. Genesis 31:17–21.
11. See Kass at p. 52.
12. Ginzberg at p. 371.
13. In the words of one contemporary commentator, he relies "on craftiness to outwit superior force" (Kass at p. 52).
14. Genesis 47:9.
15. Schulweis, p. 72.
16. Schulweis, p. 72, quoting Genesis Rabbah 67:4.
17. See *New York Times*, May 2, 1999, p. 1.

CHAPTER 8

Dina Is Raped—and Her
Brothers Take Revenge

*Now Dina, Lea's daughter, whom she had borne to Yaakov,
   went out to see the women of the land.*

*And, Shekhem son of Hamor the Hivvite, the prince of the
   land, saw her:*

he took her and lay with her, forcing her.

*But his emotions clung to Dina, Yaakov's daughter—he loved
   the girl,*

and he spoke to the heart of the girl.

So Shekhem said to Hamor his father, saying:

Take me this girl as a wife! . . .

Hamor spoke with [Jacob and his sons], saying:

My son Shekhem—

his emotions are so attached to your daughter,

[so] pray give her to him as a wife!

And make marriage-alliances with us:

*give us your daughters, and our daughters take for yourselves,
   and settle among us! . . .*

*Now Yaakov's sons answered Shekhem and Hamor his father
   with deceit,*

speaking [thus] because he had defiled Dina their sister,

they said to them:

We cannot do this thing,
give our sister to a man who has a foreskin,
for that would be a reproach for us!
Only on this [condition] will we comply with you:
if you become like us, by having every male among you
circumcised.
Then we will give you our daughters, and your daughters we
will take for ourselves,
and we will settle among you, so that we become a single
people. . . .
Their words seemed good in the eyes of Hamor and in the eyes
of Shekhem son of Hamor, . . .
[A]ll the males were circumcised, all who go out [to war]
from the gate of his city.
But on the third day it was, when they were still hurting,
that two of Yaakov's sons, Shim'on and Levi, Dina's full-
brothers,
took each man his sword,
they came upon the city [feeling] secure, and killed all the
males,
and Hamor and Shekhem his son they killed by the sword.
Then they took Dina from Shekhem's house and went off.
Yaakov's [other] sons came up upon the corpses and
plundered the city,
because they had defiled their sister.
Their sheep, their oxen, their donkeys—whatever was inside the
city and out in the field, they took,
all their riches, all their little-ones and their wives they
captured and plundered,
as well as all that was in the houses.
But Yaakov said to Shim'on and to Levi:
You have stirred-up trouble for me,
making me reek among the settled-folk of the land, the
Canaanites and the Perizzites!

For I have menfolk few in number;
they will band together against me and strike me,
and I will be destroyed, I and my household!
But they said:
Should our sister then be treated like a whore?

GENESIS 34

The vigilante punishment meted out to Dina's rapist and his entire clan crystallizes a fundamental issue that pervades the Bible and has confronted every system of justice: individual versus collective responsibility and punishment.

Even before the Dina narrative, this issue had been foreshadowed: the collective punishment of all men and women for the sin of Adam and Eve, the flood, the destruction of Sodom. These were all inflicted directly by God. The vigilante punishment inflicted by Dina's brothers on "all the males" in the clan of Dina's rapist raises the issue in the starkest of human terms. The brothers trick the men into undergoing circumcision and then take advantage of their weakness, murder them in cold blood, and take their children, wives, and wealth.[1] As mentioned in the previous chapter, Jacob rebukes his sons for what they did, but not in moral terms. He is troubled because their actions will make him look bad in the eyes of his neighbors and perhaps subject him to retaliation. His sons have violated his prudential rule of winning against more powerful adversaries by deception alone and not force.[2]

The story of Dina is unrelated to the continuing narrative of the Book of Genesis. Dina never reappears.[3] We never learn what happened to her: A

149

Midrash has her becoming pregnant and giving birth to Joseph's wife, but there is no textual support for this speculation. Nor does the narrative reveal whether she approved of her brother's actions. The retaliation that Jacob feared never materializes. The only subsequent allusion to the Dina story occurs during Jacob's deathbed testament, wherein he recalls the lawlessness and anger of his sons Simeon and Levi.[4] Why then is this isolated vignette included in the Bible? What lessons about justice are we supposed to learn from the brothers' murderous vengeance and Jacob's tactical reproach?

Several of the "defense lawyers" are quick to justify the actions of the patriarch and his children. They point to the words of the text that say that the brothers destroyed "the city which had defiled their sister," thus suggesting that all the residents of the city are in some way guilty.[5] Even Maimonides, who often questions the actions of biblical heroes, argues that all the men who were killed were guilty because they did not bring the rapist to trial for his crime. Maimonides points to the Noachide laws that govern non-Jews and, according to the commentators, prohibit seven specific acts. There are several problems with this argument. First, rape is not among the seven prohibitions, so Maimonides is forced to define Shechem's act as "robbery"—an insult to women, since it analogizes them to property. Second, the Noachide laws do not prescribe capital punishment for inaction or even for accessories. Third, even the more stringent Jewish law does not punish rape of an unbetrothed maiden by death.[6] Fourth, even if the men deserved to be executed, surely they were entitled to some legal process. Nachmonides disagrees

150

with Maimonides's justification but claims that the men deserved to die because they "were wicked" and had "thereby forfeited their lives."

As a final irony, the victims here were Jewish when they were killed, since they had been circumcised. This led one cynical rabbi to conclude that Shim'on and Levi had them circumcise themselves because no one cares if Jews are killed!

Many traditional commentators seem to presume guilt on the part of anyone who incurs the wrath of God, a patriarch, or even the son of a patriarch. If a man was punished, he must be guilty of something! If he was punished severely, he must be guilty of something quite serious. I am reminded of the joke that went around the Soviet Gulag during the time I was representing Jewish refuseniks. One prisoner asks another prisoner what he had done to warrant his ten-year sentence. "I did absolutely nothing," the second prisoner responds. "You are a liar," the first one shoots back. "For absolutely nothing, they only give you five years!"

If a commentator begins with the premise that certain biblical heroes can do no wrong, he must necessarily find fault with those who have been killed or otherwise punished by the hero. This variation on the "blame the victim" defense recurs in the story of Job and among some traditional commentaries. Job's friends are certain he must have sinned to have been punished so harshly. Traditional commentators argue that even Bathsheba's husband—who was sent to the front to die so David could marry Bathsheba—must have done something quite awful to deserve the horrible treatment he received at the hands of the hero David. This sort of backward thinking leads to the belief that all disasters are the fault of the victims. Patrick Buchanan once said that AIDS is God's revenge on homosexuals, while an ultra-Orthodox rabbi insisted that the Holocaust was God's way of punishing pork eaters.

Some contemporary commentators go so far as to argue that it is forbidden to criticize any of the great biblical figures. One must always find virtue in their actions. One talmudic sage actually says that "whoever suggests that David sinned [with Bathsheba] is mistaken." Several years ago a fight broke out in Israel's Knesset, when a Labor minister suggested that David's action had been less than pure. Nachmonides rejects this hagiographic approach and declares that "Abraham our father sinned a great sin unwittingly, that he brought his righteous wife to [the brink of] the stumbling block of sin because of his fear lest he be killed." But even those traditional commentators most willing to criticize biblical heroes always find some mitigation. Rabbi Shlomo Riskin, a contemporary modern Orthodox biblical commentator, places the views of Nachmanides in an acceptable religious context:

> [Nachmanides] may very well have believed that it is only when we can identify with the personalities of the Bible, when we see them as great human beings but human beings nonetheless, who grapple with—and sometimes even fail in their effort to overcome—the very same problems and blandishments which assail our every step, that we can truly utilize them as models and learn from their experiences. . . .
>
> Indeed, it is difficult to read the pages of the

Bible in accordance with the "literal meaning of the text" and not come to the conclusion that our Torah pictures its heroes and heroines as complex human beings, rising to great spiritual heights and descending to jealous hatreds, prone to sin, but always with the element of spirituality which enables them to rise above their weakness and accomplish great things; it is their very struggle which makes them worthy of our veneration and makes possible their emulation.[7]

Rabbinic commentators observe that "the greater a person is, the greater is his Yetzer hara" (evil instinct), and his greatness is shown by overcoming it.[8] Psychologist David Rapaport related the following contemporary midrash on this topic from the life of Moses. Before being afflicted with the plagues, Pharaoh sent his royal painters to create an accurate portrait of his enemy-to-be. He then gave the portrait to his royal phrenologists so that they could assess his strengths and weaknesses. After examining the portrait, they concluded that Moses was a weak and vain man, who would easily be intimidated and flattered—that he was no match for Pharaoh. After Moses proved that he was more than a match, Pharaoh ordered his painters and phrenologists to appear before him. "Either the portrait was inaccurate or the interpretation was wrong," he bellowed. When Moses next appeared to demand the release of the Jews, Pharaoh asked him to determine whether it was the painters or the phrenologists who were wrong and must die. Moses said both were correct: "I *am* a weak and vain man. Those are my inherent characteristics. But I have struggled mightily to overcome them."

The concept of the flawless biblical hero who can do no wrong and whose victims deserve their punishment is inconsistent both with real life and with the Jewish Bible. The Pentateuch, like all great literature, recognized that no human being is perfect. This recognition is one of the reasons why the Five Books of Moses have been so enduring and influential. Biblical heroes make mistakes; they succumb to human passions; they violate rules and commandments; often they try to rationalize, deny, or cover up their sins and crimes. But the Bible does not airbrush the blemishes of its heroes. Like Oliver Cromwell's portrait painter, it depicts its subjects "warts and all." The Jewish Bible is not hagiography, despite efforts by some defense lawyer commentators to make it such.

Those commentators who assume that the victims of Simeon and Levi's murderous revenge necessarily deserved what they got send a terrible message about justice. The message is that right and wrong are a matter of *status* rather than *action*: If the actor is of a certain status—patriarch, son of a patriarch, prophet, king, or other hero—then it follows that his actions must be justified, regardless of how unjust they may appear to be (this is ever truer of God Himself, who surely can do no wrong). It is the job of the defense lawyer commentator to figure out *why*—not *whether*—the actions of such elevated beings were justified. The corollary, of course, is that if the hero does something terrible to a nonhero, the latter must have deserved it.

The status approach to justice has been pervasive

throughout history and certainly not limited to Jews or biblical commentary. "The king can do no wrong" was a principle of common law. Status-bound justice has often been used against "the Jews" or against individuals of Jewish heritage. Early Christian theology argued that the victimization of Jews—by crusades, inquisitions, pogroms, or discrimination—was always justified by the dual collective sins of deicide and rejection of Christ. To the Nazis, everything done by a Jew was bad. Even in modern Poland it is said that if something bad has happened, "there must be a Jew behind it."

It is an imperative of justice that culpability be based on a fair assessment of the actions and intentions of individuals, regardless of their status. Those commentators who can see no evil in the actions of biblical heroes undercut justice. We must be open to the possibility that the victims of Simeon and Levi's treacherous massacre were as innocent as the Jewish victims of collective revenge over the centuries. We should not search for—or manufacture—rationalizations to justify so brutal a mass murder. Nor should we be satisfied with Jacob's tactical rebuke of his vengeful sons. If the biblical narrative is to serve as a teaching tool of justice, we must condemn Simeon and Levi's mass murder on moral grounds, while perhaps understanding the passions that led them to impose such disproportionate and collective revenge.

The Bible certainly understands the inherent human passion for vengeance. In one of the most subtle and innovative ideas of the subsequent law books, God commands Moses to "appoint . . . cities of refuge . . . that the manslayer who killed any person *by accident* may flee into."[9] Murderers were not entitled to such refuge from the "blood avenger," but accidental killers were entitled to protection until passions cooled. The Bible thus recognizes that the passion for revenge may be just as great against the accidental killer as against the premeditated murderer. To the dead victim's family, there may be very little difference. Their loved one is dead, and the person who caused his death is guilty and deserves to die. I hear that cry often when I try to argue that a killer should be found guilty of manslaughter rather than murder. I will never forget a case in which my client, a woman, shot her husband and was convicted of murder. I argued on appeal that his history of abusing her warranted a reduction to manslaughter. When I finished my argument, an older woman came over to me and pulled out a picture: "This is my son who I will never see again because of your client. She should suffer like I must." I understand why the victim's relatives are outraged at my effort to mitigate the crime that robbed them of a loved one. To understand, however, is not necessarily to justify. The Bible tries to protect the less culpable killer from the understandable passions of the blood avenger by allowing the killer to seek refuge in a designated place for a specified period of time. If the killer leaves the city of refuge and the blood avenger "finds him" and slays him, "there shall be no blood-guilt upon him." The Bible recognizes that an avenger who kills "while his heart is hot" is not as culpable as one who kills in cold blood.[10] This insight, which becomes a basic tenet of the subsequent law books of the Bible, derives from the narratives of Genesis, which feature cold-blooded, hot-blooded, and lukewarm-blooded killings.

The mass murder of the clan of Hamor by Dina's

brothers fits somewhere between hot-blooded revenge and cold-blooded deterrence. On the one hand, the brothers were understandably outraged by the crime against their maiden sister. On the other hand, what they did required a carefully planned subterfuge involving one of the most sacred rituals of Judaism—circumcision. (One midrash goes so far as to suggest that their actions have made it more difficult for potential converts to trust in the good faith of Jews who require circumcision as a condition of conversion.)[11] Moreover, there are ambiguities in the biblical narrative about precisely what had been done to Dina and what her own wishes were. Like so many of the women of Genesis, Dina remains entirely silent during the ordeal.

It is not surprising that we never hear from the rape victim herself, since during biblical times—and for centuries thereafter—rape was considered primarily a crime against the father, husband, or fiancé of the raped woman.[12] The Bible provides that "if a man finds a virgin *who is not betrothed* and lays hold of her and lies with her," his punishment is to pay *the father* fifty shekels and to marry the virgin and never divorce her.[13] The reason for this punishment is that the man, by deflowering the woman, has "damaged" the "goods" of the father, thus making his daughter less valuable as a commodified bride. The rapist must make the father whole by paying him money and relieving him of the burden of an unmarriageable daughter.[14] Paradoxically, however, according to the Bible the rapist must be punished because he "humbled" *the woman*. (The Hebrew word for "humbled" is *ena*, which comes from the same root as the word used to describe what Shechem did to Dina: *va yehaneha*.)

157

Lest there be any doubt who the real victim of rape is in the Bible, compare the punishment for raping an unbetrothed virgin—fifty shekels and permanent marriage—to that for raping a betrothed virgin: death. The betrothed virgin herself is also put to death unless she cried out, because if she submitted without protest, she is deemed to have consented, thus offending her betrothed.

Nor did this male-centered attitude toward rape die an easy death. As recently as 1964, the Georgia Supreme Court characterized rape as a crime against "the most precious attribute of all mankind"—the "purity" of woman, which is "soil[ed] for life" by rape.[15] In 1992 an Ohio court quoted a 1707 case describing "adultery [as] the highest invasion of [a husband's] property."[16]

It is against this patriarchal background that the ambiguity of the Shechem-Dina encounter must be understood. Some of the commentators divide the initial blame between Shechem and Dina. As one midrash puts it:

> While Jacob and his sons were sitting in the house of learning, occupied with the study of the Torah, Dinah went abroad to see the dancing and singing women, whom Shechem had hired . . . in order to entice her forth.[17]

Thus in one sentence the Jewish men are presented as scholars, the Gentile man as a manipulative seducer, and the Jewish woman as an easy mark.

Dina is faulted by some of the rabbis for going "out" of the confines of her father's tents. One rabbinic sage suggests that she went out "adorned like a harlot."[18] Others argue that if she had "stayed home," the way women are supposed to, "nothing would have happened to her."[19] "But she was a woman," a midrash explains, "and all women like to show themselves in the street."[20]

For whatever reason, Dina did not stay home and something did happen to her. Precisely *what* happened to her is the subject of much dispute among commentators. Most agree that the initial encounter was forced upon her against her will. Rashi says she was sodomized.[21] Ibn Ezra says it was "natural" sex, but she was "afflicted" because she was a virgin. There are even suggestions that she was a consenting partner but that the brothers still blamed the man for damaging her worth to their father. Whatever the nature of the initial encounter, the mutuality of the subsequent relationship is even murkier. We know how Shechem felt about Dina: He loved her and was willing to do anything in order to marry her. We also know he spoke to Dina "comfortingly" and that she was ensconced in his home. But because Dina never speaks, we can only surmise her feelings toward the man who initially humbled her, then spoke to her comfortingly and eventually underwent circumcision in order to marry her. The word "comfortingly" is an interactional adverb, suggesting that Dina was comforted by Shechem's words, but her reaction is never made explicit. A particularly disturbing midrash says that "when a woman is intimate with an uncircumcised person, she finds it hard to tear herself away!"[22] This early example of penis envy suggests that Dina did want to remain with Shechem, but not necessarily because of his comforting words alone.

The image of a rapist trying to comfort his victim

is a common one today, particularly in the context of acquaintance rape. Speaking comfortingly can be an effective tactic designed to prevent the victim from calling the cops. We know that batterers often speak comfortingly to their victims, promising never again to strike them, only to see the cycle continue. It is certainly possible that Dina was not comforted by what she perceived as a tactic. On the other hand, Shechem's rape of her may have reflected his own clan's primitive courting ritual—a violent and sexist practice all too common throughout history. Perhaps he had truly come to love Dina and had succeeded in comforting her, despite the initial outrage. We don't know, because we never hear Dina's voice.

It is not clear whether Shim'on and Levi knew—or even cared about—their sister's attitude toward Shechem. When Shechem took their sister without the permission of the men who owned her, *their* honor had been offended. Much depends, of course, on these unknowns. If the brothers were rescuing an unconsenting sister from forced marriage, that would be one thing. If they were kidnapping her from the man she loved and killing that man and his entire clan in the process, that would be another thing entirely.

All the Bible tells us is that the brothers resented the implication of any deal being made under which a rapist marries his victim and the victim's family obtains material remuneration. "Should our sister then be treated like a whore?" they ask rhetorically. But it is the Bible itself that treats an unbetrothed rape victim in this manner. What the clan of Shechem proposed in the Dina narrative is very nearly what the law books of the Bible later decree: payment to the rape victim's father and marriage to the rape victim.

Why should the clan then be punished by mass murder for offering to do what the Bible would later mandate? Moreover, these same brothers who were outraged that their sister was treated like a commodity later treat their own brother in much the same way, selling him into slavery. A midrash on Jacob's blessing of his sons recognizes this inconsistency:

> After Reuben had had his "ears pulled" thus, he retired, and Jacob called his sons Simon and Levi to his side, and he addressed them in these words: "Brethren ye were of Dinah, but not of Joseph, whom you sold into slavery. The weapons of violence wherewith ye smote Shechem were stolen weapons, for it was not seemingly for you to draw the sword."[23]

Another example of the Bible speaking in different voices is provided subsequent to the Dina narrative in the deathbed testament of Jacob, in which the patriarch alludes to the earlier events:

> *Shim'on and Levi,*
> *such brothers,*
> *wronging weapons are the ties-of-kinship!*
> *To their council may my being never come,*
> *in their assembly may my person never unite!*
> *For in their anger they kill men,*
> *in their self-will they maim bulls.*
> *Damned be their anger, that it is so fierce!*
> *Their fury, that it is so harsh!*
> *I will split them up in Yaakov,*
> *I will scatter them in Yisrael.*[24]

161

The fact that their rebuke comes at the end of Jacob's life—after the passions of his daughter's rape and his sons' revenge have cooled—gives added significance to Jacob's condemnation of vigilante justice. Nevertheless, the tribes of Simeon and Levi prosper, with the Levites becoming the holy priests.

The narrative is thus a Rorschach test to be interpreted anew by every generation, consistent with its experiences and needs. In fact, the Dina narrative—most particularly the relative guilt and innocence of the avenging brothers—has been subjected to very different interpretations over time. In the biblical period, when clan violence and retaliation were the norm, the actions of Simeon and Levi were praised as demonstrations of strength. In subsequent generations, when rules of law and process began to emerge, Jacob's rebuke became more prominent. Then, when intermarriage became a major concern, the narrative was interpreted as a condemnation of intermarriage. The fact that Shechem raped Dina was less opprobrious than the fact that he then tried to marry her.[25] In the post-Holocaust era there was a return, among some, to praising Simeon and Levi for taking the law into their own hands: "A pronounced revisionist strain in postwar Biblical scholarship suggests that Simeon and Levi, rather than Jacob, are the 'real heroes' . . . precisely because they picked up their swords and made war on Shechem to vindicate their sister's defilement."[26] Simeon and Levi are the "real heroes" because their "idealistic and uncompromising stance makes them the most intricate, colorful and attractive characters in the story."[27]

Not surprisingly, zealots have cited the story of Dina to justify utterly reprehensible actions, such as Baruch

Goldstein's murder of twenty-nine Muslims at prayer in Hebron. Similarly, it has been cited by Muslim and Christian extremists in support of their murderous actions.[28]

Today, some feminists point to the Dina story as speaking with a different voice about the horrors of rape than the subsequent law books of the Bible. Without justifying the mass murder of the entire clan, they praise Dina's brothers for at least understanding the humiliation of rape better than those who later punished it by a fine paid to the "real" victim—the father.

Therein lies both the glory and the danger of morally ambiguous biblical narrative. Because of its open-textured quality, it endures from generation to generation, taking on new meaning as historical experiences change, and inviting continuing reassessment of its implications. By the same token, because it is subject to multiple—often conflicting—interpretations, the biblical narrative can be cited by the devil, or at least his human counterparts, to justify the most evil of deeds.

---

1. Only two brothers, Shim'on and Levi, actually do the killing.
2. On his deathbed, Jacob is far more reproachful of Shim'on and Levi: "Their weapons are tools of lawlessness. . . . [W]hen they are angry they slay men" (49:5–7).
3. Except in a listing of descendants (46:15). A midrash has her becoming Job's second wife. Ginzberg, vol. 2, p. 226.
4. Kugel, James, *The Bible as It Was* (Cambridge, Mass: Harvard University Press, 1977), p. 233. Genesis 49: 5–7.
5. Rashi and Ibn Ezra avoid the difficult issue, since they generally limit themselves to interpretation (*pshat*).
6. See Deuteronomy 22:28–29.
7. See Riskin, Shlomo, *Confessions of a Biblical Commentator* (Ohr Torah Institutions, 1997), pp. 12–13.
8. Chasam Sofer, *Bereishis*, p. 256.
9. Numbers 35:9–34.
10. Deuteronomy 19:6.

11. *Midrash Rabbah*, vol. 2, p. 953, n. 2.

12. The voice of women is all too rarely heard in the Bible. A contemporary midrash, in the form of a fascinating novel, tells the Dina story from the point of view of the woman involved. Diamant, Anita, *The Red Tent* (New York: St. Martin's Press, 1997).

13. Deuteronomy 22:28–29. The Bible draws a distinction between a betrothed woman who has sex with another man "in the city"and "in the field." The former, who could have cried, is complicit; the latter, who could not have been rescued even if she cried out, is not. Deuteronomy 22:23–27.

14. See Hauptman, Judith, *Rereading the Rabbis: A Woman's Voice* (Boulder, Colo.: Westview, 1998), pp. 77–82; Kirsch, Jonathan, *The Harlot by the Side of the Road* (New York: Ballantine, 1997), pp. 76–99.

15. *Sims* v. *Balkcolm*, 136 S.E. 2d. 766.

16. *State* v. *Shane*, 590 N.E. 2d 272 (1992).

17. Ginzberg at p. 395.

18. Quoted in Kirsch at p. 76.

19. Ibid.

20. Ginzberg at p. 395.

21. In discussing Shechem's love for Dina, the Torah uses the word *"na'ar"* twice. A *na'ar* is a boy. Thus the literal reading of the sentence is "And he loved the boy and he spoke comfortably unto the boy" (Genesis 34:3). The editors of the Hebrew Bible regard this as a common transcription error and instruct the reader to "read it as 'na'arah,'" the young girl. Perhaps this gender confusion is what led Rashi to speculate that Shechem had "unnatural" anal sex with Dina—as if she were a boy! Saperstein edition, the Torah, p. 383.

22. *Midrash Rabbah*, vol. 2, p. 743. Maimonides makes a related observation: that one of the reasons why Jews are circumcised is to reduce their sex drive. See Stern, Josef, *Problems and Parables of Law* (Albany, NY: SUNY, 1998), pp. 88–91.

23. Ginzberg, vol. 2, p. 142.

24. 49:5–7.

25. See Kugel, James, *The Bible as It Was* (Cambridge, Mass.: Harvard University Press, 1997), pp. 237–39.

26. Kirsch at p. 95.

27. Meir Sternberg as quoted in Kirsch at p. 96. A midrash compares the Dina story to the Book of Esther, suggesting that the clan of Hamor was planning to kill the Jews, who acted in preemptive self-defense (Ginzberg at p. 399).

28. Recently an ultra-Orthodox rabbi in Israel cited approvingly the story of the biblical religious zealot Phineas, who murdered two lovers in cold blood because one of them was not Jewish (Numbers 25:6–9). The rabbi's words were understood by some as justifying the murder of intermarried couples by "real" Jews. See Kirsch at p. 91.

CHAPTER 9

Tamar Becomes a Prostitute — and the Progenitor of David and the Messiah

Yehuda went down, away from his brothers
and turned aside to an Adullamite man—his name was Hira.
There Yehuda saw the daughter of a Canaanite man—his
  name was Shua,
he took her [as his wife] and came in to her.
She became pregnant and bore a son, and he called his name:
  Er.
She became pregnant again and bore a son, and she called his
  name: Onan.
Once again she bore a son, and she called his name: Shela. . . .

Yehuda took a wife for Er, his firstborn—her name was
  Tamar.
But Er, Yehuda's firstborn, did ill in the eyes of YHWH, and
  YHWH caused him to die.
Yehuda said to Onan:
Come in to your brother's wife, do a brother-in-law's duty by
  her,
to preserve seed for your brother!
But Onan knew that the seed would not be his,

so it was, whenever he came in to his brother's wife, he let it
    go to ruin on the ground,
so as not to provide seed for his brother.
What he did was ill in the eyes of YHWH,
and he caused him to die as well.
Now Yehuda said to Tamar his daughter-in-law:
Sit as a widow in your father's house
until Shela my son has grown up.
For he said to himself:
Otherwise he will die as well, like his brothers!
So Tamar went and stayed in her father's house.
And many days passed.

Now Shua's daughter, Yehuda's wife, died.
When Yehuda had been comforted,
he went up to his sheep-shearers, he and his friend Hira the
    Adullamite, to Timna.
Tamar was told. . . .
She removed her widow's garments from her,
covered herself with a veil and wrapped herself,
and sat down by the entrance to Enayim/Two-Wells, which is
    on the way to Timna,
for she saw that Shela had grown up, yet she had not been
    given to him as a wife.
When Yehuda saw her, he took her for a whore, for she had
    covered her face.
So he turned aside to her by the road and said:
Come-now, pray let me come in to you—
for he did not know that she was his daughter-in-law.
She said:
What will you give me for coming in to me?
He said:
I myself will send out a goat kid from the flock.
She said:

Tamar Becomes a Prostitute

Only if you give me a pledge, until you send it.
He said:
What is the pledge that I am to give you?
She said:
Your seal, your cord, and your staff that is in your hand.
He gave them to her and then he came in to her—and she be-
    came pregnant by him.
She arose and went away,
then she put off her veil from her and clothed herself in her
    widow's garments.
Now when Yehuda sent the goat kid by the hand of his friend
    the Adullamite, to fetch the pledge from the woman's hand,
he could not find her.
He asked the people of her place, saying:
Where is that holy-prostitute, the one in Two-Wells by the
    road?
They said:
There has been no holy-prostitute here!
So he returned to Yehuda and said:
I could not find her; moreover, the people of the place said:
    There has been no holy-prostitute here!
Yehuda said:
Let her keep them for herself, lest we become a laughingstock.
Here, I sent her this kid, but you, you could not find her.

Now it was, after almost three New-Moons
that Yehuda was told, saying:
Tamar your daughter-in-law has played-the-whore,
in fact, she has become pregnant from whoring!
Yehuda said:
Bring her out and let her be burned!
[But] as she was being brought out,
she sent a message to her father-in-law, saying:
By the man to whom these belong I am pregnant.

And she said:
Pray recognize—
whose seal and cords and staff are these?
Yehuda recognized them
and said:
She is in-the-right more than I!
For after all, I did not give her to Shela my son!
And he did not know her again.

GENESIS 38:1–26

Until now we have seen woman as sexual commodity, conniving manipulator, and disobedient subject. Now we see her—and hear her—in a somewhat different light: as procreator of biblical man.

The Genesis story that best reflects this role is the bizarre soap opera involving sex for pay between Judah and his disguised daughter-in-law Tamar. The brief vignette, which appears in the middle of the Joseph story, is packed tightly with numerous layers, each inviting multiple interpretations.

First, the story serves as the biblical foundation for the mysterious ritual of the "Levirite marriage." This ritual, which is elaborated later in the Bible,[1] requires a brother to impregnate his widowed sister-in-law if his dead brother has left her without a male child.[2] The "Levirite (Latin for brother-in-law) marriage" is designed to protect the blood line of the dead brother, so that "his name shall not be blotted out." Indeed, the resulting male child, though genetically the son of the sperm donor, is legally the son of the dead brother, whose name he carries and whose property he inherits.

In the Tamar story, Judah—the fourth son of Jacob,

whose name will be given to the Jewish people—marries a Canaanite woman, who bears him three sons. Judah arranges for his oldest son, Er, to marry Tamar, a woman of unspecified, but probably not Jewish, heritage. The commentators struggle to make Tamar Jewish by concocting imaginative tales of her origin, because she becomes the progenitor of some of the important Jewish leaders: *"chalilah* [God forbid] that David and Mashiach [the Messiah] should be from the cursed seed of Canaan."[3] In any event, God found Er to be wicked and slew him. The commentators speculate over the precise nature of Er's evil. Rashi believes that Er committed the same sin for which his younger brother Onan was famously killed—spilling his seed so as to avoid impregnating Tamar. His selfish reason, according to Rashi, was that "he did not want her to lose her beauty through pregnancy and childbirth."[4] Whatever the reason,[5] Tamar was now childless and husbandless. So Judah instructed his son Onan to fulfill his Levirite duty by impregnating his sister-in-law.

Onan was now faced with a clear conflict of interest. If he satisfied his Levirite duty and succeeded in producing a male heir, Onan would deprive himself (and his future children) of Judah's inheritance. As matters now stood, Onan was Judah's eldest son and heir. But if Tamar had a male child, that child—Er's son by law—would become the primogenic heir, since Er's line would continue through that child.

No wonder, then, that Onan, knowing that "the seed would not be his," engaged in coitus interruptus and deliberately spilled his seed on the ground "so as not to provide seed for his brother." Rashi delicately describes Onan's actions as "threshing within, winnowing without,"[6] while another sage—Ben Tamin Ha-Mizrachi—indelicately characterizes the act as anal intercourse. The midrash employs the euphemism "he ploughed on roofs" to describe "unnatural inter-course."[7] This provoked an angry response from Ibn Ezra: "This interpretation is sheer madness. Heaven forbid that the holy seed become defiled with such filth."[8] Whatever the mechanics of the act, God was not pleased at Onan's obvious circumvention of the Levirite duty, and He slew Onan, too. This left poor Tamar with two dead sex partners and no seed.

Before we return to the plight of Tamar, we need to turn briefly to Onan, whose name carries a terrible legacy in modern religious sermonizing. The sin of onanism—of spilling one's seed on the ground—has been preached against by generations of rabbis, priests, and ministers. "If you masturbate, you will be struck dead"—or at least blinded or made bald or have hair grow on the palm of the offending hand. The humorist Dorothy Parker mocked this puritanical view by naming her parrot "Onan," because he too spilled his seed on the ground. Parker may have been no less faithful to the text than some of these traditional commentators, because masturbation was not Onan's grievous sin; it was failing to satisfy his Levirite duty. Both involved spilling one's seed for nonprocreative purposes, but there the similarity ends. According to one contemporary commentator,

Onan's name has come to be associated with masturbation, but only because of an intentional misreading of the Bible story by sermonizers of Victorian England who were obsessed with the imagined evil of masturbation. Anx-

ious to find at least some faint biblical authority for condemning it, the moral guardians of
the nineteenth century seized upon Onan as a
cautionary example of what can go wrong when
one engages in "self-abuse."[9]

Now back to Tamar. Her father-in-law, Judah, had
yet a third son, and since neither of his other sons
had managed to impregnate Tamar, Judah was obliged
to promise Tamar the seed of his youngest son, Shelah. He did so, but without intending to keep his
promise, since he was worried that sex with Tamar
carried some kind of black-widow curse. Considering
the fate of his first two sons, who can blame him? So
Judah—who is presented as rather cold and calculating; we never see him grieving the loss of his first two
sons—orders Tamar to go back to live with her father's
family until Shelah has grown up, hoping that distance will discourage her from holding him to his
promise. The dutiful daughter-in-law follows Judah's
command and moves back to her village.[10] Eventually
she realizes that she has been duped. Shelah, who has
now grown up, is never going to perform his Levirite
duty and she is going to end up a childless widow,
with no claim to Judah's fortune and no status in
Judah's clan.

With the benefit of a bit of biblical hindsight, we
realize that this could not be allowed to happen, since
Tamar is slated to become the foremother of King
David and the prophet Isaiah, as well as the Messiah.
Indeed, Tamar is the best and last hope that Judah
will have any male heirs, since his first two sons were
struck down before fathering any children and his
youngest virtually disappears from biblical view fol-

lowing this story and does not seem to have fathered any children.[11] The entire future of the Jewish people, who eventually derive from the clan of Judah, is now at risk and in the hands—or, more precisely, the empty womb—of Tamar.[12] Tamar must beget a male child from the seed of Judah.

According to midrashic commentary, Tamar had been given the gift of prophecy and knew that she was destined to become "the mother of the royal line of David, and the ancestors of Isaiah."[13] For the resourceful Tamar prophecy is no substitute for action: She must give destiny a shove in the right direction. Her actions move us to the next layer of this complex story.

Convinced that Judah will never let Shelah impregnate her, Tamar takes advantage of two facts she has just learned: first, that Judah has recently been widowed; and second, that he is about to pass on a road not far from her village.[14] Again we see a relatively cold Judah, quickly completing his obligation to mourn his deceased wife and rushing to join the sheepshearing festivities. As we know from elsewhere in the Bible, "sheepshearing was the occasion for elaborate festivities, with abundant food and drink."[15] Determined to carry the seed of Judah—if not by way of his children, then by way of Judah himself—Tamar dresses herself as a harlot and sits by the side of the road, her face covered by a veil. Judah propositions her and agrees to pay her a baby goat in exchange for sex. The midrash regards this as an extraordinary fee for such services, observing that a loaf of bread is the usual compensation for sex with a harlot. Some commentators see the baby goat as symbolic, because "it picks up the motif of the slaughtered kid whose blood was used by Judah and his brothers to deceive Jacob (as Jacob before them used a kid to deceive his father)."[16] Tamar also uses a garment—the harlot's veil—to fool Judah, much as Judah used Joseph's garment to fool Jacob.[17] Tamar agrees to Judah's proposition and demands a pledge until he can arrange to have the goat sent to her. He gives her his signet and staff, they have sex, and she becomes pregnant.

When Judah returns home, he is determined to pay his debt to the harlot and retrieve his telltale possessions. But his messenger can find no trace of any harlot near the place where Judah encountered the veiled woman.[18] In the meantime, Judah is told that his widowed daughter-in-law is pregnant, apparently from whoring around. Furious at this family dishonor, Judah demands that Tamar be brought to him and burned.[19] But the wily Tamar produces the signet and the staff and declares that "by the man to whom these belong I am pregnant."

The commentators stress that Tamar did not directly accuse her father-in-law, waiting instead for him to acknowledge his responsibility. They suggest that the dutiful daughter-in-law would not have blown the whistle on Judah if he had remained silent,[20] because she did not want to embarrass him. This seems questionable in light of the fact that she had deliberately asked for his seal, which is intended as a source of identification. Upon inspection of the seal, it would become apparent who its owner is, since a seal is the ancient equivalent of a modern credit card or driver's license.[21] It is fair to infer that she intended to use it as insurance against precisely the accusation she anticipated.

Confronted with the evidence, Judah revokes the

death sentence, contritely proclaiming that Tamar is more righteous than he, since he had broken his promise to give her to his son Shelah. This part of the story ends with a strange coda: Judah did not "know her again" (38:26).[22]

Why would the Bible go out of its way to tell us that Judah did not have sex with Tamar again? Surely the reader should assume that now that he knows the harlot on the side of the road is his own daughter-in-law, he wouldn't dream of violating the incest taboo that was later explicitly and emphatically incorporated in Leviticus 18:15. Moreover, since she is now pregnant with his—and his dead son's—child, there is no longer a Levirite obligation.[23] Perhaps the reason is precisely to emphasize that it is never proper to have sex knowingly with one's daughter-in-law, even if the woman's husband and the man's wife are now dead and even if it is intended to fulfill the Levirite duty.

On a larger level, the Tamar story tells us much about the dependent status of women during biblical times. Moreover, it seems that the author intended to praise Tamar for her resourcefulness: She plays within the rules and still gets her due. The system was heavily weighted against women in general and against childless—really sonless—widows in particular.[24] Tamar understood she was in no position to demand her rights. So she resorted to an approach common in the Book of Genesis—trickery. Indeed, if some of the later books of the Bible glorify violence, it can fairly be said that Genesis accepts trickery as a way of achieving one's legitimate rights or accomplishing one's destiny. Certainly Tamar is in the good company of Abraham (who tricked a pharaoh and Abimelech), Isaac (who tricked Abimelech), Jacob (who tricked

174

Esau twice and his father, Isaac), Rebecca (who helped Jacob trick Isaac), Lavan (who tricked Jacob), Rachel (who tricked Lavan), Jacob's older sons (who tricked Jacob),[25] and Joseph (who tricked his brothers).

As is typical in Genesis, Tamar's trickery is part of a cycle of deception. It is payback for Judah tricking her into believing that his third son would fulfill the Levirite obligation and for Onan tricking her into having sex with the false expectation of impregnation. But Tamar is not victimized by further trickery, nor is she criticized for tricking Judah into impregnating her. Indeed, she is praised even by the man she fooled and is rewarded by giving birth to twins who become the progenitors of the Jewish people and two of their greatest heroes, as well as the Messiah.

This story, like several others in Genesis, reflects ambivalence about the rules of status that prevailed in biblical times. Just as the secondborn Jacob is praised for securing his rights and destiny in the face of primogeniture, so too is Tamar praised for her determination and ingenuity in the face of societal rules that render a childless widow worthless. These, however, are not revolutionary stories. The heroes don't change the rules but instead triumph by dint of their creative manipulations of the system. Tamar does not employ violence, only guile. Her deceptions are proportional and rational. She employs self-help to avoid an unjust punishment. The Bible seems to be suggesting a precursor to the common-law doctrine of "necessity," under which ordinarily illegal actions are justified if necessary to prevent a greater evil. For example, a starving man may break into an empty home to secure food, and an endangered ship may enter a private mooring to avoid sinking. Trickery is wrong,

175

as is sex outside of marriage and especially with one's father-in-law, but if these actions are necessary to secure one's right to procreate, they may be deemed justified. The imperative of motherhood—especially motherhood of biblical leaders—trumps even the rules against incest, as it did when Lot's daughter raped their father in order to save humankind.

In addition to foreshadowing a legal defense—necessity—the story of Tamar is also the first biblical account of a criminal trial. Primitive as it is, Judah's summoning and sentencing of Tamar is a legal proceeding. To be sure, it is an Alice in Wonderland trial, with the death sentence preceding the evidence. Eventually, however, Tamar is permitted to present her case and reverse the judgment. Judah is legislator, prosecutor, judge, jury, and executioner. His word is law, and his law is arbitrary fiat. Fortunately for Tamar, he is a benevolent despot who is willing to acknowledge the error of his ways. Judah rules neither because he is righteous nor because the people have selected him, but rather because of his status as the head of his clan. In a primitive world without formal law, one's position determines rights. In such a world, guile is needed to overcome the injustices of status.

Some would say these stories of guile—more than the later tales of conquest and violence—are a metaphor for how Jews managed to get along throughout most of their history. Physically powerless to fight against discrimination and marginalization, they sometimes resorted to methods of self-help that relied on wit and artifice. Although they played by the rules established by their Christian and Muslim hosts, they learned how to use these rules—such as the prohibition against moneylending—to their advantage.

Viewed this way, the narrative of cunning and guile becomes a knife that cuts both ways. On the positive side, they are metaphors for survival in a hostile world. At the same time, they play into the stereotype of Jew as manipulator and trickster. Shakespeare's Shylock was surely a manifestation of this negative image, which continues in some places to this day.

In 1990 I became embroiled in a dispute over the nomination of a grossly unqualified political hack for a local judgeship. My colleague Harvey Silverglate joined me in testifying against the appointment. The then president of the Massachusetts Senate, who was sponsoring the nomination, was quoted by the *Boston Globe* as having said the following about us:

> Bulger contended that Dershowitz and Silverglate are "very manipulative" and "exceedingly crafty" lawyers. . . . After citing the Old Testament story of Jacob and Esau, who was tricked into selling his birthright, Bulger called Dershowitz "a true conniver."[26]

Bulger urged his colleagues to "look at their faces," as if to emphasize our ethnicity. Both the *Globe* and the *Herald* characterized his statements as ethnic stereotyping and soft-core anti-Semitism. This contemporary tale of bigotry demonstrates how some people still use the Old Testament as a source of anti-Semitic stereotyping.

Be that as it may, the story of Tamar's deception is also part of a literary tradition, most famously represented by Oedipus, in which forbidden sex is carried out behind a veil of ignorance. We see this even earlier in Genesis when Abraham and Isaac pass their wives off as their unmarried sisters.

To illustrate Ecclesiastes's point that there is nothing new under the sun, consider the following news item from 1996:

> NASHVILLE, Tenn.—The "Fantasy Man" was convicted of rape by fraud Thursday after two women described how he duped his victims into disrobing and agreeing to blindfolded sex because they thought he was their lover.
>
> Police believe Mitchell, 45, has called hundreds of women over the years. Most hung up on him. But of the 30 women who reported Fantasy Man encounters to police, eight said they had sex with the caller.
>
> Each encounter began with an early-morning phone call to the sleeping women, prosecutors said. Whispering softly, he persuaded them he was their boyfriend and asked them to fulfill his fantasy of having sex with a blindfolded woman.
>
> One woman said she had sex with Fantasy Man twice a week over two months in 1992, and only discovered he wasn't her boyfriend when her blindfold slipped off.[27]

The Tamar narrative also raises the issue of exchanging sex for property. It is not the only such story in Genesis. The bizarre vignette concerning the "mandrakes" has perplexed commentators over the millennia. Leah and Rachel are both married to Jacob, but Jacob clearly prefers the company of Rachel, for whom he had worked an additional seven years. Leah had already provided Jacob with children, but Rachel had not. One of Leah's children finds some exotic plants—called *dudaim* in Hebrew and translated as "mandrakes"—in the field and brings them to his mother. Rachel covets them because, the commentators suggest, they were thought to promote conception.[28] Leah was not in a giving mood toward her rival sister, reminding her that she had "taken away my husband." Rachel offers to exchange a night of sex with Jacob for the mandrakes, and Leah gleefully accepts. When Jacob comes home from work that night, expecting to sleep with Rachel, Leah demands that he "come in unto" her, since she has "hired" him in exchange for the mandrakes.[29] Jacob accedes and impregnates Leah once again. Shortly thereafter Rachel also conceives and gives birth to Joseph. The mandrakes apparently worked.

The traditional commentators justify both of these sexual exchanges as necessary to fulfill the woman's imperative of motherhood, especially when it is their destiny to become the progenitors of God's chosen people and His chosen leaders. As the sixteenth-century Italian commentator Obadiah Ben Jacob Sforno put it: "To some [the mandrake] incident may appear immodest. Its purpose is to indicate that the matriarchs were only motivated by the desire to bear children and produce a people that would serve God."[30] So too with regard to the Tamar episode. Not only is Tamar's sexual trickery justified as necessary to fulfill her destiny, but Judah is also acquitted of paying for sex with a harlot by the following midrash:

> He wished to go on, but the Holy One, blessed be He, made the angel who is in charge of desire appear before him, and he said to him:

"Whither goest thou, Judah? Whence then are kings to arise, whence are redeemers to arise?" Thereupon, he turned unto her—in despite of himself and against his wish.[31]

(I know some clients who wish they had thought of the "The angel of desire made me do it" defense!) Maimonides makes a somewhat more plausible defense of Judah:

> [H]arlotry was permitted in those times—just as non-kosher foods were not forbidden—before the Torah was given. Even though the Patriarchs—and presumably their families—observed the Torah before it was given, they did so *voluntarily*, so that it was conceivable that where necessary they would act according to the laws that were obligatory at the time. Consequently, if the Divine plan required Judah to cohabit with a "harlot," he would be permitted to do so.[32]

Talk about having it both ways: The patriarchs get credit when they obey the Torah, but no blame when they don't!

The Genesis stories all take place before the advent of formal rules of law (with the exception of the basic Noachide laws). The heroes and heroines must make tragic choices, balancing lesser evils against greater evils, without the benefit of legislation. The story of Tamar—like the stories of Lot's daughters, Abraham's and Isaac's wives, Rachel and Leah's mandrakes, and others—illustrates the idea of the necessary evils. There are no perfect options, but in the face of greater harm, a bit of proportional deception is deemed acceptable. Tamar's trickery paves the way for the story of Joseph, in which a series of deceptions serve as prelude to the Exodus and Sinai—and the formal legal codes.

---

1. Deuteronomy 25:5–10.
2. "The legal obligation of 'yibum' . . . was a widespread practice in the ancient Near East . . ." (Alter, p. 218).
3. Weisman, p. 363.
4. Rashi, Genesis 35:7.
5. Robert Alter speculates that Er's evil may have been nothing more than yet another instance of God's displeasure at firstborn males: "Though the first born is not necessarily evil, he usually turns out to be obtuse, rash, wild, or otherwise disqualified from carrying on the heritage" (Genesis, p. 218). This is part of God's pattern of "reversal of primogeniture in all of these stories."
6. Alter, p. 218.
7. *Midrash Rabbah*, p. 792.
8. Ibn Ezra, p. 357.
9. Kirsch, Jonathan, *The Harlot by the Side of the Road* (New York: Ballantine, 1997), p. 139.
10. "[S]he evidently remains under his legal jurisdiction, as his issuing of a death sentence against her (v. 24) indicates" (Alter, p. 219).
11. In listing the progeny of Jacob, Tamar's twins are attributed to Judah, rather than Er, and Shelah is mentioned only as one of Judah's five children (Genesis 46:12).
12. Kirsch, p. 143.
13. Kirsch, p. 147.
14. Prior to Sinai, the Levirite duty could, when necessary, be fulfilled by close family members other than a brother-in-law, but not by a married man. See Chasam Sofer, *Commentary on Bereishis* (Art Scroll, 1996), p. 257.
15. Alter, p. 219.
16. Alter, p. 220.
17. Ibid.
18. The Bible uses different words when first describing what Judah believed the woman to be and when he later describes her to his messenger. The first word—*zonah*—means ordinary prostitute. The second word—*k'deishah*—connotes some kind of a religious prostitute associated with pagan temple worship.
19. The hasty nature of Judah's judgment and his severe sentence demonstrates the need for process, which becomes evident in the Joseph story. The Chasam Sofer observes that under non-Jewish law at the time, Tamar could not be executed while pregnant. They would postpone the execution until after the birth (Sofer at p. 258). Mishnah Arachin 1:4 provides that "if a [pregnant] woman were sentenced to death, they do not wait for her until she shall have given birth, [but] if she were sitting on the birth stool, they must wait for her until she shall have given birth."
20. Genesis 38:25 (Rashi).
21. Alter, p. 221.
22. The biblical Hebrew is somewhat ambiguous.

23. At least as long as the child is a male. It is interesting that the biblical begets list the father of Tamar's children as Judah, rather than Er, who—under Levirite practice—should get the credit (Genesis 46:12).

24. Childless and sonless married women were also treated badly and would do almost anything to produce a male heir in order to elevate their status. As Rachel said: "Give me children or else I die" (Genesis 30:2).

25. Their tricking of Hamor's clan doesn't fit into this category because they used it as a prelude to mass murder.

26. December 6, 1990.

27. Associated Press, January 19, 1996.

28. Alter points to the verbal similarity between the word *"dudaim"* and the poetic word for lovemaking, *"dodimi."* The Song of Songs also makes this association.

29. Alter sees an association between Leah trading "a plant product" for sex and Jacob trading porridge for a birthright.

30. Soncino, p. 175.

31. *Midrash Rabbah*, pp. 794–95.

32. Scherman, Nosson, *The Chumash* (Brooklyn, NY: Mesorah Publications, Ltd, 1993), Stone Ed. p. 211.

CHAPTER 10

Joseph Is Framed—and Then Frames His Brothers

[Potiphar's] wife fixed her eyes upon Yosef [Hebrew for
    Joseph]
and said:
Lie with me!
But he refused, . . .
When he came into the house to do his work,
and none of the house-people was there in the house—
that she grabbed him by his garment saying:
Lie with me!
But he left his garment in her hand and fled, escaping outside.
Now it was, when she saw that he had left his garment in her
    hand and had fled outside, . . .
Now she kept his garment beside her, until his lord came back
    to the house.
Then she spoke to him according to these words, saying:
There came to me the Hebrew servant whom you brought to
    us, to play around with me;
but it was, when I lifted up my voice and called out,
that he left his garment beside me and fled outside.
Now it was, when his lord heard his wife's words which she
    spoke to him,

saying: According to these words, your servant did to me!—
that his anger flared up;
Yosef's lord took him and put him in the dungeon house, in the
*   place where the king's prisoners are imprisoned.*

GENESIS 39:7–20

[Joseph was made second in command to Pharaoh, after he
*   was taken from prison to interpret Pharaoh's dreams. In*
*   the meantime, Jacob sent his children to Egypt in quest of*
*   food.]*

Now [Joseph] commanded the steward of his house, saying:
Fill the men's packs with food, as much as they are able to
*   carry,*
and put each man's silver in the mouth of his pack.
And my goblet, the silver goblet, put in the mouth of the
*   youngest's pack, along with the silver for his rations.*
He did according to Yosef's word which he had spoken.
At the light of daybreak, the men were sent off, they and their
*   donkeys;*
they were just outside the city—they had not yet gone far—
*   when Yosef said to the steward of his house:*
Up, pursue the men. . . .

[A]nd the goblet was found in Binyamin's pack!
They rent their clothes,
each man loaded up his donkey, and they returned to the city.
Yehuda and his brothers came into Yosef's house
he was still there—
and flung themselves down before him to the ground.
Yosef said to them:
What kind of deed is this that you have done! . . .
So now,

184

pray let your servant [Yehuda] stay instead of the lad, as
   servant to my lord,
but let the lad go up with his brothers!
For how can I go up to my father, when the lad is not with
   me?
Then would I see the ill-fortune that would come upon my
   father!

GENESIS 44:1–34

Yosef could no longer restrain himself in the presence of all
   who were stationed around him, . . .
Then Yosef said to his brothers;
   I am Yosef. Is my father still alive?
But his brothers were not able to answer him,
for they were confounded in his presence.
Yosef said to his brothers:
Pray come close to me!
They came close.
He said:
I am Yosef your brother, whom you sold into Egypt.
But now, do not be pained,
and do not let upset be in your eyes that you sold me here!
For it was to save life that God sent me on before you.

GENESIS 45:1–5

Joseph is best known as the interpreter of dreams
and the economic genius—the Alan Greenspan—who
saved Egypt from famine and reunited his family in
Egypt. But Joseph is also a victim who overcomes his
victimization and turns it into triumph. Most of Genesis's other victims—Abel, Sarah, Lot, Isaac, Dina,
Shechem—are quickly forgotten or relegated to a pas-

sive role in the narrative. Joseph, on the other hand, emerges triumphant, gets back at his treacherous brothers, and emerges as the family hero. (Tamar, as well, fits into the category of a victim who overcomes.)

The story of Joseph, like that of his father, is partly about symmetrical justice—payback. Joseph is sold into bondange by his own jealous brothers—a slight improvement over the fratricide of Cain—and his father is deceived into thinking that his favorite son has been torn apart by a wild beast. The means of deception is a garment smeared with animal blood. Then Joseph is framed for a crime he did not commit by the woman—Potiphar's wife—who sought to seduce him into adultery. She also uses physical evidence against him (in much the same way Iago plants evidence against Desdemona in Shakespeare's *Othello*) and falsely accuses him of attempted rape.[1] Joseph remains silent and is placed in prison. A midrash says that Potiphar knew Joseph was innocent but had to find him guilty in order to spare his children the stigma of being born to a harlot. Joseph's punishment—imprisonment instead of death—is given as proof of this interpretation.[2] Another imaginative midrash has Potiphar buying Joseph "for a lewd purpose, but the angel Gabriel mutilated him in such manner that he could not accomplish it."[3] In any event, Joseph ends up in prison, where his dream interpretations—really prophecies—bring him to the attention of Pharaoh. Joseph interprets Pharaoh's dreams to predict seven years of good harvests followed by seven years of famine. He proposes a solution to the coming crisis and is appointed overseer of all of Egypt. A midrash declares that "God never allows the pious to languish in distress longer than three days!"[4] If only that were so.

Years later, when his starving brothers come to Joseph for food, the overseer behaves a bit as his father, Jacob, had done when his starving brother, Esau, begged for porridge. Joseph decides to play games with his brothers as part of a grand retributive scheme. He gets them to bring their youngest brother, Benjamin—who had remained at home with their father—to Egypt, promising that no harm will come to the lad. When Benjamin is brought to him, Joseph arranges to frame his younger brother for stealing. He plants a goblet in Benjamin's pack, in much the same way Potiphar's wife misused physical evidence against him. A midrash relates Joseph's hiding the goblet to his mother's secreting her father's idols and to his brothers' selling of him:

> He searched all the sacks, and in order not to excite the suspicion that he knew where the cup was, he began at Reuben, the eldest, and left off at Benjamin, the youngest, and the cup was found in Benjamin's sack. In a rage, his brethren shouted at Benjamin, "Oh thou thief and son of a thief! Thy mother brought shame upon our father by her thievery, and now thou bringest shame upon us." But he replied, "Is this matter as evil as the brethren that sold their own brother into slavery?"[5]

Joseph's macabre joke works; the brothers—even the innocent Benjamin—are terrified for their lives. Only then does Joseph pull back the curtain and reveal himself as their missing brother. A dramatic midrash says that "Joseph bared his body" to show that he was circumcised.[6] Whatever means he used to prove who he was, the brothers are relieved to learn that they had been the victim of nothing more than a retaliatory prank. From then on, the story progresses to a happy ending, as Jacob is brought to Egypt for a reunion with his long-lost son.

Jacob can now die relatively happy, but not before he blesses his children and grandchildren. Jacob saves his greatest blessing for Joseph's two sons, Ephraim and Manasseh, commanding his progeny to bless all of Israel in the following way: "May God make you like Ephrayim and Menashe." Why was this special blessing saved for the children of a marriage between an Israelite and the daughter of an Egyptian priest? Was Jacob a social climber who favored Ephraim and Manasseh because they had more material wealth and higher civil status than any of his other grandchildren? Did Jacob grant this favor to children close to the king in order to secure Pharaoh's protection of his entire family? Surely Joseph's children were not more Jewish; indeed, by current Jewish halakah they were not Jews at all, since their mother was an idol worshiper and they were brought up as part of the Egyptian nobility.

Some of the defense lawyers argue that their mother must have converted to her husband's faith and brought up the children pursuant to the covenants God had made with Abraham and Jacob. But there is little textual evidence to support this theory or to suggest that even Joseph lived in Egypt as an Israelite. Indeed, the very last words of the Book of Genesis describe how Joseph was buried, not as an Israelite (in a simple grave with only a shroud), but as an Egyptian (embalmed and placed in an ark). His father, Jacob, had also been embalmed by physicians,[7] but his body was brought back to the burial ground of his ancestors. Joseph's body, on the other hand, remained in Egypt until the Israelites made their Exodus, and then his "bones" were taken along by Moses for burial in the Jewish homeland. Since Joseph had been embalmed, the question arises: What happened to the rest of his body; why were only his bones taken out of Egypt? Perhaps the symbolic message is that although Joseph died as an Egyptian (embalmed) he was eventually buried as Jew (unembalmed, with only his bones surviving).[8] A midrash criticizes Joseph for embalming his father's corpse:

> Joseph ordered the physicians to embalm the corpse. This he should have refrained from doing, for it was displeasing to God, who spoke, saying: "Have I not the power to preserve the corpse of this pious man from corruption? Was it not I that spoke the reassuring words, Fear not the worm, O Jacob, thou dead Israel?" Joseph's punishment for this useless precaution was that he was the first of the sons of Jacob to suffer death.[9]

Perhaps these stories of Jews living among Egyptians—and assimilating some of their ways but not others—are intended to convey a message about choice. Ephraim and Manasseh, alone among Jacob's grandchildren, had the choice whether to follow the covenant of their ancestors or adopt the ways of the foreign nation where they had been born. Jacob's blessing, "May God make you like Ephrayim and

Manasseh," was the patriarch's way of recognizing that Jews throughout history will be presented with similar choices. Ephraim and Manasseh chose the way of the covenant, as did Abraham and Jacob—despite the availability and material benefits of other alternatives. It was the act of choosing to be a Jew, rather than merely being born into that heritage, that Jacob found deserving of special praise. A fantastic midrash tried to make Joseph's wife a Jew, despite the biblical text. It claimed that Joseph's wife was the daughter of his sister, Dina, by the murdered Shechem. "An angel carried the babe down to Egypt, where Potiphar adopted her as his child, for his wife was barren." Joseph "became acquainted with her lineage, and he married her, seeing that she was not an Egyptian, but one connected with the house of Jacob. . . ."[10] This is an example of a midrash seeking to conform the biblical narrative to later halakic rules, such as the matrilineal descent of Jewishness.

Jacob and Joseph elected to have their remains removed from Egypt and taken to the Jewish homeland. That decision too is praised by God. A midrash says that Jacob did not want to be buried in Egypt because he knew that Egypt would be inflicted with plagues, "and it revolted him to think of his corpse exposed to such uncleanliness."[11] But then what about Joseph, whose corpse remained in Egypt during the plagues? A midrash, as usual, has a creative answer: Joseph was buried in a "leaden coffin."[12]

Choice is rewarded over status because it entails a thoughtful weighing of options and a renewal of the covenant, which—after all—is an arrangement of mutual choice and agreement. Jacob's blessing can be seen, therefore, as a step in the direction of elevating contract, which is a matter of choice over status, which is beyond the control of the actor.

The themes of deception and false accusation, which recur throughout the Jacob and Joseph narratives, contribute to the development of justice in the Book of Genesis. Those who are falsely accused remain silent in the face of the accusation, since there is nothing they can say to clear themselves of guilt based on damning physical evidence. When Potiphar's wife accuses Joseph, the innocent young Jew does not try to cast the blame on her. When Joseph later falsely accuses Benjamin, the brothers do not try to defend themselves. Yehuda implores Joseph, "How can we speak? How can we clear ourselves?" Their frustration in the face of the planted evidence is palpable. They cannot defend themselves without accusing their prosecutor and judge. Finally Yehuda pleads for mercy and proposes a plea bargain: He will remain a slave in place of his younger brother.

It is ironic that Yehuda (Judah) should emerge not only as the advocate for justice, but also as the volunteer hostage. It was, after all, the very same Yehuda who had come so close to executing his daughter-in-law Tamar for a sin in which he himself had participated. Tamar had saved herself by preserving the evidence of Yehudah's complicity. Yehudah had apparently learned from Tamar several important lessons—both tactical and moral—about advocacy and justice. The tactical lesson he had learned was not to confront authority directly. Tamar simply produced the signet and staff, without accusing Yehuda. This led Yehuda to recognize the injustice of his hastily imposed sentence. Now it is Yehuda who is the victim of an injustice. He does not accuse Joseph of planting the goblet, though he must have suspected as much. Instead he recognizes Joseph's unchallenged authority over him and his brothers—an authority parallel to that which he had exercised over Tamar—and implores Joseph to do the right thing. Joseph was, of course, going to do the right thing regardless of the nature of his brother's plea, but not until he had taught them a lesson about how it feels to be victimized by those more powerful than you.

A midrash suggests that Joseph did not actually fool his brother Benjamin, only the brothers who sold him into bondage. Its purpose is obviously to show that Joseph would never inflict pain on an innocent bystander, only on those who deserve payback:

> Joseph ordered his magic astrolabe to be brought to him, whereby he knew all things that happen, and he said unto Benjamin, "I have heard that the Hebrews are acquainted with all wisdom, but dost thou know aught of this?" Benjamin answered, "Thy servant also is skilled in all wisdom, which my father has taught me." He then looked upon the astrolabe, and to his great astonishment he discovered by the aid of it that he who was sitting upon the throne before him was his brother Joseph. Noticing Benjamin's amazement, Joseph asked him, "What hast thou seen, and why art thou astonished?" Benjamin said, "I can see by this that Joseph my brother sitteth here before me upon thy throne." And Joseph said: "I am Joseph thy brother! Reveal not the thing unto our brethren. I will send thee with them when they go away, and I will command them to be brought back again into the city,

and I will take thee away from them. If they risk their lives and fight for thee, then shall I know that they have repented of what they did unto me, myself known unto them. But if they forsake thee, I will keep thee, that thou shouldst remain with me. They shall go away, and I will not make myself known unto them."[13]

The sinning brothers do not forsake their innocent sibling, and Joseph—realizing that his revenge has gone far enough—identifies himself and exposes the charade. Now that the old score has been settled, the brothers can move on and reunite. All is forgiven, but not forgotten, as their father will remind them in his deathbed legacy.

The Joseph narrative illustrates a world in which justice ultimately prevails, but not because of the rule of law. Justice, in the Joseph story—as in the Tamar story—depends entirely on the whims of men, the fickleness of fate, and the miracles of God.

The horror of false accusation will recur throughout Jewish history. The blood libel alone—the false accusation that Jews use the blood of ritually murdered Christian children to bake matzo—took thousands of Jewish lives during the Middle Ages.[14] The jurisprudence of the Bible's law books, especially Exodus and Deuteronomy, reflects the frustrations felt first by Joseph and later by his brothers. The bearing of false witness—which includes the planting of evidence—is made a terrible sin and crime explicitly proscribed in the Ten Commandments. Its punishment is symmetrical to the crime: You are to "do to him as he schemed to do to his brother."[15] The law also builds in other protections against false accusations, as if to recall the ease with which the powerful—Potiphar's wife and later Joseph the overseer—could plant false evidence against the powerless and the difficulty the powerless have in defending themselves against such overwhelming physical evidence.

These stories of false evidence are the first intimations of the need for a legal process—for *procedures* of law in addition to the *substantive* rules. "Thou shall not kill" does not prevent an innocent person from being falsely accused of killing. The earlier crimes of Genesis were seen by God and judged by Him. Abraham worried that the innocent would be swept along with the guilty not because the evidence was false (a procedural issue), but because God would impose collective responsibility on an entire city as he had on the entire world (a substantive issue). God responds by acknowledging—implicitly—the inherent human difficulty in distinguishing the guilty from the innocent and the need for a fair process. Later on, in the Book of Exodus, God is even more categorical: "Keep far from a false matter; and the innocent and righteous do not slay. . . ."[16]

The Joseph narrative alerts us to the most primitive kind of evidentiary problem: the deliberate misuse of evidence in an effort to frame the innocent. There are, of course, many variations on this theme. For instance, evidence can be planted against the guilty in order to make their conviction more certain. There have been numerous instances of such misconduct in modern times, most notably by New York State Troopers who were convicted of planting fingerprints against drug dealers they had difficulty catching. Mistaken identification and imperfect memory may cause the inadvertent conviction of the innocent.

Modern DNA testing makes this more difficult, but certainly not impossible. Bias by the decision maker may skew the evidence against the accused or in extreme cases may cause the decision maker to ignore plain evidence of innocence. It is impossible for any legal system to protect against all errors—either deliberate or inadvertent. But a system can create safeguards that make conviction of the innocent less likely. These safeguards are expensive, not only because they require material resources, but because they must occasionally allow the guilty to go free. For the believing person, God provides an assurance of divine retribution: "I will not acquit one who is guilty."[17] For those more skeptical about God's justice, the occasional freeing of the guilty is seen as a necessary cost of any fair system. It is the willingness of a legal system to make this trade-off—allowing some guilty wrongly to go free in order to assure that very few innocents are wrongly convicted—that marks the maturation of any jurisprudence.

The story of Joseph forms the prelaw predicate for the intricate and innovative system of legal protections found in the later books of the Bible: the requirement of two witnesses, the protection against self-incrimination, the prohibition against double jeopardy, the difficulty of imposing capital punishment, and the strong condemnation against punishing the innocent. Like much of the earlier narratives of Genesis, the Joseph story shows us what it was like to live in a world without a legal system—a world in which those with high status could, with impunity, falsely accuse those of lower status. It shows us the need for a system of justice in which all stand equally before the law and those accused of a crime have a fair opportunity to challenge the evidence against them and to demonstrate that it was planted, false, or mistaken. It leads inexorably to the later biblical rules against favoring in judgment either the rich or the poor.

Anyone who has been falsely accused of a crime will appreciate the need for a system of justice in which the accused has the right to confront the accuser on a level playing field. The Joseph narrative makes the reader empathize with the plight of the falsely accused and sets the stage for the rigorous—and often counterintuitive—safeguards of the subsequent law books. As we apply these safeguards, we hear Yehuda's plaintiff question ringing in our ears: "How can we clear ourselves?" The answer is by a fair system that places a heavy burden on the accuser and provides the accused with adequate safeguards against the kind of false evidence employed in the story of Joseph.

And so the Book of Genesis ends with a segue to the great law book of the Bible—Exodus. It begins with a story about man and woman in the state of nature, before rules or law—a world in which passions reign. It continues with stories of men and women struggling with their instincts for good and evil. It ends with a morality tale about people wrongly accused, unable to speak out against injustice and ultimately triumphing not because of the rule of law, but rather because of the fiat of man and the benevolence of God. In Exodus, Moses, the lawgiver, brings down from Sinai not only the Ten Commandments,[18] but also the detailed code of laws and legal procedures designed to govern all human behavior.[19] In order to appreciate the absolute need for a comprehensive legal system of both substantive and procedural rules, it is essential first to see how human beings behave in a world without law. Genesis shows us that world.

There is a midrash that supports this interpretation. A talmudic rabbi asks the question "Why was the Torah given to Israel?" His answer is that the people of Israel *needed* the Torah because before they received the law, they were a "wild" people.[20] A rabbinic story elaborates this theme. The angels demand that the Ten Commandments be given to the angels rather than to the Jews. God allows Moses to make the case for the Jews. Moses asks the angels whether they ever feel the temptation to murder, rob, or commit adultery. The angels respond, "Of course not. We are angels." Moses turns to God and says, "Ah-ha, the angels do not need the law. It is necessary only for humans, who are always tempted to do evil."

The Book of Genesis is about human passions and temptations in the absence of law. There are certainly enough untrammeled passions and lawlessness in Genesis to justify the need for a formal legal system. We see Cain's murder insufficiently punished and Cain eventually rewarded with the role as builder of cities. We see Lot raped by his daughters, and Dina humbled by a man who comes to love her. That man and his entire clan are then tricked and massacred by brothers who become tribal leaders of Israel. Indeed, a midrash says that the "sons of Jacob were like wild beasts. . . ."[21] We see Jacob deceiving and deceived, Joseph falsely accused and then planting evidence so that his treacherous brothers are also falsely accused. There are no explicit rules governing such behavior, and what few general rules exist are changed at the whim of the rule maker. Hardly a positive picture of the law in action.

There is another way of viewing the Book of Genesis. Although it shows a world without *systematic* rules, it is also a world groping for such rules—a world evolving toward a system of formal justice under which rules are announced in advance and applied fairly by a complex process of justice. We see a world pursuing justice, as Deuteronomy is later to command. We see the genesis of justice in the injustice of Genesis. It is to this broad subject that we now turn.

---

1. A midrash says that God placed Joseph on trial because he was vain about his beauty (*Midrash Rabbah*, vol. 2, p. 807, n. 2).

2. *Midrash Rabbah*, vol. 2, p. 812.

3. Ginzberg, vol. 2, p. 43.

4. Ibid., p. 85.

5. Ibid., p. 100.

6. Ibid., p. 112.

7. Indeed, the phrase is repeated twice, as if for emphasis (50:1–2).

8. The biblical word is traditionally translated as "bones," but it can also mean "essence" or perhaps even "remains." But it would not include a completely embalmed body.

9. Ginzberg, vol. 2, p. 150.

10. Ibid., p. 38.

11. Ibid., p. 128.

12. Ibid., p. 181.

13. Ibid., p. 98.

14. There was even a blood libel trial in Kiev, Ukraine, as recently as 1911. The defendant, Mendel Beilis, was acquitted, but only after a jury rejected the testimony of a priest who swore the blood libel was true. Bernard Malamud's novel, *The Fixer*, is loosely based on this case.

15. Deuteronomy 19:19.

16. Exodus 23:7.

17. Ibid.

18. The "Ten Commandments" is really a mistranslation of the Hebrew "Aseret Divrot"—the Ten Statements. These statements include both commandments and declarations.

19. According to Jewish tradition, God gave Moses not only the written law, but the oral law as well. See generally, Twersky, I., *A Maimonides Reader*.

20. The Hebrew word can also be translated as "fierce." The Soncino translation is "impetuous" (*Babylonian Talmud*, Beitzah, p. 25, side B). My appreciation to Dr. Norman Lamm for alerting me to this quotation.
21. Ginzberg, vol. 2, p. 99.

PART III

THE GENESIS OF JUSTICE IN THE INJUSTICE OF GENESIS

CHAPTER 11

Why Is There So Much Injustice in Genesis?

The Book of Genesis can be read as a metaphor reflecting the stages most legal systems experience on the rocky road from lawlessness to law-abidingness. It has not been a linear development. Instead, as in Genesis, we have seen progress followed by regress followed by progress—sometimes one step forward, two steps back, and then a leap forward, like the Magna Carta and the United States Constitution. Other times, as with Nazi Germany and Stalinist Russia, the leap has been backward. Occasionally it has been unclear whether a step is forward or backward, or whether there is even agreement as to what constitutes forward movement. No two systems have followed exactly the same course. But a few common themes can be identified, and they appear in Genesis.

Genesis also reflects a world in which law is largely "natural" rather than "positive." Actions and reactions derive from the nature of human beings and their Creator, not from formal codes of conduct. Any law that calls itself "natural" will necessarily be as arbitrary, variable, unpredictable, vague, and subject to multiple interpretations as is human nature or the nature of God.[1] And the nature of human beings is as varied as the number of human beings. In the single book of Genesis, we meet a motley assortment of characters, including the fratricidal Cain, the human rights advocate Abraham, and the family man Jacob. These characters do not remain constant, each showing enormous variations within their lifetime. Cain begins as a cold-blooded murderer and ends up as a builder of cities. Abraham argues with God over the lives of strangers and then refuses to argue for the life of his son. Jacob begins as a nice young man ("ish ta'am"), becomes a conniving tactician, and ends up as a caring father capable of the most perceptive and uplifting of blessings.

The human beings of Genesis, like those throughout history, share no singular nature or even common trait. A world that can produce Moses, Jesus, Hillel, and Schweitzer, as well as Hitler, Stalin, Torquemada, and Genghis Khan, is not a world that can be reduced to a singular view of human nature.

Even the God of Genesis lacks a singular nature. He is a petulant, vengeful, demanding, and petty God, as well as a forgiving, merciful, life-affirming, and even repentant God.[2]

Little about the specific *content* of the Bible's natural law can be derived from the infinitely variable nature of either the humans or their creator as described in the Book of Genesis. The open-textured quality of the biblical narratives makes it inappropriate to derive from them one-dimensional, agenda-driven "morals." No single lesson flows from these multilayered stories, and those who seek to reduce them to a proof text for a particular conclusion do not do justice to their complexity and brilliance. For example, the story of Cain and Abel has been cited by both sides of the capital punishment debate as proof that God supports their side of the controversy.[3] Likewise, the Sodom and Gomorrah story has been cited by both sides of the controversy over homosexuality.[4]

What we *can* derive from the stories of Genesis is the *need* for an agreed-upon and enforceable code of conduct with procedural safeguards against arbitrary enforcement and unfair application. The remaining books of the Bible, and the subsequent history of the Jewish people's obsession with justice, deal with these needs. In the law books of the Bible we are given the broad principles in the Ten Commandments, the specific rules of conduct—both positive and negative—as well as a directive to pursue justice actively, as if it were an unattainable grail.

In the beginning, all "law" is ad hoc. It involves random orders and threats from the powerful to the powerless. God's first command, not to eat from the Tree of Knowledge, lacks apparent reason and defies human nature. Sanctions are inconsistent and unpredictable. Indeed, the very unpredictability of the punishment is seen as a source of power. God's first threat to Adam—"On the day that you eat from [the Tree of Knowledge] you must die, yes, die"—is followed by the imposition of a very different series of punishments. Inconsistency and unpredictability also characterized the punishment of Cain for killing his brother, Abel. This is in the nature of ad hoc punishment; it is determined not by a preexisting code of laws, but rather by an evolving yet incomplete sense of justice. Also characteristic of ad hoc punishments is the pendulum swing of underreaction followed by overreaction until an appropriate middle ground of proportionate reaction is discerned. Trial and error is inevitable in any ad hoc approach to justice. God, who was able to create the physical universe in just six days, finds it far more difficult to design a system of justice by which to govern His human creatures.

Not surprisingly, therefore, God—the source of justice in Genesis—overreacts to His underpunishment of Adam, Eve, and Cain by destroying the entire world, except for one righteous family and one mating pair of every species of animal. The remarkable God of Genesis not only learns from His mistakes, but He publicly acknowledges His lack of omniscience in His own Book for all to read. He repents His creation of mankind and tries to improve upon His first draft. Then God recognizes His overreaction by promising that He will never again sweep away the innocent along with the guilty—at least not in a flood. Finally, God realizes that His ad hoc approach to punishment has not worked very well, and—for the first time—He sets out a series of rules governing all human beings, the most important of which is that he who murders another human being shall himself be punished by execution.[5]

This process of evolution from ad hoc rules and disproportionate sanctions to codified rules and proportionate sanctions has characterized most legal systems. Generally the individual cases begin to form some type of "common law" mosaic, from which a precedential pattern can be discerned. This pattern is then formalized into some sort of a code, accessible for all to see or hear.

The late Justice Hugo Black once described a king who wrote the laws in a hand so fine that his subjects could not read them. This gave the king the power to change the laws at will and to enforce his own whim. Justice Black's colleague on the Supreme Court, Felix Frankfurter, conjured up a different image to make a similar point. He contrasted our system of rule-bound justice with the kind of individualized justice administered by "a kadi sitting under a fig tree." In both colorful examples Justices Black and Frankfurter criticize justice that relies too much on the rule of man rather than the rule of law.

The rule of law is supposed to apply to all people regardless of status or station. The governing rules are announced in advance, so that all can know which actions will be punished and which rewarded. Moreover, the rules are published before people can determine who will be their beneficiaries and who their victims.[6]

Unfortunately it is impossible to create rules that anticipate all evil or good actions. Rules, no matter how complete and carefully written, will always have interstices—holes—which must be filled on a case-by-case basis. The existence of these holes will inevitably produce the need for some individualized justice. The wise King Solomon is seen as the paradigm of individualized justice, making up the rules as he goes along. But history has taught us not to expect all of our kings to be Solomonic. That is why we try to have law *makers* (legislators) who write general laws, and law *appliers* (judges) who apply the general rules to particular situations. One of the foundations of any legal system is to strike an appropriate balance between the rule of law and the rule of man and woman.

The contemporary American system of justice seeks to strike that balance by a complex system of checks and balances among the legislative (lawmaking), executive (law-enforcing), and judicial (law-interpreting) branches. We are governed by a written Constitution, which, like the Bible, combines specific rules (a president must be at least thirty-five years old) with open-textured guides to action (no one may be denied the "due process" or "equal protection" of law). Then we have statutes—federal, state, and municipal—which must conform to the Constitution. Executives—the president, governors, mayors—enforce these statutes. And the courts interpret and apply them, subject to ultimate review by the Supreme Court to determine whether they are consistent with the Constitution.

In this respect, there are parallels between the American system and the biblical system. At the pinnacle of the biblical system is, of course, the text of the Bible itself. It is like the Constitution, in that it trumps all subsequent legislation, unless it is properly amended. Christianity claims to have amended the Old Testament with the New Testament. Specific rules, such as the prohibition against eating unkosher food, were abrogated. It is interesting that in "amending" the original "constitution," Jesus used words that would be familiar to lawyers and judges: "Think not that I come to destroy the law . . . I am not come to destroy, but to fulfill."[7]

Within the Jewish tradition, the Pentateuch can never be amended.[8] But it can be interpreted in accordance with prescribed hierarchical rules. According to this tradition God gave the Oral Torah directly to Moses along with the written Scripture. Moses then transmitted it to Joshua and the seventy elders, who then gave it to others who passed it on. It eventually reached those who "compiled the Mishna" and then was studied by later generations and interpreted by reference to "thirteen hermeneutical rules, to which the Great Tribunal assented."[9] It follows from this hierarchy of authority that each generation must defer to the more authoritative views of its predecessors who were closer in time to the original source, but everyone is bound by the agreed-upon methodology of interpretation. The famous legend of the rabbis ignoring God's own voice and admonishing Him that "we pay no attention to Heavenly voice, because Thou hast long since written the Torah at Mount Sinai" is a story about who has the authority to interpret the text of a governing document. It is a story that has recurred throughout history. The foundational Supreme Court decision in *Marbury* v. *Madison*—in which the justices claimed the authority to strike down unconstitutional laws and actions—is a variation on the talmudic story. Just as the rabbis asserted the power to interpret the Torah, so too the justices asserted the power to interpret the open-textured phrases of that enduring document according to contemporary needs and realities. I have heard judges argue that the framers, by including open-textured phrases, intended the Constitution to be subject to ongoing interpretation. Today a debate rages over whether the justices should be bound by "heavenly voices" claiming to know the elusive "original intent" of the framers or whether they should interpret the Constitution to be a living, breathing document, capable of adapting to change. I have heard rabbis make similar arguments about the Bible.

The Book of Genesis contains the seeds of these enduring debates in its narratives about the path from fiat to justice—a path that is never direct and always reflects the inevitable detours of any human journey. In Genesis we see ad hoc rulings, followed by early attempts at limited codification, followed by more ad hoc rulings, followed by common-law development. Interspersed are bargains, contracts, covenants, tests, trials, changes of status, and other legal forms characteristic of developing systems of justice. We also see challenges to authority, rule breaking, cheating, reneging, renegotiating, legal technicalities, and other phenomena characteristic of human interactions with justice systems.

After a rough beginning—out-of-control crime, a flood, a promise not to do it again—God establishes a covenant with Abraham, thus changing the status of both: God becomes a constitutional monarch, binding Himself to rules; and He bestows upon Abraham—and his progeny—a special status as partner in the covenant. Then, as if to discern boundaries of this new legal arrangement, God subjects Abraham to two seemingly inconsistent tests.

Abraham passes the first with flying colors, thereby establishing as part of the common law of Judaism that it is not only permissible, it is obligatory to argue even with God about a proposed injustice. God later commands, *"Tzedek, tzedek, tirdof"*—"Justice, justice shall thou pursue." The word *"tirdof"* literally means "to chase after"—as if never to catch. Perfect justice is not an achievable static concept. It is an imperfect process. Just as "the struggle for liberty never stays won," so too the quest for justice is never achieved. The repetition of the word *"tzedek"* can now be understood as referring not only to human justice, but also to divine justice. *Chutzpah k'lapei shemaya*—humans must show chutzpah not only in demanding justice from the denizens of the earth, but also from He who rules the heavens. God willingly accepts this limitation on His absolute authority, boasting to the angels that "my children have defeated me" in argument.[10]

But there are limits to the limits. Humans can argue with God, but they cannot refuse to obey a direct order from Him. Just as an ordinary soldier can argue with his commanding officer about a battle plan, he cannot refuse to obey a lawful order. So in order to test Abraham's commitment to *this* principle of the covenant, God gives him the most difficult direct order any human being can be given: Sacrifice your beloved son. Here we see a direct conflict between the rule of law as laid down in a binding legal code and ad hoc orders from the lawgiver himself as commanded personally by God.

Abraham's special status as a covenantal partner is a double-edged sword: It gives him special rights in relation to God (he may argue with Him), but it also imposes extraordinary obligations in relation to God—he may not refuse a direct, individualized order from God, even if it is in conflict with God's general rules for the rest of humankind.[11] Kierkegaard points out the paradox that "faith" makes "the single individual . . . higher than the universal. Abraham represents faith [and] he acts on the strength of the absurd; for it is precisely the absurd that as a single individual he is higher than the universal."[12] This is both the benefit and the burden of Abraham's special status as a "knight of faith."

The role of status is pervasive throughout the Book of Genesis and is expressly recognizable in the case of Lot, who was spared on account—at least in part—of his close relationship to Abraham. Eventually status becomes subordinate to actions and intentions, as it does in the history of the law.[13]

Viewing Genesis as a book about the development of justice before the existence of a formalized legal system helps to explain why the narrative is so much about crime, sin, deception, revenge, punishment, and other

211

bad actions. The law evolves from *bad* actions and the way they are dealt with. The common law is built on the *wrongs*, not the *rights*, of humankind. It is an accumulation of stories—narratives—about how human beings deal with each other's failures. Open any law book—from the earliest year books of Anglo-Saxon law, to the volumes of Roman law, to the cases debated in the Talmud, to current Supreme Court decisions—and you will read about *injustice*. The common law of justice is always built on injustice. Just actions do not call for the same degree of response as unjust actions. Thus the genesis of justice in the injustice of Genesis is not as ironic as it may appear at first blush.

Nor is it so difficult to understand the difference between the Book of Genesis, on the one hand, and the Christian Bible and Muslim Koran, on the other. The latter two books deal less with the development of law than does Genesis. Accordingly, they need not focus on the injustice of the primary actors. Law already exists at the time of Jesus. Indeed, in Jesus' estimation it is *too* formal. He sees the need for mercy, grace and deformalization of the law.[14] He can show the way with examples of goodness and righteousness that transcend the rigidity of the law books of the Jewish Bible.

A similar point can be made about Mohammed, who lived half a millennium after Jesus. Though the Koran deals with law to a greater extent than the New Testament, it is a somewhat later system, built as it is on the Jewish and Christian Bibles. Mohammed too can lead by example, without revealing the human weaknesses characteristic of his predecessors in the Book of Genesis.

This interpretation also helps to reconcile the dif-

ferences between the God of Genesis and the God
of the later holy books. Since God is the ultimate
Lawgiver—the manifestation of all law and justice—
and since the law is first developing in Genesis, the
God of Genesis is a developing God—a God who,
like early legal systems, makes mistakes, acknowledges His mistakes, and learns by trial and error. The
God of the subsequent holy books—the Christian
Bible and the Koran—is a more perfect God, just as
His law is a more perfect law and His heroes are more
perfect heroes.

The human actors in Genesis are also developing a
sense of justice by trial and error. In the garden of
Eden, a sense of justice was neither possible nor necessary. God reigned over the garden as a benevolent
despot reigns over his compliant subjects—or perhaps
as a shepherd rules his submissive flock. Since Adam
and Eve had not yet tasted the fruit of knowledge of
right and wrong, they had no more need for human
justice than they had for shame. Shame is an ac-
knowledgment of wrongdoing, which is a prerequisite
to justice. Once they ate the fruit of knowledge, humans learned good from evil and realized that they had
freedom of choice. Such freedom carries with it the
possibility—indeed, the likelihood—that humans will
sometimes choose evil. Without the threat of punishment, it is likely that humans would prefer evil over
good, because the immediate gratifications of evil often
outweigh the short-term rewards of goodness. That is
why God looked down at the lawless antediluvian world
and saw that "great was humankind's evildoing on earth
and every form of their heart's planning was only evil
all the day." The time had come for law and order. In
the wake of the flood, God set out the first rule of law:

213

"He who sheds human blood shall have his blood shed by humans." It is noteworthy that the Bible's first prohibition against murder was based on status, rather than a rule of general applicability. "Whoever slays Cain will be punished sevenfold."[15] Ironically, the first person to be protected against murder was the first murderer, since he reasonably feared retaliation.

Now that God had announced to Noah a rule of general applicability, human beings still had the freedom to choose between good and evil, but the choice carried consequences. Put another way, both of God's initial experiments had failed. His first draft—the Garden of Eden—was a world without knowledge of good and evil. It was an idyllic world in which humans would live in perfect submissiveness to the will of God, with no need for justice, shame, or law. Humans, who were created in God's image, rebelled against this happy ignorance. They chose instead the examined life of choice between good and evil, and for this they were, quite appropriately, banished from Eden. Knowledge is incompatible with the idyllic life of Eden.

God's second experiment was a world of choice, but *without* predictable consequences—without justice. God hoped that humans who knew the difference between good and evil would choose the former over the latter, without the promise of reward or the threat of punishment. But He soon learned that the instinct for evil—the *yetzer ha-ra*—is too powerful to allow humans to live by choice alone.

God's third experiment was a world of choice *with* consequences—with primitive rules whose violation carried severe consequences. God's covenant with Noah initiated this experiment. Eventually God would see that the simple covenant He made with Noah, incorporating only the most basic of rules, was insufficient to govern the complex relationships between God and humans and among humans. He saw the need to establish a more complex covenant with Abraham and to teach His covenantal partner "to do what is right and just." This marked the beginning of the common-law process of Genesis, in which God tests the patriarchs so that they and their descendants may learn how to do justice. Like any good teacher, He challenges and provokes His student by threatening to "sweep" the innocent along with the guilty. Abraham responds by arguing that it is better to save the guilty along with the innocent. Abraham's logic may be flawed, but his instinct is right on target. Eventually the argument will become more refined, but it is a good beginning!

It is the genius of Genesis that it mirrors so closely the history of civilizations in the days before the development of formalized legal systems. It shows us a world without law, but not an entirely lawless world. In one sense, Genesis is the beginning of the common law of justice—a series of ad hoc commands, threats, punishments, rewards, tests, reprisals, blessings, curses, bargains, promises, deceptions, turnabouts, consequences, and life stories, which, when taken together, form the basis for many of the rules that became codified in the subsequent books of the Bible. Virtually all of the large jurisprudential underpinnings of these later rules can be discerned in the Book of Genesis. The themes of justice that permeate the legal codes of Exodus, Numbers, and Deuteronomy are all suggested in Genesis through the vehicle of narrative, rather than rules. As we will see in the next chapter, the narratives of Genesis are essential to explaining and justifying the subsequent rules of law.

1. I do not intend here to enter into a detailed substantive debate over the issue of natural versus positive law. To the extent natural law serves as a check on positive law, it is unexceptionable. Jewish law provides that positive rabbinical enactments cannot be expected to endure if they defy the deeply felt needs of the community.

2. Schulweis, Harold M. *For Those Who Can't Believe* (New York: HarperCollins, 1994), pp. 105–108.

3. See 134 Cong. Rec. S 15669-01 (10.13.88); 138 Cong. Rec. S 10876-01 (7/10/92); 132 Cong. Rec. H 6679-02 (9/11/86); 136 Cong. Rec. S 5186-01 (4/27/90).

4. Gomes, Peter J. *The Good Book: Reading the Bible with Heart and Mind* (New York: HarperCollins, 1994), pp. 105–108. Portions of the Bible have also been cited as proof texts on issues as far-ranging as Onanism, abortion, slavery, women's rights, gun control, and war and peace.

5. Even the earliest hints of procedural safeguards can be discerned in God's giving Adam, Eve, and Cain an opportunity to defend their actions—and in telling both Noah and Abraham of His plans for punitive destruction. See Rashi, Genesis 3:9.

6. The Harvard philosopher John Rawls has constructed a theoretical "veil of ignorance" to assure that rules of law do not depend on one's station in life. The veil of ignorance may be defined in the following terms:

> [A]ll the "players" in the social game would be placed in a situation which is called the "original position." Having only a general knowledge about the facts of "life and society," each player is to make a "rationally prudential choice" concerning the kind of social institution they would enter into contract with. By denying the players any specific information about themselves it forces them to adopt a generalized point of view that bears a strong resemblance to the moral point of view. "Moral conclusions can be reached without abandoning the prudential standpoint and positing a moral outlook merely by pursuing one's own prudential reasoning under certain procedural bargaining and knowledge constraints" (*http://caae.phil.cmu.edu/CAAE/Home/Forum/meta/background/Rawls.html*). See Rawls, John, *A Theory of Justice* (Cambridge: Belknap Press of the Harvard University Press, 1999).

7. Matthew 5:17.

8. See Maimonides's 13 principles in Twersky, Isadore, *A Maimonides Reader*.

9. Maimonides, introduction to the Mishnah Torah, pp. 1–16.

10. But see Job.

11. Once the Torah was given at Sinai, Jews were instructed to obey its written terms and not to listen to contradictory voices from heaven, from prophets, or even from God Himself. Hence the story of the rabbis arguing about the oven.

12. Kierkegaard, Soren, *Fear and Trembling* (Princeton, NJ: Princeton University Press, 1945), p. 83.

13. See Maine, Sir Henry Sumner, "Movement from Status to Contract," *Ancient Law* (New York: Scribner, 1867), p. 165.

14. Matthew 5:17–18: "Do not think that I have come to abolish the law or the Prophets; I have not come to abolish them but to fulfill them."

15. Genesis 4:15.

CHAPTER 12

Why Does the Bible Begin at the Beginning?

I recall one of my rabbis in yeshiva asking the class a question that seemed ridiculous—a real *klutz kasha!* He asked us, "Why does the Bible begin with the story of creation?" The answer seemed obvious: "Why not begin at the beginning? Isn't creation the logical starting point?" The rabbi replied that the Torah was a *law* book, not a *history* book, and law books should begin with the first laws.

The rabbi's question was not original to him. Rashi, among the most authoritative commentators on Jewish sources, poses it in his very first commentary on the Bible: What is "the reason" that the Torah "begins with Genesis"? Since the Torah is the law book of the Jewish people, the logical starting point would be the First Commandment in the Book of Exodus,[1] rather than the story of creation. Rashi observes that "it was not necessary to begin with the creation" and wonders why God made that choice.[2] Rashi then provides an entirely unconvincing and somewhat chauvinistic answer to his own question:

THE GENESIS OF JUSTICE

It began thus because it wished to convey the
message of the verse, "The power of His acts
He told to His people, in order to give them
the estate of nations." So that if the nations of
the world will say to Israel, "You are bandits,
for you conquered the lands of the seven nations who inhabited the Land of Canaan," [Is-
rael] will say to them, "The whole earth belongs
to the Holy One, Blessed is He. He created it
and He gave it to them, and by His wish He
took it from them and gave it to us."

This answer is unconvincing for several reasons:
First, there are plenty of other stories throughout the
Bible that provide justification for Israel's right to live
in the Holy Land. Second, Rashi's own question is
really broader than why the Jewish law book *begins*
with the narrative of creation. Implicit in that question is the deeper question of why a law book should
include any stories at all, instead of simply being a
compendium of the rules. Why, for example, should
it include the long lists of "begats" or the other stories—from the flood, to the binding of Isaac, to the
Jacob and Joseph narratives, to the death of Moses?
Rashi does not answer that question.

Let me propose an answer that addresses both the
narrow question of why the Torah begins with creation and also the broader question of why, if it indeed is a law book, it includes so much narrative,
especially in Genesis and the first part of Exodus.

It is precisely because the Torah is a law book that
it *should* include stories that illustrate the need for
laws and rules. As I will show in the final chapter, the
entire book of Genesis and the first part of Exodus

can be viewed as the narrative prelude to the Ten Commandments and the laws that follow the revelation at Sinai. Even after the laws are given, the narrative continues, the experiences change, and the law continues to develop.

Oliver Wendell Holmes taught us that the life of the law has been experience, not logic. So too the laws of the Bible were based, at least in part, on the experiences of the people to whom they were given. Without knowing about these experiences, we find it difficult to understand the law. That is why the narratives of Genesis had to precede the law books of Exodus, Leviticus, Numbers, and Deuteronomy. (The first part of Exodus continues the narrative of Genesis, culminating in the revelation. Thereafter the narrative continues, interspersed with laws.) Just as experience must precede law, so too must narrative precede codification. The genius of the Bible, at least from the perspective of a law teacher, is its integration of narrative and rules and its use of memory to bring home the moral component of the laws. "Do not oppress the stranger, since you understand the soul of the stranger, because you were strangers in the land of Egypt"[3] is perhaps the paradigm of such experiential codification. The theme of memory pervades the Bible and its commentaries.

Had the Torah—the great law book—simply begun with a list of rules, the reader would wonder about the basis for the rules. Some of them appear eminently logical, but the others cannot be understood without reference to the experience of the Jewish people.

The Bible is the first law book to integrate narrative and law. Previous law codes, such as Hammurabi's and Lipit-Ishtar's, simply presented a compendium of rules, without historical explanation or moral justification. Other early narratives, such as Homer's, simply presented the stories, without accompanying rules. The Bible is different. Most of the laws of the Bible develop organically out of the narratives and are justified by reference to the experiences of its protagonists. There is a genre of nonjustified laws, called *chukkim*, which are seen as testing faith, but these are the exception. It should not be surprising that the God of the Bible justifies most of His laws rather than merely declaring them. After all, this is a God who enters into covenants with Noah, Abraham, Jacob, Moses, and the Jewish people. He is also a God who allows humans to argue with Him and sometimes even to succeed in persuading Him to change His mind. As we have seen, He is a "constitutional monarch" rather than an autocrat, and His subjects are entitled to seek reasons for the laws they are told to obey.

Some biblical scholars and historians of ancient law have noted the uniqueness of the Bible in justifying its laws. They note the prevalence in the Bible of "clauses" that give reasons for the laws, such as the passage cited earlier about treating strangers fairly because "you were strangers" and "the seventh day is the Sabbath . . . , for in six days the Lord made heaven and earth."[4] In the Ten Commandments alone there are several such clauses using the words "because" (*ki*), "that" (*lema'an*), "lest" (*pen*), or "therefore" (*al ken*). Deuteronomy contains more than one hundred "motive clauses," as these forms of justificatory language are called. Professor David Weiss Halivni, a leading contemporary Jewish scholar, explained that the prevalence of motive clauses demonstrates that "biblical law is not categorically imperative, that it [generally] seeks to justify itself." He cites research contrasting these motive clauses of the Bible with other law books of the ancient Near East and concludes:

> The motive clause is clearly and definitely a peculiarity of Israel's or Old Testament law.[5]

Professor Halivni argues that this need to justify law grows out of the character of the Jewish people. He writes about the natural reluctance of the "Jewish imagination" to "accept categorical law"[6] and claims that "Jews cannot live by apodictic [absolute, declaratory] laws alone," since "making laws categorical leads to autocracy," which Jews "instinctively reject."[7] This emphasis on the natural and instinctive traits of Jews strikes me as a bit of a genetic and historical overgeneralization, but it is difficult to quarrel with Halivni's observation that the biblical approach "expresses a basic trait of Jewish law, which tends to be justificatory (one could say 'democratic') to explain rather than to impose, as opposed to the autocratic attitude of the ancient Near East."[8]

Throughout history Jewish law has been characterized by its argumentative quality: The Talmud preserves dissenting views for posterity;[9] the midrash has people arguing with angels, angels arguing with God, and everybody arguing with each other; the *pilpul*—a talmudic variation on the Socratic method—knows no perfect answer. No wonder the Bible describes the Jews as a "stiff-necked" people. But there are countertrends as well throughout Jewish history, when Jews sought authoritarian rule from charismatic rabbis and military leaders. As might be expected, Jews have argued about these trends as well.[10]

Whether it was the biblical method of justifying laws by reference to the narrative that caused Jews to become argumentative, or whether it was the argumentative nature of the Jewish people that caused the Bible to integrate the narrative into the laws, the end result has been the same: We have a Bible that is unique in its justification of the laws, and we have a people who are unusual in their reluctance to accept laws without reason. These are the seeds of democracy.[11]

What distinguishes the Torah is precisely that it is a book of rules based on remembered experiences! That is why the Torah begins with wonderful stories—stories about fallible human struggles with jealousy, temptation, vengeance, lust, selfishness, and other vices in the absence of a formal legal system.

These open-textured narratives are susceptible to ever-changing interpretations. They invite dialogue and intellectual freedom. Again, like the open-textured phrases of the United States Constitution—due process, equal protection, cruel and unusual punishment, full faith and credit, and freedom of speech—the narratives of Genesis are designed to endure through the ages. The seventy faces of the Torah can never be reduced to a single religiously correct view. Yet throughout history it has not been the devil alone who has cited these stories in support of his ignoble ends. Virtually everyone—angels and mortals alike—have quoted the Scriptures. Throughout history politicians, church leaders, and others have pointed to particular biblical stories as proof texts for their agendas. Lenin quoted Exodus, as did the Puritans and

African American slaves. None of them is demonstrably wrong.[12] None is exclusively right. The narratives of the Bible are not blueprints for liberalism, as some argue, or for conservatism, as others allege.[13] They provoke, challenge, and confront every orthodoxy: political, religious, social, economic, and legal. Simple as they appear, they raise the most profound issues of philosophy, theology, and jurisprudence. A good educator trapped with a group of students on a desert island with nothing but the Book of Genesis could teach wonderful courses on many subjects. In the next chapter we will focus on one of the transcendental questions raised by the Genesis narrative.

---

1. The first few commandments appear in the Book of Genesis (do not kill, be fruitful and multiply, circumcise males), but they are not deemed as authoritative as those that follow the revelation at Sinai. See Maimonides generally.

2. This question was first raised by a popular midrashic homily. For references to its original source, see Halivni, David Weiss, *Midrash, Mishnah and Gemara* (Cambridge, Mass.: Harvard University Press, 1986), pp. 9, 120.

3. Exodus 23:9.

4. Exodus 20:7.

5. Halivni, p. 13. In addition to the *specific* motive clauses, there are also *general* ones, such as the observation that man is made in the image or spirit of God and that Israel is a holy nation.

6. Ibid., p. 92.

7. Ibid., pp. 68, 91.

8. Ibid., p. 14.

9. In order "to provide the possibility for a future court to reopen the case" and to make sure that those who disagree with the majority realize that both views were considered (Halivni, p. 110).

10. Maimonides strongly believed in legal codification. In espousing this view, he was following the Mishnah, which was an early attempt at codification and which generally sought to state the law without long discursive justifications. Critics of this approach called its practitioners "destroyers of the world," who "deprive students of the proper mode of studying Torah," which is to "have the laws attached to the Bible (by way of Midrash) rather than to circulate them separately, as does the Mishnah" (Halivni, p. 62).

11. A legal system that sees the need to justify itself by reference to the experience of the people "signifies that it reckons with the will of the people to whom the laws are directed; it seeks their approval, solicits their consent, thereby mani-

festing that it is not indifferent to man" (Halivni, p. 14). This contrasts sharply with other ancient codes that reflect "no concern for the will of the people to whom the laws are directed. The laws are to be obeyed; they need not be understood. Motives are not necessary. The law's authority is derived from the need to have law and order, and it is the king and his entourage who decide what law and order are; the people are not privy to that decision" (ibid.).

The uniqueness of the Bible lies in its invitation to "the receiver of the law to join in grasping the beneficent effect of the law, thereby bestowing dignity upon him and giving him a sense that he is a partner in the law" (Halivni, p. 14). Without recounting the experiences that gave rise to the rules, the Jewish book of laws would be like any other legal compendium.

12. Walzer, *Exodus and Revolution* (New York: Basin Books, 1985).

13. See Dershowitz, *The Vanishing American Jew* (Boston: Little, Brown, 1997), pp. 276–80.

CHAPTER 13

Is There Justice in This World or the Next?

One of the oldest philosophical and theological dilemmas confronted by religious people is the problem of theodicy: Why do bad things happen to good people, and why do good things happen to bad people?[1] These questions, of course, present a dilemma *only* for people who believe in an intervening God who is omniscient, omnipotent, and just. As Billy Graham said in discussing John F. Kennedy Jr.'s tragic death: "God has a plan for every human being." Believers in such divine planning must struggle with the apparent injustice of so many of God's actions. For those who believe in no God, or in Aristotle's nonintervening creator,[2] there is no problem of theodicy. The world is random and there is no reason why disease, natural disasters, wars, and other misfortune should not afflict the righteous as well as the unrighteous. To expect otherwise would be to ascribe moral order to physical chaos. Indeed, because bad people are often more aggressive and more selfish, it should follow that in a godless world, good things should happen to bad people and bad things to good people more often. To the extent that human beings seek to impose justice on a random world, they try to level the natural injustice by mandating—to the extent possible—rewards for good people and punishments for bad people. Ultimately, however, natural injustice seems to outpace human justice, and, on the whole, the world appears to be an unjust place.[3]

Some people point to the reality that so many bad things happen to so many good people as the best proof of God's nonexistence (or nonintervention). Citing Einstein's famous dictum "God does not play dice with the universe," they argue if it is true that a just God would not impose random injustice, it must follow that there is no such God, since it certainly appears that our universe is the product of dicelike randomness. Once when I was teaching a class with Stephen Jay Gould, the evolution expert, I wrote on the blackboard, "Gould or God?" I argued that you couldn't have both since Gould postulates a world in which evolution is the product of random forces. Gould replied that what appears to be random to the human eye may be orderly to the divine and that in any event God is capable of randomness as well as order.

Out of a perceived need to justify God's justice, religious people have struggled for millennia to answer Job's plaintiff cry: Why me? Thoughtful religious people have devoted more time, energy, and creativity to this intellectual conundrum than perhaps any other in human history. That is probably why the redactors of the Bible included such troubling works as Job and Ecclesiastes, which address the problem of theodicy directly. Neither, of course, provides a wholly satisfying answer. Job's friends try mightily to explain why he, a righteous man, has been so afflicted. Their basic

226

answer is a variation on the naturalistic fallacy: If bad things are happening to you, you must deserve it, because God would never allow bad things to happen to a wholly good person.[4] God rejects this explanation and offers one even less satisfying: I am God. Mere mortals can't understand Me. How dare you even try! Not only does this reductionistic nonanswer trivialize the question of theodicy, it discourages humans from even seeking to confront it.

Ecclesiastes simply poses the problem, then offers little beyond a bit of hedonistic advice: Eat, drink, and be skeptical, for tomorrow you return to dust. Eventually he appends a coda—probably added by the redactors in an attempt to make Ecclesiastes religiously correct—that is hardly more satisfying: Put your faith in God and obey His commandments.

The Abrahamic religions ultimately devised a more sophisticated and elegant solution to the problem of theodicy: an invisible hereafter where sin is punished and virtue rewarded out of sight of mortals. According to this solution, God has deliberately made the hereafter invisible, in order to see whether we are willing to accept it on faith. So despite the obvious injustice we see all around us, we are told not to trust our mortal perception. In urging His followers to have faith in the unseeable justice of the hereafter, God paraphrases a Groucho Marx line from *Duck Soup*: "Who are you gonna believe, me or your lying eyes?"

The Bible goes through three phases in constructing a world of invisible justice. The early books of the Bible do not mention a hereafter. This omission is quite striking, considering the place—Egypt— where the Jews who received the Torah at Sinai had been living for so many years. The entire Egyptian civilization was based on the afterlife. Indeed, the very last sentence of the Book of Genesis describes Joseph's Egyptian burial, his embalming, and the placing of his mummified body in an ark.[5]

Yet despite (or perhaps because of) this intimate knowledge of the Egyptian focus on the afterlife, the Jewish people accepted a Torah that appears to have eschewed life after death—or at least to have ignored it.

This is not to suggest that the Bible rejects promises of reward and threats of punishment as a means of securing compliance with divine commands. The God of the Bible is a threatening and promising God. But in the Pentateuch God's punishments and rewards are *all* administered *here on earth*.

The first phase involves the threat of immediate and visible consequences here on earth. Among the threats that fit into this category is the first one God made to Adam: "On the day that you eat of the Tree of Knowing of Good and Evil, you will surely die." Subsequent threats include the following: "I will kill you with the sword and your wives will be widows and your children fatherless." "I will appoint terror over you, even consumption and fever," "bring seven times more plagues," "send beasts of the field among you, which shall rob you of your children," "send pestilence," "make your cities a waste,"[6] "smite you with . . . boils . . . itch . . . madness. . . . [T]hy life shall hang in doubt . . . and the Lord shall bring thee back to Egypt in ships."[7] Among the visible rewards are the following: "[I will] lengthen your days on the ground that God has given you." "[I]t will go well for you and lengthen your days."[8] "I will give you rains . . . , cause evil beasts to cease out of your hands,"[9] "get

228

thee high above all nations," "cause thy enemies . . . to be smitten," and "bless thee in thine land."[10] Pretty specific, both as to where and when these punishments and rewards would be imposed! The "where" is here on earth, "on the ground that God has given you." The "when" is now, in time to make your wives widows and your children orphans. There is no hint of an afterlife with postponed punishment and reward.

Later commentators argued that the hereafter, with its invisible justice, always existed, despite the Pentateuch's silence about it. But if God wanted humans to know that we will receive our divine comeuppance in a world to come, why did He keep it a secret from those He intended to be influenced by the promise and threat of postearthly consequences?[11] Surely He knows that here on earth, we see injustice all around us. Indeed, His own Bible places this observation in the mouth of Ecclesiastes: "In the place of justice, wickedness was there. . . . I have seen a righteous man perishing in his righteousness and a wicked man living long in his wickedness." God Himself is often the moving force, as with Job. (Satan taunted God into testing Job, just as the serpent—which some commentators believe was Satan—tempted Eve to eat of the tree. But just as Eve was held responsible for her actions, so too must God be held responsible for killing Job's innocent children, in order to test their father.)

Had there been a belief in the afterlife at the time of Job, God could easily have explained Job's suffering as temporal, to be remedied in the hereafter. Instead the midrash criticizes Job for denying "the resurrection of the dead."[12] Other concerns about the earthly punishment of the righteous and reward of the unrighteous, which recur throughout the Bible, could have been answered by reference to the hereafter, but they were not.

All humans observe earthly injustice all the time.[13] That is precisely why Job is such a powerful and enduring figure. Any observant person will surely notice an imperfect relationship—at best—between the sinner and the threatened death, plagues, beasts, and boils, as well as between the saint and the promises of long life and prosperity. Ecclesiastes tells us not "to be surprised at such things" or to expect otherwise. But human beings do expect more of their God than the randomness described by Ecclesiastes, whereby "all share common destiny—the righteous and the wicked" alike. "All go to the same place: all come from dust and to dust all return." There must be some reward and punishment—somewhere, sometime. If life is random, why do we need God?

God's first attempt to answer that question fails. He cannot continue to threaten the kind of immediate and visible punishment of the type specified in the Adam story and then not carry it out. People will notice that Adam lived a long life. So God began to issue threats against individual sinners without specific time frames: Your wives will be widows (though not necessarily today). You will get boils and plagues (at some point in your life). But even such postponed punishments didn't always happen. Not only did great sinners die of old age, they outlived their wives, without ever having experienced boils. So God had to take His system of punishments and rewards to the next level.

In God's second attempt to assure ultimate justice, He postpones the consequences of current actions *beyond the life span* of any particular generation, but still in *this* world. God threatens, in the Ten Commandments, to punish "the iniquity of fathers on *children*, to the *third* and *fourth* generation," and He promises to show "mercy unto the thousandth generation of them that love Me and keep My commandments." God postpones punishment and reward until after the death of the sinner and saint repeatedly throughout the early books of the Bible,[14] thus making consequences invisible *within a given generation.* He has learned that by threatening *immediate, specific,* and *visible* punishments—such as He did to Adam—He risks a loss of credibility when these consequences do not materialize. By postponing the consequences beyond the life span of one generation, He maintains the deterrent credibility of His threats.

The Bible and the midrash struggle mightily to demonstrate that God's threats and promises are in fact carried out in future generations. Particularly in the stories of Jacob and his children, the Book of Genesis provides numerous examples of people who reap what they sow. The midrash elaborates on this theme with its moralistic stories of descendants who receive payback for the vices and virtues of their ancestors. Remember Cain, whose evil "overtook him in the seventh generation," when a descendant accidentally shot him with an arrow.

This generational invisibility can survive only in a world without recorded history (or with the sort of recorded moralistic folktales concocted by the midrashic storytellers). In a world of accurately transmitted accounts, it will soon be seen that dreadful things do not necessarily befall the descendants of sinners, nor do blessings attend the offspring of saints. Indeed, after the Crusades, the Inquisition, and the

Holocaust, it was obvious that God could not keep His promise and reward the descendants of saints, for the simple reason that in many instances no descendants were left alive. Entire families, entire villages, entire communities, were wiped out—their seed forever crushed—by unrighteous people who went on to become builders of cities and respected leaders. Many Nazi murderers lived untroubled and guilt-free lives of wealth, health, and reward. Their children and grandchildren honor their memories. The victims of genocide and other human horrors crave ultimate justice, insisting that somehow, somewhere, sometime, the righteous must be rewarded and the unrighteous punished. This deep yearning for retribution helps to explain why even sixty years after the Holocaust, children and grandchildren of victims persist in their lawsuits against corporations that profited from slave labor. I understand the anger of victims when I occasionally help to free a probably guilty killer, who then goes on to live what appears to be a good life. I have felt that anger myself and continue to feel it when I see a Nazi collaborator like John Demjanjuk living a long and healthy life surrounded by loving family.

There is rarely perfect justice here on earth. There is no complete answer to the question of theodicy *in this world*, even if threats and promises are postponed for many generations.

Moreover, the concept of punishing and rewarding descendants raises troubling moral questions about individual versus familial or group accountability. It simply isn't fair to punish an innocent person for another's sin. This issue first arose when God punished Adam and Eve, not only by exiling *them* as individuals, but by inflicting painful sanctions on all working men and childbearing women. If the murder of Abel by Cain is also seen as part of the punishment of their parents, then the life of the innocent Abel was forfeited to avenge a crime he did not commit.

The flood, the destruction of Sodom and Gomorrah, and the slaughter of the entire clan of Shechem are other examples of collective or familial punishment. The subsequent law books articulate conflicting rules regarding this difficult issue. The Ten Commandments threaten punishment "to the fourth generation," while Deuteronomy, thought to be a later work, mandates that "fathers shall not be put to death for children, neither children be put to death for fathers: every man shall be put to death for his own sin." The commentators struggle to reconcile these apparently conflicting texts.[15] In addition to contradictory rules, we see inconsistent practices throughout the Bible. God commands the destruction of Amalek throughout the generations for the crimes of one generation. He threatens reprisals on the descendants of sinners and rewards on the descendants of just people. Sometimes the collective punishment is vertical (down through the generations), other times it is horizontal (within one generation, but extending to the entire family, clan, or city). Yet paradoxically, God appears to agree with Abraham that the innocent should not be swept along with the guilty.

Even today we have conflicting attitudes toward parental responsibility for the acts of their children. In the wake of the shootings at Columbine High School there were calls for expanding the civil and criminal liability of parents. Following the defeat of Nazi Germany, there were calls for collective sanctions against the German people. But in the end, the decision was made to punish only those individuals whose guilt could be proved.[16] The Allies refused to employ the concept of *Sippenhaft*—punishment of kin—which had been widely used by the Nazis.

Eventually Jewish law accepts the *principle* that it is wrong to punish (or reward) anyone for the sins (or good deeds) of another; punishment and reward, if they are to be just, must be individualized.[17] This principle, which develops over time, is easier to articulate in theory than to apply in practice. Whenever we punish an individual for his crimes—by execution, imprisonment, fine, or other sanction—we inflict harm on his innocent family, friends, associates, employees, and others within his circle. The corollary to this reality is that when we reward an individual for his good deeds, some of that reward may benefit those who did not themselves earn it. Some degree of collective punishment and reward may be inevitable in any system of individualized justice, but there is an important difference between systems in which collective sanctions are an explicit part of the process and those in which they are an inevitable by-product. The movement from collective responsibility—of the family, the clan, the tribe, the city, the nation, the race, the religion, and so on—toward individualized responsibility is reflected in the Book of Genesis. It has not been a linear movement in history, because the emotional pull of collective accountability remains powerful.

Thus, God's second attempt to assure His followers that there is ultimate justice in this world fails for two reasons, one empirical, the other moral. Empirically it becomes clear, once recorded history is developed, that descendants do not necessarily reap what their ancestors have sown. Morally we are troubled by

a system of justice that relies on vicarious accountability. So the theologians of Judaism, Christianity, and
Islam had to accept the solution offered by other religions—namely, a world to come in which the righteous are rewarded and the unrighteous punished.
Justice would indeed be served, but in a world no
human could see and from which no human could return or report. An elegant solution to an otherwise in-
soluble problem.

The sharp difference between the earthly promises
and threats of the early books of the Bible and the
otherworldly punishments and threats of the talmudic commentators is beautifully illustrated by a chill-
ing story about a second-century rabbinic sage named
Elisha, the son of Abuyah, who became a disbeliever
after he saw, with his own eyes, that one of God's
most explicit promises was not kept. Tradition has it
that Elisha was studying on Sabbath in the valley of
Gennesar when he saw an evil man climb to the top
of a palm tree and take a mother bird along with her
young. He thus violated two commandments: to keep
the Sabbath and to send away the mother bird. Yet
nothing happened to him. After the Sabbath, Elisha
saw a young boy climbing a tree to retrieve some bird
eggs. His father instructed him to send away the
mother, and the young boy did so, thus obeying the
two commandments, which explicitly promise long
life. Yet as soon as he descended the tree, the good
boy was bitten by a snake and killed. Rabbi Elisha
cried out against this betrayal: "There is no justice,
and there is no judge."[18]

According to the tradition, Rabbi Akiva—the greatest sage of his time—responded to Rabbi Elisha's apostasy by explaining that despite the seeming explicitness

of the text, the promise of a long and good life is not in this world, but rather "in the world to come," which is "wholly good" and "whose length is without end."[19] It is also, of course, a world invisible to those on earth, and thus any promise or threat involving this world is not subject to observation or verification.

The story of Rabbi Elisha is telling for a number of reasons. No rational person would believe a promise of reward and punishment in this world, where the young die, the righteous are punished, and the unrighteous are rewarded—all in plain view of everyone. Rabbi Elisha was the reasonable skeptic, believing his own eyes and concluding that the first mechanism of biblical sanction—immediate consequences here on earth—was demonstrably false. Ecclesiastes recognized the injustice of life and the emptiness of death yet accepted God. King David blinded himself to the injustice of life by declaring that he had never seen a "righteous person abandoned or his children wanting for bread."[20] But those who did not live as privileged kings saw a real world full of iniquity. As a result, Judaism had to accept the prevailing view of other—sometimes competing—religions of the day. The sages searched the sources, particularly the prophetic writings, and declared that despite the pregnant silence of the Pentateuch, there *is* life after death, with reward and punishment. Rabbi Eleazor was certain that "wherever there is not judgment [below] there is judgment [above]."[21] Maimonides elaborated on this theme and attempted to reconcile the world to come with the rather explicit language of the Bible specifying earthly punishments and rewards:

Hence, all those benedictions and maledictions promised in the Torah are to be explained as follows: If you have served God with joy and observed His way, He will bestow upon you those blessings and avert from you those curses, so that you will have leisure to become wise in the Torah and occupy yourselves therewith, and thus attain life hereafter, and then it will be well with you in the world which is entirely blissful and you will enjoy length of days in an existence which is everlasting. So you will enjoy both worlds, a happy life on earth leading to the life in the world to come. For if wisdom is not acquired and good deeds are not performed here, there will be nothing meriting a recompense hereafter, as it is said, "For there is no work, no device, no knowledge, no wisdom in the grave" (Ecclesiastes 9:10). But if you have forsaken the Lord and have erred in eating, drinking, fornication, and similar things, He will bring upon you all those curses and withhold from you all those blessings till your days will end in confusion and terror, and you will have neither the free mind nor the healthy body requisite for the fulfillment of the commandments so that you will suffer perdition in the life hereafter and will thus have lost both worlds—for when one is troubled here on earth with diseases, war or famine, he does not occupy himself with the acquisition of wisdom or the performance of religious precepts by which life hereafter is gained.[22]

Thus the narrative of justice, so demonstrably false here on earth, can be continued in a world whose existence no one can disprove. Hence the leap of faith, without which traditional religion becomes impossible.

Judaism, which is based on a covenant between God and His people, could not easily endure without a world to come in which God could keep His promises out of the view of humankind. In the mortal world, God's promises—long life, defeat of enemies—are repeatedly broken. As the tenth-century sage Saadia Gaon put it hopefully, if not somewhat desperately: "In this world we see the godless prosper and the faithful suffer. There *must*, therefore, be another world in which all will be recompensed in justice and righteousness." A contemporary evangelist made the same point in a recent television appearance concerning the murder of innocent children. The Reverend Robert Schuller insisted that there *has to be* an afterlife with eternal justice.[23] This is a common religious reaction to inexplicable tragedy. A variation on this theme is presented by a prominent Conservative rabbi, speaking in the political language of our times: "The world to come is a form of protest against a wretched status quo in which poverty, illness, and wars crush the human body and soul."[24]

A poignant Yiddish story by the nineteenth-century writer I. L. Peretz illuminates the need for an afterlife in a wretched world of poverty and oppression. A man named Bontsha has lived the most horrible of lives—poverty, sickness, parental abuse—but never complained, either to God or to his fellow man. His death goes unnoticed on earth. The board marking his grave is blown away. In heaven, however, his arrival is greeted with great ceremony. Even the prosecuting angel can find nothing bad to say about him. The divine Judge pronounces His decree for Bontsha:

> There in that other world, no one understood
> you. . . . There in that other world, that world
> of lies, your silence was never rewarded, but
> here in Paradise is the world of truth, here in
> Paradise you will be rewarded. . . . For you
> there is not only one little portion of Paradise,
> one little share. No, for you there is everything!
> Whatever you want! Everything is yours!

Bontsha smiles for the first time and speaks: "Well then, what I would like, Your Excellency, is to have, every morning for breakfast, a hot roll with fresh butter."[25]

This Yiddish story is an elaboration of the New Testament's promise "The meek shall inherit the earth" and the rich will have difficulty making it into heaven. The scales will be balanced, the playing field leveled, and justice achieved. Those who were despised on earth for their virtues shall flourish in the world to come. That is the leap of faith the Abrahamic religions can offer to offset the obvious injustice of this cruel world.

But not all the sages have been prepared to make the leap of faith from the injustice of this world to the perfection of the next. Rabbi Judah Low, the great scholar of Prague, took a more rationalist view in the sixteenth century: "A foundation of religion cannot be something that is not discernible to experience." That is why, he surmised, the Torah "avoided the hereafter." Other commentators have suggested that the generation of Jews who left Egypt were not ready to accept an afterlife, perhaps because they had suffered so much from the Egyptian obsession with the world to come. So the oral tradition "discovered" it when the Jews were ready for it.

A midrash, written after rabbinic Judaism accepted the afterlife, has Jacob and Esau debating this issue in the context of Esau's selling of his birthright:

> Esau: "Is there a future world? Or will the dead be called back to life? If it were so, why hath not Adam returned? Hast thou heard that Noah, through whom the world was raised anew, hath reappeared? Yea, Abraham, the friend of God, more beloved of Him than any man, hath he come to life again?"

> Jacob: "If thou art of opinion that there is no future world, and that the dead do not rise to new life, then why dost thou want thy birthright? Sell it to me, now, while it is yet possible to do so. Once the Torah is revealed, it cannot be done. Verily, there is a future world, in which the righteous receive their reward. I tell thee this, lest thou say later I deceived thee."[26]

The discovery of an afterlife, which neatly solves all the problems of theodicy, made it unnecessary for God to continue to threaten or promise consequences in relation to future generations. Punishing and rewarding future generations may be necessary in a world that includes no intimation of an afterlife, because sometimes it is simply not enough to threaten the life of a sinner, especially when he is old and near death.[27] More severe punishment may be needed. A God who can threaten eternal damnation and promise eternal salvation does not need to threaten a sinner's children or promise reward for the descendants of the righteous.

In one sense, threats and promises to be carried out against future generations are the *functional equivalent* of threats and promises to be carried out in the hereafter: Both are unseen by the sinner or saint; both provide answers to those who see sinners rewarded and saints punished in their lifetimes. In a world in which punishment and reward are bestowed on future generations, it is possible to believe in divine justice—at least for a while—despite the obvious empirical evidence to the contrary. Maybe *this* sinner has not been punished, but his descendants will surely be punished for him—if not in the first or second generation, then sometime in the future. Similarly, in a world in which punishment and reward are bestowed on the sinners themselves, but in the invisible hereafter, it is possible to believe, despite evidence that in this world sinners are often rewarded and saints punished. Maybe he has gotten away with it *here*, but just wait until he reaches the pearly gates. Both the indeterminate future rewards and punishments for descendants here on earth and the promise of salvation and purgatory in the hereafter share an invisibility to the generation witnessing injustice, and invisibility permits faith to overcome empirical doubt.

If "justice must *be seen* to be done"—as a legal principle pronounces—then both God and man fail in the never-ending quest for justice, because justice is too rarely seen here on earth. If justice may be achieved in the next world or in the next generation, then we can continue to have faith in its eventual accomplishment. To turn a phrase, therefore, justice must *not* be seen to be done, else it will rarely be done, because it is so rarely seen. The Book of Proverbs categorically assures its believers to "be sure of this: the wicked will not go unpunished, but those who are righteous will go free."[28] But no one with eyes, ears, and mind can be sure of that, since they experience its opposite every day. Either the assurance is false (as Ecclesiastes concludes); or it is a reference to future generations (as the Ten Commandments suggest); or it is a promise about the world to come (as Maimonides assures us). There is no other possibility. Nor can the answer ever be known with certainty. It will always be a matter of faith, not of proof.

It is no accident, therefore, that as the Abrahamic religions move from exclusive reliance on punishment and reward in *this* world to a belief in the *hereafter*, there is a parallel movement away from punishing and rewarding descendants for the sins and good deeds of those who are personally responsible. Eventually Judaism is able to accept the important principle of individual accountability precisely because it comes to believe in a world to come in which all scores are personally settled by God. I don't know whether or not there is a hereafter—no one does. But I must commend its creator—divine or human—for solving the puzzle of how a just and intervening God can permit so much injustice in this world.[29]

Regardless of how strongly some people may believe in punishment and reward after death, no society has ever been willing to rely exclusively on this leap of faith to deter earthly misconduct. Every society imposes earthly punishment on criminals, in addition to the purgatory threatened by religion. (No one, it seems, is willing to take Pascal's wager to the point of leaving it to God alone to punish all sin.)

Is There Justice in This World or the Next?

Earthly punishments require earthly rules. It is to these rules, and the influence of the Genesis stories on them, that we now turn.

---

1. *Webster's Tenth Collegiate Dictionary* defines theodicy as the "defense of God's goodness and omnipotence in view of the existence of evil." A variant on this question is, why are good deeds so often punished and bad ones rewarded?

2. Aristotle, *Metaphysics*, Book XII, Part 8.

3. The problem of why good people are punished and bad people rewarded has multiple aspects. There is the problem of theodicy, which asks the question How can God, who is deemed responsible for all good and evil, bestow both with such apparent unfairness? But there is also the human analogy to divine theodicy: Why do human beings in administering justice (broadly defined to include not only legal, but political, social, and economic justice as well) produce so much unfairness? The latter is included in the former, since God is thought to control human as well as natural injustice, but the former is not necessarily included in the latter, since humans do not exert much control over natural disasters.

4. "The naturalistic fallacy states that it is 'logically impossible for any set of statements of the kind usually called descriptive to entail a statement of the kind usually called evaluative'" (John R. Searle, *Speech Acts: An Essay in the Philosophy of Language* [Cambridge: Cambridge University Press, 1977], p. 132). See generally, Moore, George Edward, *Principia Ethica* (Cambridge: Cambridge University Press, 1960).

5. See p. 189 supra.

6. Leviticus 26.

7. Deuteronomy 28.

8. See also Deuteronomy 17:20 ("so that he may prolong his days in his kingdom, he and his children, in the midst of Israel").

9. Leviticus 26.

10. Deuteronomy 28.

11. Commentators suggest that there are a handful of veiled allusions to the hereafter in the Pentateuch, but they are there only if you are looking very hard for them, and even so, the question persists: Why did God hide them in veiled allusion, rather than make them clear for all to see?

12. Ginzberg, vol. 2, p. 227.

13. Maimonides addresses this issue directly, arguing that the earthly rewards and punishments cataloged in the Bible do occur, but they "are not the *final* reward [or] the last penalty" (Twersky at p. 82, emphasis added).

14. For example, God commands the destruction of the nation of Amalek throughout the generations for the crimes of one generation.

15. The former may reflect divine justice, while the latter imposes limits on human justice. Rashi distinguishes between minor children and mature children who stand on their own. The halakhah also distinguishes the age at which a parent ceases to be responsible for his children's crimes and sins. According to some commentators, thirteen is the age of responsibility to human courts, whereas twenty is the age for the heavenly court.

243

16. It can be argued that the German people—certainly those who lived in West Germany—were collectively rewarded by the Marshall Plan.

17. See generally, Elon, Menachem, ed., *The Principles of Jewish Law* (Jerusalem: Encyclopedia Judaica, 1975).

18. Rabbi Milton Steinberg has written a moving novel about this episode entitled *As a Driven Leaf* (Northvale, N.J.: J. Aronson, 1987).

19. Rabbi Akiba elaborated on this view elsewhere: God "grants ease to the wicked and rewards them for the few good deeds which they have performed in this world in order to punish them in the future world." Similarly, he punishes the righteous in this world for their few wrongs in order to "lavish bliss" upon them in the world to come (*Midrash Rabbah*, vol. 1, p. 257). Pretty clever! That explains all the injustices we see in this world.

20. Numerous commentators have tried heroically to rationalize David's invocation of this variant on the naturalist fallacy. Let me offer the following interpretation. David himself witnessed God's injustice against an innocent child—his own. God kills the offspring of his illicit liaison with Bathsheba, thus demonstrating that the offspring of the unrighteous are punished, despite God's promise in Deuteronomy that children will not be put to death for the sins of fathers (24:16). Now that David has grown old and has become righteous, he has seen his children rewarded. He is making an observation about his own checkered life. See Psalms 44, 73, 79, and 82 for somewhat different perspectives.

21. *Midrash Rabbah*, vol. 1, p. 216.

22. Twersky at p. 82.

23. *Larry King Live*, March 22, 1999.

24. Harold, Schulweis, *For Those Who Can't Believe* (New York: HarperCollins, 1994), p. 183.

25. Peretz, I. L., "Bontsha the Silent," in *A Treasury of Yiddish Stories*, ed. Irving Howe and Eliezer Greenberg (New York: Penguin, 1990), pp. 223–30.

26. Ginzberg, p. 320.

27. See Dershowitz, *Just Revenge*. (New York: Warner, 1999).

28. 11:21; see also 12:17, 26:27.

29. Talmudic and Midrashic efforts to impose an afterlife on the stories of Genesis are understandable theologically, but they do an injustice to the power of these stories whose poignancy derives, in significant part, from the injustice of life and the finality of death. To understand Genesis as it was written requires the reader to accept the weltanschauung of its time, rather than to impose, postfacto, a concept—the afterlife—which came to be accepted only in subsequent books.

CHAPTER 14

Where Do the Ten Commandments Come From?

The narratives of injustice that typify the Book of Genesis not only raise the most profound questions about justice in this world and the next, they also foreshadow many of the specific rules that follow in the Books of Exodus, Leviticus, Numbers, and Deuteronomy.

When viewed against the background of the narrative of Genesis, the revelation at Sinai is not the dramatic break with the past that some traditional commentators attribute to it. For Maimonides, prior to Sinai there were no binding laws. But if the Book of Genesis tells the story of the developing legal system—ad hoc rules, common law, statutes, and so on—then Sinai does not represent so dramatic a break with the past. It is a culmination of a process begun in the Garden of Eden and continued with Cain, Noah, Abraham, Jacob, Dina, Tamar, Joseph, and the other actors in the opening narratives of the Bible.

Familiarity with these narratives is a prerequisite to understanding the more formal codes of law revealed at Sinai, since these laws are a reaction to the anarchy of the narratives. Many of the laws make explicit or implicit references to narratives, and commentators often tie them together.

To the extent that Sinai does not represent as much of a dramatic break with the past as a culmination of a long process of development, it reflects not only the history of the law, but its historiography as well. We tend to look back at great moments, such as the Magna Carta and the American Constitution, as if they were dramatic breaks with the past. Careful study, however, often discloses that they were actually the inevitable and predictable culminations of developments over time. Because historians crave landmarks and watersheds, they often exaggerate the significance of dramatic singular events that are the culminations of a long, gradual process of adumbration. Magna Carta, for example, summarized and codified developments that were already recognized as part of the common law. Once we had Magna Carta, it became less important to focus on the prior Year Books in order to extract from them the principles that would come to be codified in the great charter.

This is not to trivialize the dramatic moments historians count as significant. It is to understand that these moments do not arise out of nothingness. In history there is never a tabula rasa. We always write on a tableau on which much has already been written, erased, and rewritten—even if the tableau is oral.

Many traditional commentators disagree, arguing that the Ten Commandments and the other rules emerged full-blown from the revelation at Sinai. The reluctance of some traditional commentators to acknowledge the close association between the early narratives and the subsequent rules reflects a theological dogma. If the revelation of Sinai is to retain its centrality, it is essential that the laws revealed at Sinai emerge fully formed from the mountaintop. To see these laws foreshadowed in earlier stories—even stories about God—is to diminish the drama of Sinai.

Even the most traditional of commentators are forced to trace some of the rules to Genesis. For example, Maimonides, who most stridently makes the case for the centrality of the revelation at Sinai, must acknowledge that the Jewish prohibition against eating the sinew of the thigh vein derives from the story of Jacob wrestling with the angel of God and straining the hollow of his thigh, since the narrative explicitly makes the connection: "Therefore the children of Israel do not eat the sinew . . . unto this day, because he touched the hollow of Jacob's thigh."[1] This particular association between narrative and rule is largely symbolic[2] and has little to do with justice. The association between other narratives and rules of justice is far clearer.[3]

Virtually all of the substantive and procedural rules that are decreed in the subsequent law books of the Pentateuch flow from the stories of Genesis. Each of the Ten Commandments can be traced to at least one of the earlier narratives. The more specific rules—positive and negative, substantive and procedural—often have sources in the stories as well. At the very least, they have roots in the common problems addressed in both the narratives and the rules.

Jews and Christians number the Ten Commandments differently. For Jews, number one is not even a commandment. (The Hebrew for the Ten Commandments is the Ten *Statements—Divrot.*) The first statement is a declaration of faith: "I am the Lord thy God." It is immediately followed by a summary of the

247

earlier narrative: ". . . who brought thee out of the land of Egypt, out of the house of bondage." It could well have continued: ". . . into which I placed you by sending Joseph to Egypt and having him summon his brothers and father." After all, this was not the first time God had revealed Himself. He had previously made covenants with Jacob, Abraham, and Noah. Thus the First Commandment grows directly out of the earlier narratives.

Christians begin with the theological commandments—"Thou shalt have no other gods before me," "Thou shalt not make unto thee a graven image," "Thou shalt not bow unto them or serve them," "Thou shalt not take the name of the Lord thy God in vain"— all of which have their sources in the shift from idolatry to monotheism narrated in the Abraham story. According to a midrash, Abraham's father, Terach, was a maker of idols, and one day Abraham then "took a hatchet in his hand, and broke all his father's gods," except for the biggest one.[4] When his father saw the smashed idols he became angry, but Abraham denied breaking them, blaming it on the largest of the idols in whose hand he had planted a hatchet. Terach accused Abraham of lying. To prove that the large idol had been framed, Terach argued:

> Is there spirit, soul, or power in these Gods . . . ?
> Are they not wood and stone? [H]ave I not my-
> self made them?

Abraham responded:

How, then, canst thou serve these idols in whom there is no power to do anything? Terach then took the hatchet from the hand of the large idol and smashed it,[5] thus demonstrating his rejection of false gods, graven images, and idol worship. Hence the commandments against these theological sins.

The Fourth Commandment—"Remember the Sabbath to keep it holy"—derives explicitly from the creation narrative. Indeed, the commandment concludes: "For in six days the Lord made heaven and earth, and all that is in them, and rested on the seventh day; wherefore the Lord blessed the Sabbath day and hallowed it."

The Fifth Commandment—"Honor thy father and thy mother"—has roots in the stories of dishonor cast upon parents in Genesis. Jacob tricks his feeble father; Shim'on and Levi dishonor their father by deceiving and murdering the clan of Shechem; Joseph dishonors his father by deceiving him into sending his youngest son to Egypt; Rachel dishonors her father by stealing his idols and covering up her theft; Cain dishonors his parents by killing their son; Lot's daughters dishonor their father by getting him drunk and raping him; Noah's son dishonors his father by seeing his nakedness and then telling his brothers; even Abraham may have dishonored his father by tricking him into giving up his idol worship. Indeed, it can be said that the Book of Genesis is a collection of stories about children dishonoring parents. Clearly, human beings needed a commandment from on high to resolve their intergenerational conflicts.

The Sixth Commandment—"Thou shalt not murder"—has its roots in God's command to Noah, "Who so sheddeth man's blood by man shall his blood be shed." This rule is derived from another narrative: "For in the image of God made He man." The Book of Genesis relates the stories of several murderers and attempted murderers: Cain, Shim'on, Levi, and Abraham. Yet none is punished by death, despite the Noachide covenant. The need for a clear directive is apparent.

The Seventh Commandment—"Thou shalt not commit adultery"—is a bit more difficult to trace directly to a specific narrative. There are, of course, numerous stories of forbidden sex (or at least close calls)—Sarah and Rifka with the kings; Lot with his daughters; Tamar with her father-in-law; Reuven with his father's mistress;[6] Potiphar's wife with Joseph—enough to warrant a specific prohibition in the Ten Commandments.

The Eighth Commandment—"Thou shalt not steal"—also has roots in the narrative. The midrash traces this prohibition to the Garden of Eden, where God tells Adam: "Of every tree of the Garden thou shalt freely eat: here He commanded him against theft."[7] Adam and Eve violated this command by taking fruit from a prohibited tree. There are other stories of stealing in Genesis, including Rachel's theft of her father's idols. Rachel may have believed that it was permissible to steal idols in order to prevent idol worship—an act of religiously motivated civil disobedience akin to the blocking of an abortion clinic—but the commandment is absolute.

The Ninth Commandment—"Thou shalt not bear false witness against thy neighbor"—derives directly from Potiphar's wife bearing false witness against Joseph and Joseph then bearing false witness—even as a pretense—against his own brothers. Yehuda's desperate question "How can we clear ourselves?" is answered by this prohibition and by the subsequent procedural safeguards that rest on this commandment.

Moreover, the earliest biblical narratives support the right of an accused person to a defense—at least against God. God gives Adam and Eve an opportunity to defend themselves and gives Cain the same right. Abraham defends the people of Sodom. God also insists on coming down to earth to see for Himself whether the Sodomites deserve destruction. Heresay is not good enough even for God. He insists on direct eyewitness observation. But the clan of Shechem is given no opportunity to defend itself against human vengeance. Nor are other victims of human injustice. The need for procedural safeguards against false accusations by human beings is evident.

Finally, the catch-all commandment against coveting one's neighbor's house, wife, manservant, maidservant, ox, ass, "nor anything that is thy neighbor's," is a general protection against the evil impulses (*yetzer ha-ra*) that cause theft, adultery, murder, and the bearing of false witness. The narrative of Genesis is all about these evil impulses and the need to check them by specific rules, laws, and commandments. It was obviously not enough for God to encounter Abraham so that "He may command his children and his household after him that they may keep the way of the Lord, to do righteousness and justice. . . ."[8] Such generalities had failed to produce an end to lawlessness, deception, even murder. More specific rules, with prescribed sanctions, were necessary. The narratives of Genesis made the need for the Ten Commandments, and the laws that followed them, abundantly clear.

A midrash associates each of the Ten Commandments specifically with the Joseph narrative. It takes the form of an explanation for why Israel carried the dead body of Joseph alongside the newly acquired Tablets of the Law. In the Tablets it is written:

> I am the Lord thy God, and [Jacob] said, Am I in the place of God? Here it is written, Thou shalt have no other gods before My face, and he said, I fear God. Here it is written, Thou shalt not take the name of the Lord thy God in vain, and therefore he did not swear by God, but said, By the life of Pharaoh. Here it is written, Remember the Sabbath day, and he said to the overseer of his palace on Friday, Slay and make ready, meaning for the Sabbath. Here it is written, Honor thy father and thy mother, and he said, when his father desired to send him to his brethren, Here I am, although he knew it was perilous for him to go. Here it is written, Thou shalt not kill, and he refrained from murdering Potiphar when Potiphar's wife urged him to do it. Here it is written, Thou shalt not commit adultery, and he scorned the adulterous proposals of Potiphar's wife. Here it is written, Thou shalt not steal, and he stole nothing from Pharaoh, but gathered up all the money and brought it unto Pharaoh's house. Here it is written, Thou shalt not bear false witness against thy neighbor, and he told his father nothing of what his brethren had done to him, though what he might have told them was the truth. Here it is written, Thou shalt not covet, and he did not covet Potiphar's wife.[9]

Beyond the Ten Commandments, perhaps the most influential legal principle associated with the Bible is the "talion,"[10] first articulated in the Book of Exodus[11] in the following terms:

> *If any harm follow, then thou shalt give*
> *life for life*
> *eye for eye*
> *tooth for tooth*
> *hand for hand*
> *foot for foot*
> *burning for burning*
> *wound for wound*
> *stripe for stripe.*

This principle of "measure for measure" or strict proportionality between the harm caused and punishment inflicted has been the source of much controversy since it was first articulated. Its purpose can best be discerned by going back to the nature of the world that preceded and gave rise to it—the world of Genesis. At the beginning of that world, punishment was anything but proportional. God was too lenient on Cain, too harsh on the victims of the flood and the brimstone, too unpredictable in relation to Adam and Eve, and too harsh in His testing of Abraham.

Human justice was similarly disproportional, as evidenced by the mass slaughter of the entire clan of Hamor for the sin of Shechem.

The Jacob and Joseph narratives show a world moving toward some sense of symbolic symmetry in which people reap what they sow. Jacob wove a web of deceit that entangled those around him. Joseph tricked those who tricked him. God later inflicted plagues on the Egyptians that paralleled the harms they inflicted on the Hebrews, culminating in the killing of the firstborn Jewish males. Still, the punishment generally exceeded the crime, though the law was plainly moving in the direction of adopting the talion as the overarching substantive principle of justice. Finally, we see its codification in words that demand precise proportionality, thus imposing a strict limitation on punishment. Prior to introduction of the talion the principle of disproportionate revenge had been the norm throughout the world: You kill one, we kill an entire city; you blind me, I kill you; you wound me, I torture you and your family. Now the punishment must fit the crime, and it may not exceed the harm caused. Even before the rabbinic authorities mitigated the rigors of the talion by interpreting the taking of limbs as monetary compensation, the principle itself—harsh as it sounds to the contemporary ear—constituted a major step *forward* in the eternal quest for justice, fairness, and proportionality, since it imposed strict limits on punishment. To the ancient ear, the rule sounded like "*No more* than one life for a life, *no more* than one eye for an eye," and so on.[12] It marked the end—at least in theory—of the retaliatory blood feud with its characteristic destruction of entire clans, villages, and families. What Dina's brother did to the clan of Hamor could no longer be justified by the rhetorical question: "Should one deal with our sister as with a harlot?" Following the adoption of the talion, the answer to that question was limited by the rule of proportional justice.

The Bible, read literally, sends a complex message about law enforcement. The *substantive* law is somewhat harsh—an eye for an eye, death for a wide range of sins and crimes, including some that would seem trivial to contemporary sensibilities. The *procedural* law, on the other hand, made it extraordinarily difficult to convict people of the harsh substantive offenses. The end result was a system under which—at least in theory—few could be convicted and exposed to the harsh penalties, but those few who were convicted could be punished excessively. The deterrent message of such a system is that while any given violator may get away with it, those who are convicted will receive a punishment sufficient to frighten anyone contemplating wrongdoing. We follow a similar approach today in enforcing our tax laws, prosecuting few but punishing those who are convicted excessively in order to send a credible deterrent message.[13] Experience teaches that this kind of a system does not always work effectively, since most potential criminals don't believe *they* will actually be caught and convicted. A system in which punishment is both more certain and more moderate works better. The rabbis of the talmudic period realized this and moderated the substantive punishments by substituting monetary damages for the "eye" and "limb" of the talion while at the same time making it far easier to punish factually guilty offenders who were acquitted under the rigorous procedural requirements of the Bible. By thus interpreting the talion, they would appear to have violated the literal words of the Bible.

For example, Exodus 21:24 is clear that an "eye for an eye, a tooth for a tooth, a hand for a hand, a foot for a foot, a burn for a burn, a wound for a wound, a bruise for a bruise" does *not* mean monetary compensation. The very same chapter explicitly specifies "monetary compensation" for *other* wrongs.[14] Indeed, an eye for an eye is specifically *contrasted* with monetary payments: "[I]f no harm follow, he shall surely be fined. [B]ut if any harm follow, then he shall give life for life, eye for eye," and so forth.[15]

The procedural requirements of the Bible are equally clear, particularly its protection against double jeopardy: "Do not execute one who is innocent or one who has been acquitted."[16] Yet the rabbis devised an approach designed to circumvent the express procedural protections of the Bible. If a person was acquitted of murder because only one witness had seen him kill—the Bible requires two witnesses—he was not set free, as the Bible commands. Instead he was placed in a locked room, where he was fed a lethal concoction of water and grain calculated to cause his stomach to burst.[17] Contemporary society has come up with a term for such extralegal punishment: It is called "vigilante justice," which in reality is an oxymoron.

The rabbis justified this extrabiblical punishment as necessary to prevent lawlessness. They may have been right, but that would have implied that the Bible was wrong! The rabbis could not, of course, acknowledge that the biblical procedures were too stringent, so they came up with a series of rationales for why their approach was consistent with Scripture. Nevertheless, killing a defendant who has been found not guilty by the formal legal system simply cannot be reconciled with the explicit biblical command "Do not execute one who is innocent or who has been acquitted."[18]

It is difficult to identify any genre of later biblical rules, from the most general to the most specific, which does not have its source in the early—pre-Sinai—narratives of the Bible. The prohibition against placing a stumbling block in the way of the blind—which has been interpreted as a broad directive to be

256

fair—has its source in Jacob's deception of his blind father. The rules that require two witnesses protect against false accusation. The biblical law is particularly harsh when it comes to bearing false witness, because, as we have seen, Genesis is so rife with tales of false accusation and injustice. "Thou shalt not utter a false report; put not thy hand with wicked to be an unrighteous witness. Thou shalt not . . . bear witness in a cause to turn aside after a multitude to prevent justice."[19] "Keep thee far from a false matter; and the innocent and righteous slay thou not."[20] The principle of the talion was explicitly imposed on the bearer of false witness. His punishment was the precise punishment that would have been inflicted on the victim of his false testimony.[21]

Even many of the ritual laws have sources in the narrative of Genesis—ranging from circumcision, which God directly commands Abraham to perform on every male throughout the generations;[22] to the kosher laws, which begin with Noachide prohibition against eating blood,[23] continue with the sinew, and then later develop in the law books into a catalog of specific dos and don'ts; to sacrifices, which begin with the story of Cain and Abel[24] and then continue to Noah and to Abraham and his progeny. General ethical prescriptions, which begin with God's directive "to do righteousness and justice"[25] and continues to the grand admonition, "Justice, justice, shall you pursue,"[26] also trace their sources to the narratives of unrighteousness and injustice in Genesis.

The genesis of justice is in the narratives of injustice found in the Book of Genesis. There are also examples of justice and nobility, but these are to be expected in a book of religious narratives. What is re-

257

markable is how the Bible uses stories of injustice to teach about the need for justice. This inspired collection of tales tells the story of the law's development throughout the ages: Lawlessness and injustice provide the impetus for change and improvement. Understanding the complexities of justice—historical and contemporary—requires an understanding of the passions of the people of Genesis. We continue to strive, through law and other social controls, to suppress the *yetzer ha-ra*—the evil inclinations—that all humans possess and to encourage the *yetzer ha-tov*—the good inclinations—that most humans also possess. This story is told in Genesis. It will continue as long as Adams and Eves are tempted by serpents, Cains are enraged by jealousy, Abrahams fight for justice, Jacobs succeed by deception, Tamars are blamed for men's passions, Josephs are falsely accused, and God does not always bring about visible justice.

In other words, the story of Genesis will continue until the end of humankind.

---

1. Genesis 32:33.

2. The rabbis call a vague, symbolic association between a narrative and a rule *asmachta*.

3. Maimonides struggles to find the source for the commandment to circumcise males in the subsequent law book, where it is in fact found: Leviticus 12:3. But it is found earlier in God's covenant with Abraham: Genesis 17:11.

4. Several midrashim elaborate on Abraham's break with his father's idolatry. See *Midrash Rabbah*, vol. 1, p. 310. See also Ginzberg, Louis, *The Legends of the Jews* (Baltimore, MD: Johns Hopkins University Press, 1998), p. 214.

5. *Midrash Rabbah*, vol. 1, pp. 214–15.

6. 35:22.

7. *Midrash Rabbah*, vol. 1, p. 131.

8. Genesis 18:19.

9. Ginzberg, vol. 2, p. 183.

10. 21:23–25.

11. The Code of Hammurapi adumbrated this concept, but without regard to individual culpability. For example, Hummurapi ordered the killing of the daughter of a man who has killed another's daughter. See Plant, W. Gunther, Ed., *The Torah: A Modern Commentary* (New York: Union of American Hebrew Congregations, 1981), p. 574.

12. But monetary compensation is not mentioned for these specified wrongs. Traditional "translations" of the Bible sometimes insert the words "compensation of" before the words "eye," "tooth," and so on. See Samson, Raphael Hirsch, *The Pentateuch* (New York: Judaica Press, 1996). This denies the reader who does not understand Hebrew the distinction between p'shat (literal translation) and d'rash (rabbinic explanation). Although the rabbis themselves believed that monetary compensation *is* the p'shat, the reader should be permitted to decide for him or herself. In some parts of the world, even today, the blood feud persists and sometimes mandates "a 2-for-1 or even a 3-for-1 payback." "The Curse of Blood and Vengeance," Scott Anderson, *New York Times Magazine*, December 26, 1999, pp. 29, 33, 57.

13. See generally, George P. Fletcher, *Reflections on Felony Murder*, 12 Sw. U. L. Rev., 413; 427–29 (1981).

14. Exodus 21:32–37; 22:1–8. Sometimes "double restitution" is required.

15. Numbers 35:31–32 prohibits the taking of money for the life of a killer. Commentators cite this in support of the conclusion that monetary compensation is permissible for injuries short of death. An extensive debate on this subject appears in Bava Kamma 83b–84a. The rabbis conclude that the Torah intended monetary compensation for non-lethal injuries.

16. Exodus 23:7.

17. Mishna Sanhedrin 9:5. Elon, Menachem, *The Principles of Jewish Law*. (Jerusalem: Encyclopedia Judaica, 1974).

18. Exodus 23:7. The Hebrew used the prefix ve- in listing "the innocent *or* who has been acquitted." ve- means "and" rather than "or," thus allowing the argument to be made that the commandment covers only an innocent person who has been acquitted, rather than a guilty one.

19. Exodus 23:1–2. The stumbling block reference appears at Leviticus 19:14.

20. Exodus 23:7.

21. Deuteronomy 19:19.

22. Genesis 17:12.

23. Genesis 9:4. Even the laws of ritual slaughter of animals is said to derive from the manner by which Abraham began to slaughter Isaac: "If the deduction from the verse was made as a true law, then an immovable object is absolutely unfit..." (*Midrash Rabbah*, vol. 1, p. 496, n. 5). In addition, the concept of substituting an animal for a human sin sacrifice derives from this story. Idem. at p. 499: "Sovereign of the universe! Regard it as though I had sacrificed my son Isaac first and then this ram instead of him."

24. Genesis 4:3–5.

25. Genesis 18:19.

26. Deuteronomy 16:20.

Index

Index

Index

repents of making humankind, 62–63

test of Abraham, 109–10, 114, 124, 125, 126

variability of, in Genesis, 204

Goldstein, Baruch, 162–63

Gould, Stephen Jay, 226

Graham, Billy, 225

Hacohen, Maron, 131

Hagar, 129*n*–130*n*

Halivni, David Weiss, 220–21, 223*n*

Ham, 99–100

Hammurabi's Code, 219, 259*n*

Hamor the Hivvite, 147–48

Harvard University

Law seminar on biblical sources of justice, 7–9

student who altered transcript, 44

Hasidim, concept of *daat torah*, 126

Hays Office, 58, 59*n*

Heschel, Abraham Joshua, 17, 76*n*

Hillel, 128

Holmes, Oliver Wendell, 219

Holocaust, 55, 74, 80–81, 93*n*, 99, 109–10, 127, 131*n*, 144, 152, 232

collective sanctions and, 233–34

Homosexuality, 205

Ibn Ezra, Abraham, 9, 14–15, 21*n*–22*n*, 159, 170

Illinois, State of, death penalty convictions of innocent people, 88–89

Inherit the Wind (play), 55

Inquisition, 100

Isaac (Yitzhak), 74

binding and attempted murder of, 101, 103–29

offers wife to save himself, 98, 138, 178

trauma of, 124

tricked on deathbed, 124, 132–35, 137–38, 139, 249

trickery or guile of, 174

Isaiah, 171, 172

Ishmael, 109, 129*n*–130*n*

Jacob (Yaakov), 3, 204

believes Joseph has been killed, 140–41, 175

blessing on Ephrayim and Menashe, 188–90

burial of, 189

character of, 137, 142, 143, 174–75

cheating of Esau, 4, 132–35, 137–38, 139–40, 143, 175, 187, 240, 249

conditional faith of, 7, 81, 143

covenant with God, 72–73, 220

deceptions turned against him, 139–41, 143–44, 197

long-term, symmetrical justice and, 144–45

loves Rachel, tricked into marrying Leah, 135–36, 139–40, 175

midrash on, 137–38, 139–40

midrash on blessing of his sons, 151

reunion with Joseph, 188

sons Simeon and Levi slaughter the Hamorites (condemnation of), 140, 142, 150, 154, 155, 156–57, 162, 163*n*, 197, 249, 254

wrestling with God and kosher law, 247

Jaha, Lamija, 144

Jerome, 138

Jesus, 1–2, 17–18, 208, 212

Jewish people, 13

altruism versus self-serving behavior, 128–29

Index

Index

metaphors in Bible, 17

on Sarah, 109

sexism of, 129*n*

thirteen principles, 216*n*

on Torah study, 3

variation of Pascal's wager, 108–9

Malum in se versus *malum prohibitum*,
53

Marbury v. Madison, 209

Masada, 131*n*

Masturbation, 170–71

McNaughton rule of legal sanity,
52–53

Messiah, 102*n*, 169, 171

Midrash(im), 9, 10, 17

  Abraham and father's idols,
248–49, 258*n*

  Abraham's willingness to sacrifice
Isaac, 105–9, 114–29, 130*n*

  Adam and Eve story, defense,
43–44

  Adam, mitigation of offense, 36,
47*n*

  on afterlife, 240

  Aggadah, 17, 23*n*, 52

  associating all commandments
with Joseph narrative, 251–52

  bird held by hunter metaphor, 54

  Cain's crime, 56–57, 59*n*

  Cain's protection, 51

  "defense lawyers," 11–12, 31, 65,
105, 114, 150, 154

  on Dinah and her rape, 150–51,
158–59, 162–63, 164*n*

  on flood, 65, 68*n*, 82

  God errs in making humans, 63

  on Ham, 99–100

  on Jacob's birth, 137–38

  on Jacob's blessing of his sons,
161

  on Jacob's burial, 190

  on Job, 76, 76*n*

  on Joseph, 198*n*

  on Joseph's corpse, 190, 198*n*,
251–52

  on Joseph framing Benjamin, 187,
192–93

  on Joseph's wife, 190

  on Judah and sex with harlot,
179–80

  on Lot's wife, 100

  on Moses, 153–54

  on murder in general versus
Abraham's ordered sacrifice of
Isaac, 118–19

  on Onan, 170

  on overly-broad prohibitions, 35

  on Rachel, 140

  serpent and Eve, 31

  "Socratic" commentators, 12

  subtle skeptics, 13

  on Tamar, 172

  on Torah, giving of to Israel, 197

  on Torah study, 3, 15–16

  traditional categories, 16–17, 23*n*

Minyan, 88

Mishnah, 58*n*–59*n*, 93*n*, 208, 223*n*

Mishpatim, 6, 41

Moabites, 100, 102*n*

Mohammed, 1–2, 17–18, 212

Molech, 116

Morality, 39–40, 108–9, 112

  better instinct (*yetzer ha-tov*), 123,
126

  relativism and, 112

Moses, 13, 47*n*, 153–54, 189, 196–97,
198*n*, 208

Motive clauses, 220–21, 223*n*

Murder

  accidental, 156

  attempted, 122–23, 131*n*

  Cain's, 48–58

  child, 110–11

Index

Index